THE INTERNATIONAL CRISIS OF THE CARIBBEAN

THE INTERNATIONAL CRISIS IN THE CARIBBEAN

ANTHONY PAYNE...

THE JOHNS HOPKINS UNIVERSITY PRESS
Baltimore, Maryland

First published in the United States of America, 1984, by
The Johns Hopkins University Press
Baltimore, Maryland 21218

First published in Great Britain by
Croom Helm Ltd

ISBN 0-8018-3239-X
Library of Congress Catalog Card No 83-49193

Printed and bound in Great Britain

CONTENTS

To my parents

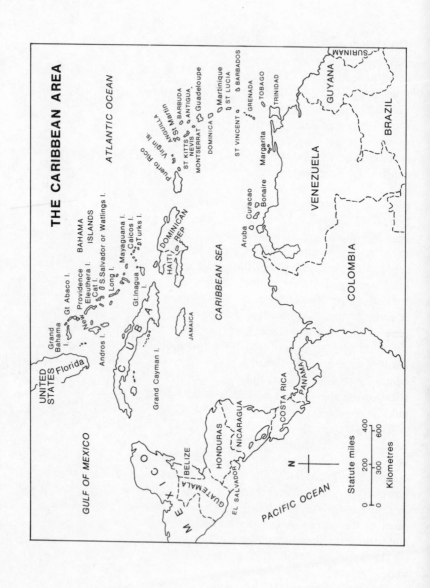

THE CARIBBEAN AREA

PREFACE

The Caribbean is currently a cockpit of international conflict and competition. In the telling phrase of the US State Department, it is 'a circle of crisis'. Certainly, in the light of the past, there is a crisis. The traditional model of international relations in the area has been one of unquestioned and largely unquestioning US hegemony, qualified only by the delegation of authority to the original European powers in respect of particular parts of the region. This is not to say that US control has never been challenged. Unsuccessful attempts to break away from the constraints of US imperialism occurred in British Guiana in the 1950s and early 1960s, and in the Dominican Republic in the mid-1960s; the most successful and celebrated took place in Cuba in 1959. However, the Cuban revolution had no immediate successor in the Caribbean, which has meant that, until recently, these cases remained relatively rare and isolated exceptions to a familiar pattern of acquiescence in US domination. For the most part, the rest of the world was indifferent to Caribbean politics; sometimes it was curious, sometimes amused, but hardly ever concerned. This is the mark of what has changed. A series of unsettling political developments, seemingly increasing in pace as the 1970s proceeded, forced other countries, not least the United States, to take notice of the new instability of the region. The result is that the Caribbean is now recognised as a battleground on which the rivalries of great and middle powers, the competing merits of alternative ideologies and development strategies and the ambitions of individual leaders are all being fought out.

This book provides an introduction to this situation. It describes the background to the major problems of development facing the Caribbean and explains how they created the potential for an intensified competition for influence in the region, involving several external powers. The positions and policies of these powers are then examined in the body of the text. Finally, there is offered a concluding assessment of the nature of the international crisis surrounding the region, and some suggestions of policies that might lead to its resolution.

The immediate inspiration for the book came from a period of some eighteen months working as a 'specialist adviser' to the House of Commons Foreign Affairs Committee during the course of its inquiry into the Caribbean and Central America in 1981 and 1982. The

Preface

demands of the inquiry forced me to think hard about the international politics of the region and made me realise how little understood it was. I should stress, however, that the book is not in any way based on confidential papers to which the Committee had access, nor does it reflect the views of anyone connected with the inquiry. Indeed, should they alight upon it, some of the members of the Committee will no doubt be horrified by my analysis. I thank all of them, nevertheless, for involving me in their work.

I also need to thank several other people. They include Brendan Evans and other colleagues at Huddersfield Polytechnic, who taught more intensively so that I might have the time to write; my fellow Caribbeanists, Colin Clarke, Paul Sutton and Tony Thorndike, who commented on all or part of the manuscript for me; Jackie Hepworth, who typed the whole text very efficiently; and, as always, my wife, Jill, who looked after our two boys and me with her usual unequalled care and attention during the period in which this book was written.

AJP
Huddersfield

1 INTRODUCTION: THE IMPERIAL MOULD

Books about the Caribbean commonly begin with an attempt to define the region. They do so with good reason, for the Caribbean poses genuine problems of identification and demarcation. It displays such an enormous variety of historical connections, social patterns and cultural traditions that it can easily seem as if no common characteristics can possibly attach to the region as a whole. In practice, the Caribbean means different things to different people, with the result that there does not even exist an agreed view of which countries constitute the region. Several alternative definitions compete, each deriving from a particular political perspective. Indeed, the very process of defining the region, especially by outsiders, is almost unavoidably a political act in its own right.

For the social scientist, the best approach to this problem is made via a blend of geographical and historical analysis. One must never forget that the Caribbean is a sea and not a continent. From this view-point definition is simple: the Caribbean consists of all the islands located within the Caribbean Sea. They make up a huge archipelago, which runs some 2,500 miles from the southern tip of Florida in the north to the coast of Venezuela in the south, facing Central America to the west and the Atlantic Ocean to the east. The archipelago is composed of two groups of islands, the Greater and Lesser Antilles. The former comprises the four relatively large islands of Cuba, Jamaica, Puerto Rico and Hispaniola, which is divided politically between the states of Haiti and the Dominican Republic. The latter curves from the Virgin Islands in the north to Barbados and Trinidad and Tobago in the south, and includes all the intervening Leeward and Windward Islands: namely, the Commonwealth territories of St Kitts-Nevis, Anguilla, Antigua-Barbuda, Montserrat, Dominica, St Lucia, St Vincent and Grenada; the French territories of Martinique and Guadeloupe; and three of the Dutch islands that partly comprise the Netherlands Antilles — St Eustatius, Saba and St Maarten. Also generally included within the conventional geographical definition of the Caribbean are a few other very small islands: the Turks and Caicos Islands to the north of Hispaniola, the Cayman Islands to the west of Jamaica, and the remaining islands of the Netherlands Antilles — Aruba, Bonaire and Curaçao — which lie off the Venezuelan coast.

1

From this point onwards, however, problems of inclusion and exclusion begin to arise. By virtue of being islands located in the Caribbean Sea, the Bahamas archipelago ought certainly to be considered as part of the Caribbean, but often it is not or, at best, it is treated only as a marginal member of the region. In some hands, too, the geographical approach is extended to include all those territories whose shores are washed by the Caribbean Sea. By this measure, the region would include Yucatan province of Mexico, Belize, Honduras, Guatemala, Nicaragua, Costa Rica, Panama, Colombia and Venezuela. This wider notion of the Caribbean Basin has lately enjoyed considerable popularity in certain political circles, but it is artificial in anything other than narrow geographical or partisan political terms.

This is made clear by the introduction of some historical considerations. Most of the islands of the Caribbean have been forged out of the mould of imperialism. They have grown up as plantation societies, hewn around the institution of slavery, and they still bear many of the scars of that experience. This gives them a particular identity and separates them in important ways from many of their neighbours. The Bahamas, for example, have not experienced the effects of a history of plantation, and to this extent merit their marginal role as far as inclusion within the Caribbean is concerned. The Central American countries have never had their entire societies reconstructed according to the demands of imperialism, even though, like the Dominican Republic and Cuba, they suffered the consequences of Spanish conquest. Historically, they have never looked towards a Caribbean destiny and even now few of their centres of population lie on the Caribbean coast. The one notable exception to this is Belize, formerly British Honduras. After the early exploitation of its forests by Spanish settlers, it became a British colony in 1862 and thereafter had much in common with other British Crown colonies in the Caribbean. These political and administrative links usually cause Belize to be considered a Caribbean country, even though it has never had a plantation past.

Although the question of historical experience suggests the effective exclusion of the circum-Caribbean territories of Central and South America from any working definition of the Caribbean, it also demands the inclusion of others not embraced by the geographical method. These are the territories of the three Guianas: the former British territory of Guyana, the former Dutch territory of Suriname and the French territory of French Guiana or Cayenne. Their shoreline is the Atlantic, not the Caribbean, and they belong to the continent of South America. Yet their history is similar to that of the islands of the

Caribbean; they have suffered the experience of plantation economy and they have long considered themselves Caribbean territories.

This blend of geographical and historical analysis thus provides the most satisfactory definition of the Caribbean: the Greater and Lesser Antilles and other islands in the Caribbean Sea with the addition of Belize and the three mainland territories of the Guianas. Conceived in this way, the region possesses an intellectual coherence which not only pertains to the past, but is still apparent in the contemporary era. The broad historical experience of imperialism has left behind a legacy which simultaneously divides and unites the Caribbean, but still makes it possible to talk about the region as an entity.

Political Fragmentation

In political terms, the impact of imperialism upon the Caribbean has always been extremely divisive. From the outset, it imposed upon the Caribbean conflicts which derived solely from the rivalry and competition for power of leading European states. Following its discovery by Colombus, the region was dominated for more than a century by Spain, a period of heremony which has shaped the character of countries such as Cuba, Puerto Rico and the Dominican Republic. In the seventeenth century, Spanish power was challenged by British, French and Dutch colonisers. Uninhabited islands were claimed for one or other of the European powers and some inhabited ones, such as Jamaica, were seized from Spain. A period of intermittent warfare between the European powers followed throughout the eighteenth century, during which many of the smaller islands, such as Grenada and St Lucia, changed hands several times in accordance with the ebb and flow of the fighting. The conferences which brought wars to an end exacerbated the process, as Caribbean islands were again regularly swapped between the powers as the currency of victory or defeat. Indeed, for over half a century, from approximately 1760 to 1815, the Caribbean was one of the main areas of the world in which intra-European conflicts and power struggles were pursued. Moreover, by the end of the nineteenth century, the emerging power of the United States was beginning also to bear upon the region and in 1898, at the end of the Spanish–American war, when it acquired effective control of Cuba and Puerto Rico, it joined the ranks of those imperial powers which had a stake in the Caribbean.

The consolidation of imperial rule following these struggles further entrenched the divisions established during the initial phase of conquest. Each territory was administered in accordance with the practice of its particular imperial master. Across the Caribbean, different legal and governmental systems were established in different languages within different cultures. Lines of communication were directed towards the metropolitan capital, rather than other parts of the Caribbean region. Generally speaking, as well, the European powers made little effort to bring about a greater sense of unity amongst their possessions in the area. British colonial administration, for example, was marked by occasional attempts to achieve a closer union between its Caribbean possessions, chiefly for reasons of economy, but it never displayed a consistent concern for this question and certainly gave no thought to co-operation with other regional states beyond its imperial domain. As a result, all the territories of the region have tended to develop strongly parochial and insular political cultures.

Finally, the process of decolonisation in the Caribbean has served to divide it still further. Each imperial power approached this matter in its own way and its own time. The result has been to create an astonishingly fragmented political landscape in the contemporary Caribbean. Quite apart from the varied social and cultural legacies of different imperialisms, the region is now divided between territories at three levels of political development: the independent states, the semi-independent and the remaining dependencies.

The first category, those states that are fully independent, comprises sixteen countries. Three of the original Spanish colonies gained their formal independence in the nineteenth century: Haiti in 1804 following a slave rebellion, the Dominican Republic in 1865 and Cuba in 1898, although the latter two had to pass through periods of US control before independence came to have any meaning. These countries apart, the modern wave of independence began in the 1960s, when in 1962 Jamaica and Trinidad and Tobago, and in 1966 Barbados and Guyana won their independence from Britain. A second wave of decolonisation by Britain followed with the Bahamas achieving independence in 1973, Grenada in 1974, Dominica in 1978, St Lucia and St Vincent in 1979, Antigua-Barbuda and Belize in 1981, and St Kitts-Nevis in 1983. In the middle of this period, in 1975, Suriname also attained independence from the Netherlands.

The second category incorporates three countries which are in some way semi-independent. Of these the largest is Puerto Rico, which since 1950 has been a self-governing 'Commonwealth' associated with the United States. Under this arrangement, Puerto Rico is self-governing in most local matters, but its defence and foreign relations are handled by the United States and it is part of the US currency and customs area. The same applies to the US Virgin Islands, which the United States bought from Denmark in 1917, except that the extent of internal autonomy is less than in Puerto Rico. In the Commonwealth Caribbean, the various British Associated States among the Leeward and Windward Islands also enjoyed full internal self-government whilst relying upon Britain for defence and the conduct of external relations, but they have at last disappeared with the achievement of independence by St Kitts-Nevis in September 1983. In a similar intermediate category still is the Netherlands Antilles, which is a federation of the six widely-separated Dutch islands in the region. It is internally self-governing, but the Kingdom of the Netherlands is still responsible for defence and foreign affairs.

The third category is represented by the remaining dependencies in the region. Five are British territories — Anguilla, the British Virgin Islands, the Cayman Islands, Montserrat and the Turks and Caicos Islands — and three are French. These are the territories of Martinique, Guadeloupe and French Guiana (Cayenne), which are French overseas 'départements' and are thus juridically part of metropolitan France with the right to participate directly in French elections. There are no remaining Spanish or Dutch colonies in the area.

Economic Unity

By contrast, the impact of imperialism on the Caribbean in economic terms has been broadly similar across the region, creating a kind of unity in terms of political economy. This is not to imply that important economic differences do not exist between the Caribbean territories.[1] Some are obviously larger than others in area and population and are better endowed with resources. Some states have quite advanced manufacturing sectors, other are still reliant upon agriculture as the main economic activity. In a variety of ways the region's economies inevitably reveal divergent characteristics and structures. Yet it remains true that the basis of a genuinely Caribbean political economy can still be detected. It resides in the common fact, noted by the sociologist Malcolm Cross, that all the countries of the region have either 'had to, or still have to, come to terms with the uniquely New World experience of being dependent suppliers of tropical primary products for Western European or North American markets'.[2]

Historically, as is well known, the contemporary economies of the Caribbean were formed as appendages of European metropolitan economies in the era of mercantilist expansion. The metropole provided organisation and decision-making, capital, transport, supplies, markets and even transplanted labour from Africa, relegating the Caribbean to the mere locus of production. The local economy was composed more or less entirely of a sugar-producing plantation sector, exporting the crop to European markets in largely unprocessed form. The ending of slavery and the loss of preferences, particularly in the British market, in the middle of the nineteenth century seriously undermined the Caribbean sugar economy, but did not cause its complete collapse.

A number of adjustments were made to the structure of the pure plantation economy. Everywhere the plantation sector was rationalised, many estates and factories were consolidated and inefficient ones fell into disuse. In Haiti, for example, the system effectively came to an end. In other parts of the region, notably in the under-populated territories of Trinidad and Guyana, the introduction of indentured labour from India, China, Portugal and elsewhere shored up the plantation sector for another century or so. More important, though, was the emergence of a new sector in the regional economy — a peasant class consisting largely of ex-slaves growing food for themselves and their families as well as the domestic market and, later in the century, pioneering the production of new export crops, like bananas, cocoa, coffee and spices. The growth of this new sector was given additional impetus in the last years of the nineteenth century by the long depression in sugar caused by the subsidisation in Europe of beet sugar.

The present century has witnessed further diversification of the Caribbean economy, but as yet no major transformation of the plantation inheritance. Although agriculture has fallen as a contribution to gross domestic product in a number of Caribbean countries in recent years, the economies of the smaller Commonwealth Caribbean territories, the French islands and the poorer countries of the Dominican Republic and Haiti remain heavily dependent on their agricultural sector. Since it is more labour-intensive than any other industry, its role in providing work is particularly critical: as late as the 1960s, it provided over 40 per cent of the labour force in several Caribbean countries. In terms, too, of export earnings, many territories are highly reliant on one or two basic agricultural crops. In St Kitts, for example, 80 per cent of export revenue is derived from sugar, and in Dominica almost as high a percentage from bananas. Moreover, within the agricultural sector, the plantation is still dominant, especially in the export sphere. Although peasants usually own the vast majority of farms, their holdings are small, typically less than five acres. It is the much smaller number of plantations which control the greatest proportion of farm land, and the best-quality land too. Plantations are certainly fewer in number than they were, even at the beginning of the twentieth century. They have tended in the modern era to become concentrated in the hands of large, foreign-owned corporations, such as Booker McConnell Ltd, which owned, until relatively recently, the bulk of the sugar plantations in Guyana, and Tate & Lyle, which operated for many years in other parts of the Commonwealth Caribbean. Costs of production generally remain high and special arrangements still need to be negotiated in external markets, if substantial earnings are to be achieved. In short, the plantation sector remains fundamentally unreformed in virtually all the countries of the Caribbean.

Nevertheless, other sectors have been developed in recent years in an effort to overcome the region's dependence on its traditional monoculture. In some Caribbean territories more modern export industries located in the mineral sector have emerged. Trinidad is the only Caribbean country with significant reserves of oil and gas, but Aruba, Curaçao, Puerto Rico, the Bahamas and St Croix in the US Virgin Islands are all substantial refiners of imported oil. Jamaica, Guyana, Suriname, Haiti and the Dominican Republic produce between them approximately 40 per cent of the world's output of bauxite, the ore from which aluminium is made, and ferronickel is mined in both Cuba and the Dominican Republic. However, these industries were all initially developed by foreign corporations, which has limited their contribution to the economic development of the Caribbean. For example, as a consequence of foreign ownership, the lucrative processing of bauxite has only been undertaken within the region on a fairly limited scale. All these industries have tended also to be highly capital-intensive, the entire Caribbean bauxite industry being reckoned to employ only some 20,000 people. Although mineral industries have often come to dominate a country's exports, as bauxite has in Jamaica, they have generally made little contribution to procuring jobs. Indeed, their effect on employment has in one sense been negative: the high wage rates paid in the new mineral sector have raised the reserve price of labour and thus encouraged people to sacrifice low-paid agricultural employment in order to join the ranks of the urban unemployed.

The panacea most widely adopted in the Caribbean in the post-war period as a means of providing employment has been the promotion of manufacturing industry. Puerto Rico was the pioneer with its policy of attracting foreign companies to establish manufacturing plants in the Caribbean on the basis of offering a range of tax and investment incentives. In the 1950s, this strategy of 'industrialisation by invitation', as it became known,[3] was copied by Jamaica and Trinidad, and subsequently by nearly all the countries of the area. It worked to the extent that foreign capital responded predictably and flowed into the Caribbean in massive amounts, bringing in its wake a number of highly visible manufacturing industries. The contribution made to gross domestic product by manufacturing rose quickly to over 25 per cent in Puerto Rico and some 15–20 per cent in the larger Commonwealth Caribbean territories. However, the industries established have been largely 'final-touch' enterprises, based upon the assembly of imported inputs which have relatively little value added and have failed to penetrate export markets. They have produced few jobs and have often been itinerant in their commitment to the Caribbean. All too frequently, when the incentive plan has expired and local taxation comes into force, the company has found it profitable to move its entire operation to another locale offering a new package of inducements. Haiti, the Dominican Republic and some of the smaller Commonwealth Caribbean islands have benefited from firms moving on from Puerto Rico and even Jamaica, but the Caribbean economy as a whole has lost.

The last new industry into which the Caribbean has lately moved in a major way is tourism. In some territories, even more than manufacturing, this has been heralded as the road to prosperity. Although the tourist industry is most developed in the larger northern Caribbean islands closest to the American market, such as Puerto Rico and Jamaica, it is most critical of all to some of the smallest islands in the region, where it is the main generator of foreign exchange and a major employer. Barbados, the Bahamas, the Netherlands Antilles, Antigua and St Lucia all fall into this category. The trouble with tourist development is that it is extremely vulnerable in times of recession in the developed economies and to bad publicity at any time. In the particular case of the Caribbean, where the industry has been geared to a particularly affluent sector of North American and European society, it can only compete if it maintains the highest standards of accommodation and hospitality. This has meant that foreign capital and foreign imports, especially of food, underwrite the industry, producing the diseconomies of inflated import bills and extensive profit repatriation. The industry has to a considerable extent become an enclave within the Caribbean economy, having few linkages with, and contributing little to, the development of the rest of the local economy.

These various attempts to diversify the Caribbean economy were generally quite successful in the 1950s and 1960s in the single matter of engendering economic growth. Several territories, notably Puerto Rico, Jamaica, Trinidad and the Bahamas, grew at an annual rate of about 5 per cent during this period, which is, conventionally speaking, a good economic performance. These apparent successes should not, however, conceal either the fixed constraint upon long-term economic viability represented by the small size of most Caribbean territories or the many immediate problems of development which had not been removed from the face of the regional economy by the growth of a few countries. Indeed, in the Commonwealth Caribbean it has been officially admitted that in many essential respects the post-war era of fast growth represented only 'a continuation of the centuries-old pattern of West Indian economy; growth without development; growth accompanied by imbalances and distortions; growth generated from outside rather than within'.[4]

Specifically, there still existed several serious weaknesses in the structure of the political economy of the Caribbean which extended in their way across the whole region. William Demas, the President of the Caribbean Development Bank and an eminent and experienced economist, has itemised the most prominent weaknesses as follows:

1. a very large food import bill, consequent upon the stagnation and decline of domestic agriculture;
2. a heavily undiversified and specialised structure of production, with dependence on a single or limited number of export products such as sugar, bananas, coffee, citrus, oil and natural gas, bauxite and alumina, and tourism;
3. corresponding dependence on a very wide range of imports, not only of capital goods but also intermediate and other consumer goods;
4. the vulnerability and uncompetitiveness of the high-cost, low-productivity export agricultural sector;
5. the lack of economic linkages between different sectors of each national economy and the paucity of linkages between economies across the region, whether measured by the size of intra-regional trade or the existence of joint productive ventures;
6. the failure of the manufacturing sector to achieve significant levels of extra-regional exports;
7. the marked external orientation of economies in the region and the dominant role played by foreign capital;

8. a low rate of national savings in all sectors and the taste for foreign goods and inappropriate patterns of consumption;
9. above all, alarmingly high levels of unemployment (ranging from 10 per cent to 30 per cent of the labour force) and low-paid under-employment.[5]

The last point, in particular, highlights the fact that, whatever were the purely economic achievements of the post-war model of political economy adopted in the Caribbean, it was a social failure. Distribution of income in the region was notoriously uneven, both between countries, where in 1973 the range extended between the US Virgin Islands with an average per capita income of US $5,910 and Haiti with an equivalent figure of US $130, and within countries, where it was, and still is, a common Caribbean phenomenon to find opulent suburbs and squalid shanty towns in close proximity. It could certainly never be claimed that the modern development of the Caribbean economy worked to the benefit of the people of the region across all classes. A minority gained considerably, but for the majority the benefits that 'trickled down' to their level of the social spectrum were minor at best and negligible at worst. As a result, large numbers were prompted to take advantage of the plentiful opportunities, which existed in the 1950s and 1960s, to emigrate to Europe and North America taking with them valuable and badly-needed skills. To sum up, then, at the beginning of the 1970s it still had to be said that across the region, notwithstanding its political fragmentation, continuing economic dependence and lack of development remained the outstanding feature of the Caribbean social and political scene.

Notes

1. For basic data on the various territories that comprise the Caribbean, see the Appendix at the end of the book.
2. M. Cross, *Urbanization and Urban Growth in the Caribbean* (Cambridge University Press, Cambridge, 1979), p. 5.
3. By the group of New World economists formed during the 1960s at the University of the West Indies. See N. Girvan and O. Jefferson (eds.), *Readings in the Political Economy of the Caribbean* (Institute of Social and Economic Research, Kingston, 1971), p. 1.
4. Commonwealth Caribbean Regional Secretariat, *From CARIFTA to Caribbean Community* (Commonwealth Caribbean Regional Secretariat, Georgetown, 1972), p. 14.
5. W.G. Demas, 'The Caribbean and the New International Economic Order', *Journal of Interamerican Studies and World Affairs*, vol. 20, no. 3 (1978), p. 242.

2 CONTEMPORARY PATTERNS OF CHANGE AND INSTABILITY

The international economic crisis sparked off by the massive oil price rises of 1973-4 severely shook the flimsy basis on which nearly every Caribbean economy rested. Only Trinidad and Tobago, which is a relatively minor oil-producing country by world standards, was able to benefit from the new high price of energy brought about by the action of OPEC. The rest of the region was faced with hugely increased import bills which they were unable to pay on the basis of earnings achieved from their own commodity exports and light manufacturing industries. Balance of payments deteriorated, foreign exchange reserves fell and governments faced serious budgetary problems across the Caribbean. As the recession intensified, even those commodity prices which had gone up temporarily in the wake of oil fell back, further depressing production levels and thus exacerbating the problem of unemployment. Large-scale migration was no longer available as a means of alleviation, with the result that the number of people without work grew sharply. At the same time, to make the situation worse, inflation was imported from the industrialised world. The economic problems facing the region were quite suddenly immense and pressing, and for the most part beyond the managerial capacity of the traditional and conservative governments which predominated in the Caribbean.

The result was to set in motion a process of change which quickened as the 1970s unfolded and made the Caribbean an area of widespread political instability. Many countries in the region became increasingly dubious of Western values and began to search around for new strategies of development and new models of political organisation. No clear pattern and no precise direction of change emerged, although the broad trend was to move to the left to reject in some way the traditional order within the region.[1] As can be seen, the process has now embraced nearly all the countries in the Caribbean.

Guyana: the 'Co-operative Socialist' Republic

Guyana was in the vanguard of the process of change in the Caribbean. In 1970, with the racial violence and the general political discontent of

11

the previous decade apparently contained, the People's National Congress (PNC) government of Forbes Burnham declared Guyana to be a Co-operative Socialist Republic. This novel ideology was conceived as a means of allowing the Guyanese people a greater role in the operation of their own economy in order, as the slogan had it, 'to make the little man a real man'. It was proclaimed as a local alternative to the rival systems of capitalism and Communism, based upon the particular historical and psychological make-up of the Guyanese people. The government highlighted accordingly the importance of co-operatives and promoted their expansion, setting up a separate Ministry of Co-operatives and National Mobilisation. The spirit of co-operativism also underlay the ambitions of a new development plan which aimed to 'feed, clothe and house' the nation by 1976.

In pursuit of its new ideology, Burnham's government also set out to gain greater control of the various foreign interests which dominated the Guyanese economy. It began pragmatically seeking schemes of joint ownership, but when negotiations with the Canadian-owned Demerera Bauxite Company faltered in 1971, the government nationalised the entire operation amidst declarations that this was the first step in the building of socialism in Guyana. Nevertheless, Burnham did not embark upon further nationalisations until 1974: by that time he had acquired a two-thirds majority in Parliament by means of widespread fraud of the electoral process and had enunciated the new doctrine of the paramountcy of the party, by which it was deemed that henceforth all organs of the state, including the government, would be considered as agencies of the ruling PNC and subject to its control. Thus entrenched, the government took over the US-owned Reynolds Bauxite Company, which gave it full control of the country's bauxite industry, but alerted the US government to the sort of policies being developed in Guyana. During the following couple of years the nationalisation policy was further extended until eventually, in 1976, it embraced the vast and varied holdings of Booker McConnell Ltd. According to the government's own figures, the company, which was the country's largest sugar producer, provided 40 per cent of Guyana's exports and 35 per cent of gross domestic product. So extensive were its operations that, in the colonial era, it was often said that in reality British Guiana was Booker's Guiana. As a result of this take-over and the institution of other measures of state control in the distribution, communications and public transport sectors, in banking and in the import trade through the formation of an official External Trade Bureau, the government could claim that by the end of 1976 it owned and controlled 80 per cent of the economy.

In parallel with its apparent shift towards socialism in domestic affairs, the Burnham government moved towards a more radical position in foreign policy. A commitment to non-alignment surfaced as early as 1970, when diplomatic relations were established with the Soviet Union and Guyanese representatives played an active role in the Non-Aligned Summit Conference in Zambia. In 1972, Guyana established relations with China and Cuba and developed warm relationships with both powers. The Chinese government immediately granted Guyana a large interest-free loan and negotiated an economic assistance programme; in 1973 Fidel Castro visited Georgetown, his first visit to an independent Commonwealth Caribbean state. Guyana was also actively involved in the formation of the International Bauxite Association, in support of wars of liberation in Africa and in the diplomacy attached to the Third World's demand for a 'New International Economic Order'. Not surprisingly, in the light of these moves and the measures of nationalisation, especially in the bauxite industry, relations with the United States cooled, despite the fact that in the internal political struggles of the 1960s Burnham had been the man backed by Washington. In 1976 Burnham even alleged that there existed a CIA conspiracy to destabilise his government because of its firm and active commitment to co-operative socialism.

In short, Guyana appeared for a while to possess one of the most radical governments in the whole of the Third World, let alone the Caribbean. That image has since been completely destroyed. Burnham and the PNC remain in power, but have had to resort to increasing coercion and numerous abuses of democracy to preserve their position and have singularly failed to bring about the development of the country's economy which has now been cast into a deep slump by a combination of world recession and government mismanagement. In retrospect, co-operative socialism can be seen to have been, in the words of an eminent Guyanese critic, merely 'an ideological rationalisation for the development of state capitalism in Guyana'.[2] Yet in the mid-1970s observers were widely persuaded of the sincerity of Burnham's move to the left. The opposition Communist party, the People's Progressive Party, offered him 'critical support', the US State Department was undoubtedly concerned at the direction of policy and several academic observers within Guyana testified to the reality of the government's commitment to socialism. In the wider geopolitical context, the inaccuracy of this analysis hardly matters; even as a rhetorical disguise for the consolidation of power by an avaricious ruling clique, the

Burnham government's loud advocacy of an alternative approach to development delivered a considerable shock to the prevailing *status quo* in the Caribbean.

Jamaica: the Adoption of 'Democratic Socialism'

A further challenge developed in Jamaica, where the People's National Party (PNP) government, led by Michael Manley, which came into office in 1972, pursued a policy of reform in accordance with the ideology of 'democratic socialism'. From the moment that he became leader of the PNP in 1969, in succession to his father, Manley had demonstrated a clear understanding of the nature of the political economy produced by the post-war era of expansion in Jamaica. He was aware that the social benefits of economic growth had been thinly spread and that there existed pockets of alienation within the urban environment which on more than one occasion in the 1960s had exploded into violence. By addressing himself to this discontent and adopting a dynamic approach to such issues as unemployment, poverty and political participation, Manley was able to lead the PNP to victory in the 1972 elections. The result reflected broad support from the young, the unemployed, large sections of the working class and peasantry, most of the professional and administrative middle class and intelligentsia, and even some newer members of the capitalist class disaffected by the failures of the previous government, and it could only be interpreted as a decisive mandate for change in Jamaica.

By this time Manley had also developed a coherent vision of the changes he wished to introduce in both domestic and foreign policy. He himself was a social democrat, educated in the Fabian tradition. All his thinking disavowed, either explicitly or by implication, Marxist-Leninist notions of class struggle and proletarian dictatorship. It rested instead on what he has called the 'single touchstone of right and wrong',[3] the notion of equality, which he proceeded to make the foundation of socialism in Jamaica. He has written:

Social organisation exists to serve everybody or it has no moral foundation . . . the fact that society cannot function effectively without differentials in reward together with the fact that men are manifestly not equal in talent must not be allowed to obscure the central purpose of social organisation. This is, and must always be, the promotion of the welfare of every member of the human race.[4]

Manley was aware, however, that the nature of economic dependence was such that PNP's programme of domestic reform could be secured only if his government was able to negotiate better terms for Jamaica in all its dealings with the international economy, and so Jamaican socialism acquired a clearly articulated international dimension, requiring radical revision of the direction of post-independence Jamaican foreign policy.

The first two years of the PNP government brought a number of significant social reforms, but no fundamental break with the previous pattern of Jamaican politics. However, the year 1974 was a turning-point for the Manley administration. The international economic crisis badly dislocated the Jamaican economy and forced the Manley regime to take radical action to repair the damage. The first sign of this change of gear came in January 1974, when the government announced its intention to renegotiate the tax agreements signed with the American and Canadian companies which owned the island's bauxite and alumina industry. After four months of inconclusive talks Manley abrogated the old agreements and imposed a novel method of raising revenue, a production 'levy' on all bauxite mined or processed in Jamaica set at a percentage of the selling price of the aluminium ingot. This increased the revenue obtained by the government from bauxite by some 650 per cent in just two years and greatly alarmed the companies, with whom Manley also set in train discussions on the subject of government purchase of majority control in local operations. Along with Guyana, Jamaica also played a leading role in the formation of the International Bauxite Association. This particularly disturbed the US administration, which at the time was fearful of the effects of such Third World cartels on Western economic interests. The United States was also concerned by Manley's active involvement in the Non-Aligned movement and by his developing friendship with Fidel Castro, which led him to give Jamaica's support for Cuban involvement in the Angolan civil war. These various moves raised real, if unfounded, doubts in government circles in Washington about the extent of Jamaica's continued commitment to the West.

These reservations were deepened when, in 1974, the government announced that Jamaica was henceforth to be considered one of the socialist countries of the world. Although it was widely publicised, the manifesto setting out the 'democratic socialist' principles which were in future to guide the government in fact contained little that was new. The aim of the announcement was to mobilise the Jamaican people more actively behind the government's strategy at a time when support seemed to be falling. However, although the direction of the government's policy was not noticeably changed by the declaration of support for socialism, that was not true of external perceptions of its position. Domestic and international opposition to Manley's regime increased, culminating in the period leading to the election in December 1976 in what has come to be called a campaign of 'destabilisation'. The election was won in triumph by Manley amidst considerable anti-imperialist fervour, and for a while afterwards it looked as if Jamaica was going to embark upon a complete disengagement from the capitalist world economy. In the event, Manley retreated, only to be forced by the continuing problems of the economy into negotiations with the International Monetary Fund, from which moment onwards the Jamaican economy was locked into a disastrous, but yet inescapable, deflationary spiral. Manley's socialist experiment was broken on the back of the IMF connection and eventually came to an end in electoral defeat in October 1980. Yet, for a time, it had held centre stage in the Caribbean, and undoubtedly it contributed further to the decay of the traditional order within the region.

Puerto Rico: the Emergence of 'Independentista' Politics

Ever since it was established in 1952, Puerto Rico's semi-colonial Commonwealth relationship with the United States rankled with a tiny minority of the islanders, who consistently favoured independence. Support for this option grew in Puerto Rico in the 1960s, but still remained at a very low level. Part of the problem was that, when Commonwealth status was introduced, the United States had succeeded in persuading the United Nations General Assembly to remove Puerto Rico from the list of remaining colonies. As such, it was not covered by the famous Resolution 1514, passed in 1960, which proclaimed that colonialism 'in all its forms and manifestations' must be ended. However, in 1972 Cuba took the initiative and placed the Puerto Rican situation before the UN Committee on Decolonisation. The Committee formally recognised the right of the people of Puerto Rico to self-determination and in the following year 'requested' that the US government refrain from taking any measures which might obstruct full and free exercise of that right. The United States denied that Puerto Rico was a colony and maintained that the issue was an 'internal' one of no concern to the international community. There the matter rested until

1978, when the emergence of 'independentista' politics on the island itself brought the issue again to the attention of the United Nations.

Like the rest of the Caribbean, Puerto Rico was badly affected by the international economic crisis of the 1970s. As a result of the difficult conditions, many of the companies which had established themselves in the island in the 1940s and 1950s to enjoy the tax exemptions and low-wage labour began to transfer their operations to more attractive investment havens, such as Haiti and Taiwan. Unemployment in Puerto Rico reached an official level of 20 per cent, although including underemployment the real figure was probably closer to 40 per cent. The cost of living also rose sharply, largely because almost everything consumed on the island is imported. The result was that by the middle of the decade no less than 70 per cent of the population was sufficiently impoverished to be eligible for US food stamp coupons. The 'economic miracle' which Puerto Rico had long enjoyed was manifestly at an end, and the country's clientelistic relationship with the United States increasingly in question. In 1978, in contrast to the attendance of just the usual few committed advocates of independence, representatives of all the major political parties and many leading religious, educational and cultural organisations in Puerto Rico chose to appear before the UN Decolonisation Committee to convey varying degrees of dissatisfaction with their country's political status to the international community. They were motivated primarily by concern about the state of the economy, but nevertheless specifically raised such issues as the territory's inability to participate in international organisations, the government's lack of control over immigration, the subordination of the island's claim to a 200-mile zone to US national policy, and other manifestations of the semi-colonial character of Commonwealth status. The hearings lasted several days and culminated in a resolution which stressed that only through a complete transfer of power from the United States to the people of Puerto Rico could the latter be able to decide freely their political future. The resolution went on to call upon the United States to present a plan to the Committee for the eventual political independence of the island.

However, the debate about political status within Puerto Rico was not quite so simply conceived. The ruling New Progressive Party of Governor Carlos Romero Barceló favoured statehood, namely the incorporation of Puerto Rico into the United States as the 51st state, whereas its chief rival, the Popular Democratic Party, led by ex-Governor Rafael Hernández Colón, still backed Commonwealth status. Between them they dominated public opinion, which was evenly divided between the two options. The election of November 1980 was a very close contest; Barceló narrowly held on to office, but was forced to abandon a planned referendum on the statehood issue. By contrast, the two parties which advocated independence won little support.

In these circumstances, the independence issue spilled over into sporadic guerrilla activity. Since August 1978, when two policemen were kidnapped and one of them killed, pro-independence and revolutionary guerrillas have been responsible for a series of attacks, including bombings of US property and military personnel on the island. Several groups exist, the most prominent being the so-called Macheteros who, in January 1981, just after the election, blew up 10 US fighter planes at the Muniz airbase in San Juan. Other, more peaceful protests have been regularly organised by fishermen against US naval use of the island of Vieques which lies just off the coast of Puerto Rico. In the face of these pressures, the United States government has made no concessions in the way of independence, moving instead in the opposite direction towards support for statehood. It has, nevertheless, been disturbed by the movement of the Puerto Rican question from being a private internal affair of the United States to an issue of international concern.

Grenada: the New Jewel Revolution

The forces of change which were steadily beginning to undermine the traditional order in the Caribbean achieved their next and most dramatic triumph in Grenada, where, on 13 March 1979, some 200 ill-armed men belonging to the so-called People's Revolutionary Army overthrew the island's government and carried out the first successful revolution in the history of the English-speaking territories of the region. The novelty of this act briefly captured international attention and the events leading up to the revolution became well known. Grenada had moved to independence in 1974 under the leadership of Eric Gairy, a flamboyant and mystical figure who had dominated its politics for more than twenty years. The island had subsequently been governed with such a mixture of brutality, inefficiency and corruption that it gained notoriety even beyond the Caribbean. The only effective and lasting opposition to Gairy's regime came from a small radical party called the New Jewel Movement (NJM), which had to contend with organised manipulation of the elections by the government and savage physical assaults on its leaders by the police and Gairy's personal 'Mongoose Gang', a group of hired thugs. When word reached the NJM in March

1979 that Gairy had organised the assassination of eight of the movement's most prominent leaders whilst he was off the island, it was clear that all the avenues to change in Grenada had been eliminated except that of violent revolution. The insurrection was launched and a People's Revolutionary Government (PRG) was set up under the NJM leader, Maurice Bishop.

The new government was revolutionary in purpose as well as name. It immediately set itself the daunting task of overcoming Grenada's long-standing underdevelopment, embarking on a series of radical new policies. On the domestic front, the most urgent necessity was simply to get the Grenadian economy functioning again after the almost total collapse engendered by the mismanagement of the Gairy regime. The PRG worked hard to do this by first restoring order to the country's finances, borrowing sensibly from external sources and instituting new plans for modernising the island's fishing industry, developing agro-industry and extending the country's tourist potential. These various economic initiatives were sensibly conceived and quickly brought benefits to the Grenadian people. Yet they were largely ignored by critics and opponents of the PRG, who sought to undermine the new regime by focusing attention upon two particular aspects of its policy.

The first concerned Grenada's foreign policy, which became formally one of non-alignment. As Bishop told a mass rally in the capital, St George's, to mark the first anniversary of the revolution, 'we are not in anybody's back yard . . . the Grenadian people reserve the right to choose their friends and pursue their own path of development'.[5] Grenada accordingly established diplomatic relations with a wide range of countries and accepted aid from such diverse sources as the EEC, the IMF, Canada, Cuba, Mexico, Venezuela, and various Arab states. Many observers nevertheless felt that the real basis of Grenada's new foreign policy was alliance with Cuba. The link-up between Cuba and the new government began in the immediate aftermath of the revolution and arose out of the latter's urgent need to protect its position against the threat of a counter-revolution led by the deposed prime minister and his friends. Bishop initially called upon the USA, Britain and Canada to provide military assistance to deter such threats, and turned to Cuba only when he received negative replies from Grenada's traditional allies. Following this request, diplomatic relations between the two countries were quickly established at ambassadorial level and Cuba subsequently provided technical assistance in a number of areas, notably in connection with the building of a large new international airport on the island. To the annoyance of the US government, the relationship between the two regimes became very close.

The other issue which was in the forefront of the debate about Grenada following the revolution was the degree of commitment felt by the new regime to democracy. Critics of the PRG were quick to allege that its aim was to establish a single-party dictatorship in Grenada. This fear derived partly from the Cuban connection, but was also given credence by a number of other acts of the new government, such as the closing of the island's main newspaper and the holding without trial of a number of 'political prisoners', supporters of the former Gairy regime. Undoubtedly, though, the main weapon of those who attacked the PRG's democratic credential was the government's failure to hold elections after it came to power. By way of defence, the PRG argued that the 'type of democracy where people walk into a ballot box and vote for two seconds every five years is often not real democracy at all'[6] and claimed instead to be building in Grenada a system of 'participatory democracy', involving the wider mobilisation of the people within community education councils, health councils, youth groups, voluntary work organisations and eventually village assemblies. It was not easy to evaluate the progress that had been made in this direction, but certainly no one was able to doubt the new spirit and sense of popular involvement which characterised the Grenadian people after the revolution.

In sum, the Grenadian revolution greatly alarmed conservative opinion inside and outside the Caribbean. It showed what could be done, even on a small island, by a group of young, well-educated, middle-class men and women who had been genuinely appalled at the way Grenada had previously been governed and who passionately believed they could do better. Critics condemned the new regime as Marxist, citing as evidence the fact that PRG leaders addressed each other as comrade, and expressed a warm admiration for Cuba. Undoubtedly, there were those in the government who believed in the so-called 'non-capitalist' path of development, but in public they defended the government's commitment to the mixed economy. In practice, the main characteristic of PRG rule was a determined nationalism, which is, of course, radical in its own right in the context of Caribbean history.

The Eastern Caribbean: 'a Sea of Splashing Dominoes'

The revolution in Grenada had an obvious impact on the other small islands of the Eastern Caribbean. It created a sense of insecurity on the part of governments and a sense of the possible on the part of small radical groups sharing the political philosophy of the New Jewel Movement. The combination appeared fertile. Within months, Dominica and St Lucia had also acquired new governments whose initial predisposition suggested that Grenada had indeed set in motion a marked shift to the left in Eastern Caribbean politics.

In Dominica, the situation seemed not unlike that in Grenada. Since July 1974 the premier and leader of the dominant Dominica Labour Party (DLP) had been Patrick John, an erratic and intolerant man with a propensity for oppressive rule. Despite the impassioned objections of opposition leaders, John succeeded in leading Dominica to independence in November 1978, whereupon their worst fears were quickly confirmed as the government, no longer inhibited by the British connection, passed new laws restricting press freedom and banning civil servants and other workers in essential services from taking strike action. The crisis reached a climax in June 1979, when armed troops opened fire and killed one man and a small child during a demonstration against these laws in the island's capital, Roseau. This led to the calling of a general strike and the formation of a Committee for National Salvation, comprising business and church leaders, trade unions and opposition political parties on both the left and the right, which called upon John to resign. A period of violence and confusion followed, in which John manoeuvred to hold on to power, even though his government had disintegrated, but which was finally ended when an interim government was formed under the leadership of the former DLP minister, Oliver Seraphine. Although the new government was a coalition of all the political forces in Dominica hostile to John's authoritarian rule, prevailing opinion had it that Seraphine himself was 'left of centre', and included within the government were Atherton Martin, the progressive leader of the Dominica Farmers' Union and 'Rosie' Douglas, a leading member of the radical Dominica Liberation Movement. A significant change in the political complexion of the Dominican government seemed, in other words, to have occurred.

Meanwhile, in St Lucia, the pro-Western government of John Compton was coming up for re-election in conditions of relative economic depression. Its main opponent was a revitalised St Lucia Labour Party (SLP). During the early part of the 1970s the SLP had been joined by a number of the island's youthful radical leaders, men like George Odlum and Peter Josie. They had become politically active in the late 1960s in left-wing and Black Power organisations like Forum and

the St Lucia Action Movement, and brought to the SLP a large following from those days as well as a more critical approach to the economic
dependence engendered by the Compton government's open strategy
of development. By 1979 the SLP had acquired not only a new leader,
Allan Louisy, a highly respected former judge of the West Indies
Associated States Supreme Court, but a new deputy leader, Odlum
himself. It was therefore no real surprise when, in the election in July,
the SLP won a considerable victory. Compton no doubt hoped that the
credit for leading St Lucia to independence a few months earlier would
rub off on his party. In the event, his defence of his record in office and
his allegation that Odlum, Josie and others were 'Communists' were no
match for the enegetic and radical SLP campaign, based on the theme
of 'returning St Lucia to the St Lucians'. The victory of the Labour
Party was immediately interpreted inside and outside the Caribbean as
another indication that, following upon events in Grenada and
Dominica, the little islands of the Eastern Caribbean were moving
sharply to the left.

That line of analysis was further reinforced when, within a week or
so of the election, Louisy, Odlum and Josie, representing St Lucia, and
Seraphine and Martin, representing Dominica, met with Bishop and
members of the PRG in a 'mini-summit' in Grenada. The left-wing
character of the gathering was apparent in the 'Declaration of St
Georges', which the leaders issued at the end of their discussions.
Amidst proposals for the development of closer relations between the
three states, it set 'popular democracy, respect for the rights of
workers, and social and economic justice for the masses' as the main
domestic objectives of the participating governments, declared its
opposition to imperialism in all its forms, gave full support to liberation
movements in Africa and Central America, and endorsed 'an independent and non-aligned approach to foreign policy relations with all
countries'.[7] Moreover, at the conference, it was reported that placards
were displayed reading 'Cato next', a reference to Milton Cato's government in St Vincent, where left-wing forces were gathering their
strength. A vocal radical group also existed in Antigua, and it did seem
for a time as if further moves to the left could be effected in these
other islands. It was in this atmosphere that US State Department
spokesmen began to talk of the Caribbean as 'a sea of splashing domi-
noes'.

In reality, such fears were misplaced. In Dominica, in October 1979,
following the devastation caused by Hurricane David, Seraphine dismissed Martin and Douglas from his government, saying that he had

been constantly embarrassed by their 'communistic ideas' and that the international donors who were helping in the reconstruction of Dominica were anxious to know the ideological position of the country. Seraphine's government subsequently displayed no hint of radicalism and was defeated in elections in July 1980 by the conservative Dominica Freedom Party. In St Lucia an unseemly internal quarrel broke out in the government between Louisy and Odlum over the former's failure to honour an apparent pre-election agreement to take up the position of Governor-General so as to allow Odlum to become prime minister. The administration utterly failed to live up to its radical promise and resorted to almost incessant feuding, conceding power to Compton once more in elections in May 1982. In St Vincent and Antigua, furthermore, elections came and went in 1979 and 1980 respectively with left-wing groups failing to win a single seat in either country. Although they may perhaps be said to have laid the foundations for a later and more substantive challenge to the ruling order in their territories, it was clear that whatever 'left-wing tide' the United States thought was flowing through the Eastern Caribbean had for the moment subsided.

Suriname: Revolutionary Military Government

The next country in the region to break its traditional pattern of politics was the former Dutch territory of Suriname, where in February 1980 a military coup took place, overthrowing the existing elected government of Henck Arron. Suriname had had a difficult introduction to independence. In the two years prior to 1975 there had taken place a remarkable exodus of people to the Netherlands, involving over a third of the population and robbing the new state of indispensable administrative and managerial skills. By the end of the decade Arron's government seemed to have lost the ability to act, let alone foster development. It was riddled with nepotism, deeply divided on ethnic lines and possessed a majority of only one in Parliament. Social and economic conditions in the country deteriorated and the government's unpopularity grew. For more than a year before the coup, there had been discontent in the country's small army over pay, promotions and the demand for recognition of a soldier's trade union. The climax came when the leaders of the union were brought to court charged with mutiny. Before a verdict could be given, the rebel soldiers moved: they freed their colleagues, arrested Arron and his Cabinet and established a nine-member National Military Council (NMC). The average age of the rebels was 30 and the rank typically that of sergeant. Few had any previous political experience. They had no clear programme, talking only vaguely in terms of 'breaking down the old structures holding the country back', and chose instead to pass the task of government to a new interim administration, headed by a surgeon of Chinese extraction, Henk Chin-a-Sen. His Cabinet was composed mainly of civil servants, doctors and lawyers, carefully chosen to reflect the complicated racial structure of the country and the soldiers' hostility to corruption, but still broadly representative of Suriname's traditional bureaucratic establishment. The left had only a token presence and thus, at best, the initial effect of the coup was to replace a right-wing with a centrist government. The moderate political character of the new regime seemed to be confirmed in August 1980, when one of the members of the NMC, Sergeant-Major Daysi Bouterse, arrested several of his colleagues, including the chairman of the council, on the grounds that they were plotting a Communist take-over allegedly with the help of Cuba. As a result of this internal coup, and the accompanying suspension of Parliament, Bouterse emerged as the new 'strong man' of the military government.

Since then, the course of military rule in Suriname has been unpredictable. At the beginning of March 1981, close to the first anniversary of the coup, Bouterse surprised everybody by announcing that three of the accused left-wing soldiers had been freed and rehabilitated as 'allies of the first hour' of the military government. That was not all: Bouterse went on to speak of the emergence of a new sense of direction in the NMC, declaring that the country would henceforth follow a clear socialist path. He ended his statement with this ringing peroration – 'long live Socialism! long live the revolutionary process! long live the Suriname revolution! Suriname will win!'[8] Even before this dramatic declaration, some signs had existed of a move to the left by the regime. Relations between Suriname and Cuba were good enough for the former to be officially represented at a congress of the Cuban Communist Party and for non-resident diplomatic ties to be established between the two countries. In reality, though, Bouterse had promised more than he could immediately deliver. On the international scene, he associated Suriname with the Non-Aligned Movement and in July 1981 attended a Socialist International meeting in Grenada, but at home it was clear that the struggle for the future ideological direction of the country was still being vigorously pursued. Quite apart from alleged counter-coup attempts, for which the regime had constantly to be on the alert, many of the civilian elements in Chin-a-Sen's government were dubious about the proclamation of socialism. They were reluctant to break with the West, in particular the Netherlands which had already showed itself ready to use the provision of a large US $1.8 billion aid programme to its former colony as a means of bringing pressure to bear upon the soldiers. Moreover, Chin-a-Sen was concerned to push ahead with the preparation of a new constitution and the holding of elections. In the face of these obstacles and in the absence of any effective grass-roots political organisation which could sustain the revolutionary process, Bouterse found himself unable to make much headway in bringing about radical change in the domestic sphere. Proposals to enable the government to assume more effective control of the country's natural resources and to establish better health care and wider educational provision were advanced, but only limited success was achieved in implementation.

The growing frustration of the left at its inability to take full control of events in Suriname led to a new and even more bitter power struggle within the country. A Revolutionary People's Front, composed of trade unions, progressive parties, student and farmers' organisations, intellectuals and military cadres, was established in December 1981 as a means of sustaining the regime's left-wing policies, and Chin-a-Sen himself was dismissed two months later. In reply, the Dutch suspended aid talks and the right in the country provoked an unsuccessful counter-coup, the leader of which was subsequently executed by the government. Anti-regime strikes and demonstrations greeted the arrival of Maurice Bishop on an official visit in October 1982, and a further counter-coup was attempted just before the end of the year. The government reacted to this in a violent fashion, killing at least 20 of its most prominent opponents and, in so doing, drawing upon itself international condemnation. In short, the Suriname revolution has developed into a bloody fight for survival. After three years Bouterse has few results to show for his efforts to develop socialism. He has been preoccupied with the internal struggle within the government and has gradually lost the support which was fairly widely given to the original seizure of power. A conservative 'liberation council', led by former prime minister Chin-a-Sen, now exists in the Netherlands to organise the continuing campaign against the beleaguered military government.

Guadeloupe and Martinique: the Growth of Nationalism

There was also some signs of a growth of nationalism in the French island territories of Guadeloupe and Martinique. Since they were established as 'départements' of France in 1946, the people of these territories have traditionally been content to enjoy the benefits of their close association with the home country. Compared with the other islands of the Eastern Caribbean, average per-capita income is high, education free and compulsory up to the age of 16, welfare benefits quite extensive and the development of the infrastructure of a modern economy impressive. In this environment, it was for a long time almost impossible to arouse any dissent against French rule. The radio carried virtually no news of the rest of the Caribbean and most local political parties, even socialist ones, were strongly tied to their counterparts in metropolitan France. In short, the pressure to assimilate and, if necessary, emigrate to France was overwhelming. Aime Césaire, the left-wing mayor of Fort-de-France in Martinique and founder of the Parti Progressiste Martiniquais (PPM), put it well in observing that 'French West Indians have sold their souls against a full stomach'.[9]

However, helped by economic stagnation and growing unemployment in the 1970s, the message of the new Caribbean radicalism at last began to be heard. By the end of the decade, discussion of the possibility of independence was taking place openly in Guadeloupe and Martinique. A series of bombings in Guadeloupe, beginning in March 1980 and lasting over a year, drew further attention to the case for independence. They were carried out by the Groupe de Libération Armé (GLA) and were directed against French property and personnel on the island. The violence was condemned by other more nationalist or left-wing parties in Guadeloupe, who preferred to fight their cause by more peaceful methods, but it unquestionably served to draw the French government's attention to the sort of problems that were developing in their Caribbean colonies.

The bulk of the population remained, and still remains, generally unsympathetic to the independence movement, voting predominantly for ex-President Giscard d'Estaing in the French presidential elections of May 1981. Yet the rate of abstention in voting was as high as 60 per cent in Guadeloupe, and not much less in Martinique. This scarcely indicates a very high level of support for the current political arrangements of the islands and has been taken by the new government of President Mitterrand as a sign that some steps must be taken to bring about greater autonomy in the government of Guadeloupe and

Martinique. It has proposed a decentralisation plan which has been well received for the most part by the left. The PPM in Martinique, for example, resolved to drop the issue of the political status of the island in the light of the Mitterrand proposals. The scheme, however, has been aggressively opposed by the local whites, who control the island economies through their plantations and import/export businesses and are hostile to any thought that their power might be eroded by slackening of ties with France, even a socialist-dominated France. For the moment, therefore, the independence issue, which came to the fore for a while in 1980–1, has been diverted into a debate about the powers to be given to new assemblies that are to be established in the two islands.

Haiti: Mass Asylum

Haiti fits into the emergent pattern of change and instability in the Caribbean a little differently. It is the poorest and most underdeveloped country in the Western hemisphere, possessing a combined rate of unemployment and underemployment of some 80 per cent, an illiteracy level of 85 per cent, a mortality rate of 50 per cent for children up to the age of 4 years old and a 40 per cent rate of homelessness. Despite such appalling and long-existent social and economic conditions, the dictatorship of the Duvalier family has lasted over a quarter of a century and still does not face any real threat to its power. There seems no prospect of a revolutionary overthrow of the government or even the emergence of a sustained insurgency campaign. An undercurrent of violence, the occasional bombing and some protests on the streets are all that exist by way of opposition. Anything more substantive is inhibited by the repressive apparatus of the regime, including the infamous 'Tontons Macoutes'. Unlike other parts of the Caribbean, Haitian politics have definitely not been characterised in the 1970s by a move to the left or a flirtation with socialism.

Yet, in this period, the country's political system generated an unusual crisis which greatly added to the instability of the Caribbean. It concerned migration. For nearly a century Haitians have migrated in great numbers to the Dominican Republic, where they have traditionally cut cane on the large sugar plantations, working in brutal and dehumanising conditions. More recently, they have fled to the Bahamas, where it is estimated that some 25,000 Haitians now reside, representing a tenth of the population of those islands, to the French West Indies and, increasingly, to the United States, the most obvious magnet in the hemisphere for poor and oppressed people. However, in contrast to the ease with which Cubans, Indo-Chinese and other peoples fleeing communist regimes have gained asylum in the United States, the Haitians encountered difficulty after difficulty. The official assumption was that the former were political refugees who were worthy of support for reasons of international politics, the latter merely economic refugees who should be deported back to their place of origin. Though admitting that 'Haiti has a long history of authoritarian rule . . . and the most serious types of human rights abuses', the State Department's view was that 'determination of a particular asylum claim . . . is not a general referendum on human rights in the home country'.[10] Instead, the question that had to be asked was: 'does this particular individual have a "well-founded fear of persecution" based on race, religion, nationality, membership in a particular social group or political opinion if he or she were to return to the home country?'[11] The United States maintained that returning Haitians were not persecuted and accordingly refused most requests for asylum from Haitians. In short, the deteriorating social and economic conditions in Haiti were insulated from international attention.

However, the situation changed dramatically in 1980. In July 1979, the US District Court for Southern Florida ruled in a case brought by the Haitian Refugee Centre that Haitians were denied due process of law by the US Immigration and Naturalisation Service and ordered that no Haitian claiming political asylum in the United States should be deported. The same court subsequently judged that poverty in Haiti was indeed a function of the political system, a result of the Duvalier family's efforts to maintain power. In 1979, the government of the Bahamas also announced its intention to begin deporting all illegal Haitian immigrants on the islands. Prompted by these two events and the growing distress of the economy, an extraordinary exodus of Haitians to the southern shores of the United States took place during the spring and summer of 1980. They numbered approximately 11,000, travelling in overcrowded and flimsy sailing boats. Many died on the way, most arrived exhausted. The problem was the more serious for the US government because it coincided with the Mariel boat lift, the huge exodus of Cubans to the United States, in April of that year. In the light of the new court order, the government had to take responsibility for the arrivals, housing them at considerable cost in a number of detention camps up and down the country and in Puerto Rico, the unpleasant conditions of which in turn aroused criticism on humanitarian grounds.

In this grim fashion, underdevelopment and political tension in the Caribbean was literally brought home to the US government. On coming to office, the Reagan administration took a tough line, reaching an agreement with the Duvalier regime that allowed the US coastguard to intercept and return to Haiti the seemingly endless convoys of boats carrying people trying to get away from the destitution in which most Haitians lived. The aim was to unload the refugee problem upon the Haitian government itself, in return for which the United States promised increased aid, economic assistance and general political support. It also insisted that a genuine effort be made to reform the corrupt system of government in Haiti and urged the appointment of a former World Bank official, Marc Bazin, as Minister of Finance. Bazin set about house-cleaning, but quickly came into conflict with the entrenched financial interests of President Duvalier's own family and was dismissed in July 1982, after a mere five months in office. From the US point of view, the deployment of patrol boats off the northern coast of Haiti stems the inflow of refugees in the short term. However, US efforts to engender reform and greater economic development in Haiti have not succeeded and do not appear likely to do so. As a result, the underlying problem which gave rise to the mass asylum crisis has been left to fester and worsen.

Belize: the Attainment of Independence

Belize has long been something of a special case within the Caribbean. Situated on the Central American mainland, divided ethically between Creole and Mestizo elements, it has remained aloof from many of the main trends in Caribbean politics. It was granted internal self-government in 1964, only to find its independence subsequently delayed — to British irritation as much as Belizean — by the threats of invasion of neighbouring Guatemala, if full sovereignty was granted before the settlement of a long-standing border dispute. Successive Guatemalan governments have claimed a large part of Belizean territory on the grounds that Britain failed to honour a commitment given in a treaty in 1859 to build a secure access to the Caribbean Sea for Guatemala. The territory's premier, George Price, worked laboriously for many years to bring about a solution to the problem, but achieved no success until the mid-1970s, when the changing political situation in the Caribbean, and more particularly in Central America, began to create diplomatic opportunities that he could exploit. Urged on by two able socialists, Assad Shoman and Said Musa, whom he had taken into his Cabinet in the 1970s, Price sought to internationalise the dispute in an effort to win the support of uninvolved countries for Belize's cause. He did not shy away from accepting the help of socialist governments, such as that of Cuba, or left-wing Caribbean allies such as Jamaica under Manley and Grenada after the revolution.

This diplomacy was rewarded by the steady collapse of international support for Guatemala's claim, especially in Central America. The revolutionary Sandinista regime, which overthrew the Somoza dictatorship in Nicaragua in July 1979 and which was carefully courted by Price, came out openly in Belize's favour; Panama and Venuezela also gave up their defence of Guatemala's position and Mexico reiterated earlier support for Belize. Because of its long-standing support for the resolutely anti-Communist government of Guatemala, the attitude of the United States administration was critical. Even though under President Carter relations with Guatemala cooled and arms sales were stopped, the US remained suspicious of Price and his party, fearing that an independent Belize could become a Cuban foothold in Central America, a belief openly encouraged by opposition groups in Belize who feared independence under the leadership of Price. In a UN vote on Belizean independence in November 1979, the United States therefore abstained. Only at the beginning of 1981, when the crisis in El Salvador was at its height, did it finally accede to Belize's imminent independence. It did not want another Central American problem at that moment and was already perhaps thinking of Belize's potential as a base, not only with respect to the situation in El Salvador, but also in connection with the growing strength of left-wing guerrillas in Guatemala itself. Despite the fact that, at the last moment, Guatemala reneged upon a compromise settlement agreed with Britain and Belize, Belize at last became formally independent in September 1981, although it was still protected by a British garrison.

The whole ideological spectrum of Caribbean politics was represented at the celebrations: from Cubans to Americans. Price has been considerably radicalised by the dispute and the left in his government consistently urge him to establish close relations with Cuba and to align the country generally with progressive forces in Central America and the Caribbean. Yet Guatemala's continuing claim upon Belizean territory cannot be forgotten. Aware of Britain's keenness to withdraw its troops, Price, to the anger of such as Shoman and Musa, signed a military agreement with the United States shortly after independence and entered into secret talks on the possibility of a US airbase being established in Belize and US troops being stationed there, ostensibly for 'jungle training'. For the present, Belize treads a careful path, adopting a stance on the international issues confronting the region which Price calls 'middle of the road', but which is nevertheless a long way from the overarching conservatism of all political opinion in Belize in the 1960s.

Dominican Republic: a Shift to the Left

In 1982, the current of opinion shifting Caribbean politics to the left reached even the Dominican Republic. To some extent the ground was laid for this four years earlier, when Antonio Guzman, the candidate of the moderate Partio Revolucionario Dominicano (PRD), was elected president in succession to the very conservative figure of Joaquin Balaguer, an associate of the former dictator, Rafael Trujillo. When the early results showed the PRD in the lead, the army threatened to intervene and were only dissuaded from doing so by the sharply expressed disapproval of President Carter and the US government. Despite promising land reform, Guzman — himself a prosperous cattle rancher — made slow progress in breaking up the large holdings, such as those of the US multinational, Gulf and Western, which characterise the agricultural sector in the Dominican Republic. There grew dissatisfaction within some parts of the PRD at the performance of the administration, focusing in particular on its failure to bring about substantial improvement in the living standards of urban workers and peasants, its inability to stem inflation and reduce unemployment and its alleged personal nepotism.

The discontent came to a head in 1980 when, with dollar reserves at their lowest level in recorded history and the economy as a whole in a crisis, it became clear that Guzman intended to renege on a party commitment to amend the constitution to prohibit presidential re-election in order to run for office again himself. The internal opposition to this was so strong that Guzman was forced to back down, leaving the party a choice for presidential candidate in the 1982 election between the existing Vice-President, Jacobo Majluta, and the former party President, Salvador Jorge Blanco, who was Guzman's rival for the nomination in 1978. Majluta was an economist with close links with US business interests, whereas Jorge Blanco was the leader of the PRD's left wing and was well respected in such bodies as the Socialist International. In an unprecedented exercise in intra-party democracy in the Dominican Republic, Jorge Blanco was selected by a clear majority of grass-roots party members.

The 1982 election took place against a background of growing social tension provoked by the government's helplessness in the face of the deteriorating condition of the economy. Unemployment, already some 25 per cent, was growing; thousands of peasants were staging land occupations in the south of the country; a number of strikes were being threatened; and demonstrations against rising bus fares were broken up by the police. In this situation, Jorge Blanco's chief rivals for the presidency were former President Balaguer, the candidate of the conservative Partido Reformista (PR), who by this time was advanced in age, in ill health and nearly blind, and another former president, Juan Bosch, the candidate of the socialist Partido de la Liberacion Dominicana (PLD). Bosch was the first post-Trujillo elected president, governing for seven months in 1963 until his overthrow by a military coup which led to civil war and US military intervention in 1965. Against these two representatives of the past conflicts of modern Dominican political history, Jorge Blanco, who is himself best characterised as a social democrat, ran an effective populist campaign. His long-term objectives were defined in ambitious terms: to embark on the elimination of poverty, to reduce unemployment, to improve housing conditions. Land reform was included, although it was to consist mainly of settling small-holders on parcels of state land, rather than breaking up large estates. Indeed, a pledge was given not to nationalise Gulf and Western. In foreign affairs Jorge Blanco's programme backed peace, non-intervention and friendly co-operation with all countries, although it was unspecific on the question of establishing diplomatic relations with Cuba.

During the campaign, some observers argued that the PLD would be the principal beneficiary of dissatisfaction with the Guzman government. But Jorge Blanco had been successful in his efforts to disassociate himself from the conservative wing of his own party and emerged the winner, polling 46.7 per cent of the vote, compared with 39.1 per cent for Balaguer and 9.8 per cent for Bosch. Jorge Blanco is no radical. He has already shown himself reluctant to confront the powerful vested interests in industry and agriculture that stand in the way of a solution to the grievous social and economic problems of the Dominican Republic. Yet he is perhaps the most committed reformist to have won power in the country for nearly two decades and he may find that hopes of change, once aroused, cannot be easily or quickly stilled.

Summary

The changes which have taken place in Caribbean politics in the ten years since 1973 have clearly altered the face of the region. Contrary to the over-simplistic interpretations popular in the West, they have not all derived from the inspiration of ideology and they certainly do not represent a simple victory for Communism, socialism or any other variant of left-wing thinking. The old foundations of Caribbean politics and government have undoubtedly been shaken, but the pattern produced is diverse and complex. What really characterises the region is a sense of 'groping about' for some better alternative than the traditional policies of the past. The phrase may be inelegant, but it does accurately describe the indecision which beset the various governments. Under the pressure of the economic crisis that began in 1973-4, there was set in motion a search for any possible option that might lead to more sustained economic development than had been previously achieved, no matter where and in connection with whom it might be found. In this search, many Caribbean countries were led in new directions and made new friends. In particular, as the validity of the orthodox model of free enterprise was increasingly questioned in a variety of countries, so the West's wider political influence over the region similarly came to be called into doubt. Several powers were alert to the situation and began to try to assert their influence on the region's development. The Caribbean has thus become an arena of international competition between a range of regional and extra-regional powers whose policies the remaining chapters of this work now aim to explore.

Notes

1. For a fuller discussion, see A.J. Payne, *Change in the Commonwealth Caribbean* (Royal Institute of International Affairs, London, 1981), pp. 47-8.
2. C.Y. Thomas, 'Guyana: The Rise and Fall of "Cooperative Socialism" ' in A.J. Payne and P.K. Sutton (eds.), *Dependency under Challange: The Political Economy of the Commonwealth Caribbean* (Manchester University Press, Manchester, 1984), p. 100.
3. M. Manley, *The Politics of Change: A Jamaican Testament* (André Deutsch, London, 1974), p. 17.
4. Ibid., p. 18.
5. *Caribbean Contact* (Bridgetown), April 1980.
6. *New Jewel*, vol. 2, no. 11 (13 March 1980), p. 5.
7. 'The Declaration of St Georges', *Bulletin of Eastern Caribbean Affairs*, vol. 5, no. 3 (1979), pp. 32-4.
8. *Caribbean Contact*, April 1981.

9. Ibid., July 1981.
10. Testimony of Stephen E. Palmer, Jr, Deputy Assistant Secretary of State for Human Rights and Humanitarian Affairs, before the Subcommittee on Immigration, Refugees and International Law of the House of Representatives Judiciary Committee on 17 June 1980, cited in G.D. Loescher and J. Scanlan, ' "Mass Asylum" and US Policy in the Caribbean', *The World Today*, vol. 37, no. 10 (1981), p. 390.
11. Ibid.

3 UNITED STATES: DECLINE AND REASSERTION OF HEGEMONY

The most obvious feature of the international politics of the Caribbean over the last decade has been the decline of the traditional hegemony of the United States over the region. In general terms, of course, it is the case that in the aftermath of Vietnam and Watergate, and in the midst of the continuing world economic recession, the existing hierarchical order characterised by the predominance of the United States has been seriously threatened all over the world. In this respect, what has happened in the Caribbean has been no more than part of a wider process. Viewed against the past, however, the challenge to the authority of the United States appears especially marked in its own 'backyard'. The emergence of competition for power in an area such as the Caribbean undoubtedly constituted a major loss of influence for the United States. In the last few years, however, successive US administrations have sought, by a variety of methods, to restore their country's traditional dominance over the region. For this reason, therefore, discussion of the various powers competing for influence in the Caribbean must still begin with the United States itself.

United States' Interests in the Caribbean

As in other parts of the globe, perceptions of US interests in the Caribbean have changed over time. They have been affected by changes on the ground in the region, differing interpretations of global trends, developments in American public opinion and variations in the relative power of presidents and other policy-makers, both within and between administrations. Yet, from every perspective, US interests in the area have been seen to be extensive and at all times, including the present, they have been treated with importance by Washington. They can be divided into the following four overlapping categories — political, strategic, economic and human interests.

Political Interests

US interests in the Caribbean are primarily political, understood in the widest sense of the term. They embrace the fact that the United States

35

possesses two 'semi-colonies' in the region, Puerto Rico and the US Virgin Islands, but extend well beyond this consideration to a concern with the political direction of the entire Caribbean area, and indeed beyond that to the hemisphere as a whole. Since the days of the Monroe Doctrine, the United States has regarded itself as the leader of the countries of the Western hemisphere and is viewed as such by other world powers.[1] It perceives its own standing as a great power and its credibility in the eyes of the Soviet Union to be dependent upon its ability to maintain and demonstrate control of its own hemispheric community. In official eyes, any weakening of this political control reduces Soviet perceptions of US strength, weakens European and NATO perceptions of US leadership and undermines the Third World's faith in the Western model of development. Much therefore hangs upon US dominance of the Western hemisphere, including the Caribbean, which is deemed to be one of the core elements of the system.

On this basis, US governments have long interested themselves in the internal political affairs of all the countries of the Caribbean. Their main concern has been to secure the emergence of pro-American governments, which can then be defended in the interests of political stability. There have been times when particular administrations have tried to encourage the growth of freedom and representative democracy in the Caribbean, but these have been outweighed by frequent instances of US support for oligarchic or dictatorial regimes which align themselves diplomatically with American interests. On several occasions, too, in situations of conflict US governments have intervened, militarily and by other means, in the politics of Caribbean states in order to ensure the outcome they have desired.[2]

From this perspective, the presence of a Soviet-backed Communist regime in Cuba, just 90 miles from the southern tip of Florida, is the most profound irritant to the United States. It represents an undeniable and highly visible breach of hemispheric solidarity which successive US governments over the last twenty years have feared might gnaw away at US credibility the world over. In the early days of the Cuban revolution, attempts were made to bring the regime down, and if US policy has of late come to accept the reality of Cuba's position in the hemisphere, it has definitely not tolerated what it has seen as active Cuban efforts to subvert other governments in the Caribbean in favour of Communist alternatives. As such, United States concern about the political stability of the Caribbean is greater at present than for some time.

Strategic Interests

Strategically, the Caribbean's proximity to the United States has long given it a unique position in US national security considerations. It constitutes the vulnerable southern flank of the land area of the United States itself. Although it might be argued that in the nuclear age this is a less relevant consideration than in previous eras, the military import- ance of the Caribbean to the United States should not be under- estimated. The US possesses major bases at Guantanamo Bay in Cuba, Fort Buchanan and Roosevelt Roads in Puerto Rico, and in the Panama Canal zone, quite apart from several smaller air and naval installations throughout the region. A variety of military testing and training activities take place which would be costly and, in some cases, impos- sible to move, and communications and surveillance facilities have been established in several territories, particularly in the Eastern Caribbean. In addition, the US Navy's Atlantic Undersea Test and Evaluation Center in the Bahamas is critical to the development of American anti- submarine warfare capabilities. In terms of the deployment of military hardware, therefore, the Caribbean is of obvious value to the United States.

However, the region is of strategic importance in another sense too. It is a vital maritime route for a whole range of valuable commodities and raw materials coming to the United States from Guatemala, Venezuela and the Caribbean islands, as well as for all sea-going vessels approaching the Panama Canal. The importance of this is not always realised. Former US ambassador to Barbados, Sally Shelton, felt it necessary in a speech in 1980 to remind her audience that more petroleum passes through the Caribbean each day than the Straits of Hormuz.[3] It is mainly in this light that the US views with concern the military presence which the Soviet Union enjoys in the Caribbean, courtesy of Cuba. The fear relates not so much to the possibility of Soviet or Cuban aggression against the US mainland, for nuclear missiles were removed from Cuba in 1962 and neither the Cuban navy or ground forces are sufficiently powerful seriously to endanger the defence of the United States.[4] Rather, it is the threat to supply lines and communications more generally which worries the US govern- ment, especially since the Soviet Union began to expand its naval presence in the Caribbean during the course of the 1970s. The Soviets are able to use modern docking facilities in Cuba, including the sub- marine base at Cienfuegos, from which it is possible that they might — in one rather extreme scenario — attempt to disrupt the flow of oil and other strategically important minerals to the United States.[5]

Economic Interests

US economic interests in the Caribbean are not insignificant, but they count for less in American perspectives than the region's wider political importance. US investment in the area has been estimated at US \$2 billion, but has declined in relative size as Caribbean governments have more and more taken controlling interests in US-owned enterprises. US exports to the Caribbean consist mainly of manufactured goods, but since the region is basically poor, demand for such products remains limited. It is the presence of vital minerals which gives the Caribbean its main economic significance to the United States. Their availability so close at hand represents an undoubted convenience, even if it is the case that the region is far from being the only source of such raw materials. Of the minerals found in the Caribbean, bauxite is the most important to the United States, as nearly 50 per cent of US bauxite imports now comes from Jamaica and some of the rest from other Caribbean countries. In addition, oil is important, since over 50 per cent of US imports are refined in the area from Middle Eastern and African crude. The Caribbean became a major oil-refining area in the 1950s, owing to its useful location between important sources of supply and the huge US market, its deep water anchorages, its cheap labour and its then colonial status. Even after independence, US multinational corporations have been able to extract highly profitable deals from small island governments desperate for some form of economic growth. The Caribbean is not a major producer of oil itself, only Trinidad having substantial reserves, but a considerable amount of exploration is taking place in Suriname, Barbados, the Dominican Republic and Guyana amongst other places. With the rise in oil prices and developments in offshore deep drilling techniques, it is becoming increasingly viable to exploit the potential reserves of the Caribbean. This is likely to lead to the deepening of US economic interests in the region in future and, by extension, to a greater concern, even than at present, with the policies adopted by regional governments towards foreign investment and the foreign ownership of local resources.

Human Interests

The United States also has a human stake in the Caribbean, based on the impact of regional developments on the lives of individual Americans and US communities. Hundreds of thousands of American citizens live, work and, in particular, take holidays in the Caribbean. At the same time, as many citizens of the Caribbean live, work, visit or study in the United States, and an increasing number seek to make it their permanent home. In fact, almost 20 per cent of the population of the Caribbean in 1945 has now emigrated from the region, many, if not most, to the United States. Thus, in a sense, it can be said that the United States is becoming a Caribbean nation. In recent years the US government has also been particularly worried by the massive illegal influx of Caribbean refugees, largely, although not exclusively, from Haiti and Cuba, driven to American shores by economic or political desperation. This has undoubtedly imposed severe social as well as economic problems on cities like Miami, where the new immigrants have tended to congregate. The State of Florida, for example, spends more money on hospital services for Haitians who have arrived illegally than the US spends on foreign aid to Haiti. In response, attempts have been made to tighten up immigration requirements and increase the number of patrols off the southern coast of the United States. However, these are viewed only as short-term expedients which do not get to the source of the problem, namely, the condition of Caribbean society. The United States thus sees the growing scale of migration of Caribbean peoples to America as a further reason for its involvement in regional affairs, and one which bears directly and immediately on the quality of American life.

The Traditional Hegemonic Approach

From the point of view of the United States, the Caribbean has always been a very secure region. Since the end of the Spanish–American war in 1898, it has lived under effective US hegemony. Until the Second World War, the United States shared certain responsibilities in the area with the European powers, but they were steadily forced to concede economic supremacy to the United States and generally maintained little military capability in the region, certainly not sufficient to challenge the United States. European interests were primarily in other parts of the world, and thus the defence of the Caribbean was left largely to the care of the United States.[6] The British concession to the United States of a number of military bases in its Caribbean territories in 1940 in exchange for the supply of a number of out-of-date destroyers further reinforced this dominance.

In the period after 1945, US supremacy was unquestionable. The decimation of both enemy and allied forces in the war meant that US military power in the region could not conceivably be challenged. Economically, all the European powers were exhausted and unable even to re-establish many of their long-standing commercial ties with the area. The Soviet Union was only beginning to develop the position of a world power and, until the Cuban revolution, had no interest in or connection with any state in the Caribbean, beyond the formal establishment of fraternal relations with the small number of official Communist parties. Within the region itself, nationalist politics were developing only slowly, and mostly via constitutional means. In these circumstances, the United States became rather over-confident of its hold upon the Caribbean. US attention turned away from the area and focused on such questions as the balance of power in Europe and the Middle East and the political problems of South-East Asia.

Only during the 1960s, following the emergence of the Soviet Union as a rival to American world supremacy, did US policy-makers pay any sustained attention to the Caribbean — and then only in a 'cold war' context. Their own perceptions of the nature and significance of US hegemony over the Caribbean led them to see any challenge to the political *status quo* in the region as the consequence of Communist subversion. This attitude derived from a general view of international relations, but was given additional sustenance in the Caribbean by the revolution in Cuba in 1959 and the territory's subsequent close alliance with the Soviet Union. In the years immediately following this event, the United States claimed to see new 'Cubas' appearing all over the Caribbean and responded in the traditional way of hegemonic powers — by intervention in the affairs of the offending state.

In this period, three cases of US intervention in the Caribbean stand out. The first concerned Cuba itself and involved a series of nefarious CIA operations aimed to bring down the Castro regime, including the disastrous 'Bay of Pigs' invasion of Cuba by US-sponsored Cuban exiles in April 1961. The second instance of intervention was less overt. It took place in Guyana in 1963/4, when American trade union and CIA influence was used to foment dissent against the elected Marxist government of Cheddi Jagan. The third was in many ways the most dramatic of all, the invasion of the Dominican Republic by 20,000 US marines in 1965 for fear that the return to power of a moderate nationalist government under the leadership of Juan Bosch would open the way to Communist take-over. In a nationwide broadcast President Johnson made no attempt to hide the thinking that lay behind the invasion. 'The American nations', he said, 'cannot, must not, and will not permit the establishment of another Communist government in the Western hemisphere'.[7] As far as he was concerned, this was an entirely legitimate aim, consistent with the division of the world into competing spheres of

US and Soviet influence. This narrow perspective completely dominated US hemispheric policy in the 1960s and allowed no other considerations to affect the nature of the relationship of the United States with the Caribbean or any other sub-region within the hemisphere.

During the Nixon–Kissinger–Ford era, as détente began to replace the cold war as the determining framework of American foreign policy, US attitudes to change in the Caribbean softened somewhat, but still did not develop to the point where a coherent policy for the region was thought out and followed. Towards Cuba, a policy of 'low-intensity containment', rather than active subversion, was increasingly adopted.[8] Political and economic isolation were conceived as means to make the cost of maintaining the Soviet alliance too expensive for Cuba to continue. Towards the rest of the Caribbean, *ad hoc* responses were made in the face of situations which were deemed to threaten US interests. In some cases, these were supportive of regional governments: the US was ready to display naval support for the government of Trinidad in 1970, when it was challenged by a black power movement. In others, they were designed to bring pressure to bear upon radical political tendencies: the US, for example, sought in the mid-1970s to persuade the Manley government in Jamaica to moderate both its campaign against US-owned bauxite companies operating in that territory and its generally pro-Cuban, pro-Third World foreign policy. The approach adopted was more subtle than in the past and, above all, was covert in character. In a recent account of his period in office, Manley himself has given a revealing description of a meeting with Kissinger during a short vacation spent by the Secretary of State in Jamaica towards the end of 1975. 'Suddenly he raised the question of Angola and said he would appreciate it if Jamaica would at least remain neutral on the subject of the Cuban army presence in Angola. I told him that I could make no promises but would pay the utmost attention to his request.'[9] Kissinger then apparently brought up the separate matter of a Jamaican request for a US $100 million trade credit. 'He said they were looking at it, and let the comment hang in the room for a moment. I had a feeling he was sending me a message'.[10] These were very different tactics from those that the US was prepared to employ in the 1960s. It is important to remember, of course, that in the latter part of this period the whole of American foreign policy was being subordinated to the internal and external effects of Watergate and the failure of the Vietnam adventure. The crisis concerning the ethics of intervention by the United States was at its height in 1975 and 1976. As one Caribbean foreign affairs analyst pointed out, 'one need only compare the

debates in the American Congress then with the sense of confidence
and legitimacy with which Arthur Schlesinger writes of the American
determination of the nature of the Guyanese regime in 1964 to get a
sense of the difference in political climates'.[11] What had changed here,
however, was more a perception of US ability to act in the Caribbean
than the long-standing and deeply entrenched view of the region's
subservient place in the US hemispheric system. In general, Washington
still paid relatively little attention to a region that, on the surface,
appeared secure.

Post-Vietnam Revisionism

Nevertheless, the collective impact of Watergate and, in particular,
Vietnam did in time set in train a broader reappraisal of the basis of
American policy amongst the foreign policy establishment. A number
of important lessons were drawn – that the 'cold war' era was past; that
concern with Communism should no longer be an obsessive preoccupation; that overt and forceful intervention in the affairs of other nations
was immoral and ought to be replaced by greater respect for the
national autonomy of all states; that the United States ought never
again to place itself on the 'wrong side of history' by supporting foreign
autocrats against popular movements of reform; and that, in the most
general sense, US national interests ought to be associated more openly
with universal or globalist goals like 'development', 'fairness' and the
pursuit of 'human rights'.

These revisionist sentiments were well expressed by Zbigniew
Brzezinski, whose book, *Between Two Ages*, spelled out their implications for US policy towards the Western hemisphere in general and the
Caribbean in particular. Brzezinski argued that the traditional hegemonic approach was inappropriate to the changed reality of declining
ideological competition, declining nationalism, increased global interdependence and rising Third World expectations. In his view, the
United States should review the priority it had long attached to anti-
Communism and hemispheric security. It should instead concede that
'in the new global age', geographical contiguity 'no longer need be
politically decisive', should adopt a 'more detached attitude towards
revolutionary processes' and take an 'increasingly depoliticised approach'
to aid and trade.[12] In sum, Brzezinski rejected the old 'spheres of
influence' approach to international politics and favoured the adoption
of a global strategy for the management of interdependence.

His arguments were further elaborated in two reports issued in 1974 and 1976 by the so-called Commission on United States–Latin American Relations, headed by Sol Linowitz. They reiterated the globalist framework outlined by Brzezinski and argued that the US approach to Latin America should in future be free of paternalism, respectful of sovereignty and tolerant of political and economic diversity. Several specific recommendations then followed from these assumptions. They included renegotiation of the Panama Canal Treaties, the liberalisation of trade and the multilateralisation of aid, the promotion of human rights and the abandonment of military intervention as a weapon of hegemonic assertion. Indeed, it was argued by Linowitz that, in the light of détente, the United States should 'keep local and regional conflicts outside the context of the super power relationship' and no longer 'automatically' see 'revolutions in other countries and intra-regional conflicts . . . as battlefields of the cold war'.[13] Despite the Commission's commitment to globalism, it did recognise that Cuba was a special problem in the context of US policy towards the hemisphere. It urged the normalisation of relations with Cuba and the strict control of anti-Castro activities on the North American mainland, but at the same time it suggested that the United States would be bound, in turn, to require certain concessions from Cuba promising restraint in its foreign policy before this process could be fully developed.

In this last respect, it could be said that traditional considerations of national security did remain a part of the new foreign policy revisionism. They had, however, undoubtedly been redefined in a way that cast moral doubt upon the previously unquestioned presumption of US hegemony over the Caribbean and the hemisphere as a whole. The old belief that what was good for the United States was good for the world had been neatly reversed: universal moral values were to be the new determinant of American foreign policy.

Carter the Liberal

These ideas had already begun to have some impact on United States foreign policy towards the end of the Kissinger–Ford era, but they came into their own under the presidency of Jimmy Carter. They were consonant with Carter's political image as an honest family man and closely reflected his own instinctively moralist approach to international relations. Brzezinski himself was appointed the President's National Security Adviser, Cyrus Vance, a former director of the

Council on Foreign Relations, which had also been centrally involved in the post-Vietnam reappraisal of policy, was made Secretary of State, and Andrew Young, a firm friend of the Third World, was sent to the United Nations as United States' permanent representative. A number of other important ambassadorial and State Department posts also went to revisionist thinkers.

The change of mood was quickly apparent in the new priority which the Carter administration attached to the Caribbean. Several high-ranking officials, including Vance and Young, as well as the President's wife, Rosalynn, were despatched to the region in order to establish a series of personal contacts with leading Caribbean figures, and career diplomats were appointed to posts in the region instead of the usual political appointees for whom foreign service in the Caribbean had traditionally been the reward for presidential-campaign contributions. In the State Department itself, a policy re-evaluation was set in motion under a specially designated Caribbean Task Force, and on Capitol Hill the reappraisal was given valuable support by the House Sub-committee on Inter-American Affairs, headed by Dante Fascell, a Democratic representative from Florida. From this process emerged the view that US policy towards the Caribbean should in future be based upon five principles. These were repeated many times in the speeches and statements of members of the administration and were as follows:

1. significant support for economic development;
2. firm commitment to democratic practices and human rights;
3. clear acceptance of ideological pluralism;
4. unequivocal respect for national sovereignty;
5. strong encouragement of regional co-operation and of an active Caribbean role in world affairs.[14]

What particularly struck the Carter team was the fact that the Caribbean was passing through a time of rapid change. More and more states within the region were becoming politically independent, but were not possessed of the capacity to cope with the serious economic problems which still beset them. To be effective, US policy needed to show awareness of this and to align itself with those progressive and democratic forces which were working towards enhanced social, political and economic development. In these circumstances, the United States should be willing to tolerate a degree of ideological pluralism, as represented in the region in the mid-1970s by the governments of Guyana and Jamaica. Sally Shelton summed up the administration's view.

'While we believe', she said, 'that a free enterprise system is best for spurring fast across-the-board development, we do not try to dictate the proper mix between the public and private sectors in each Caribbean country. This is for the peoples and governments of those countries to decide.'[15]

True to its word, the Carter administration began to revise American policies towards the Caribbean. In the political sphere, it sought *rapprochement* with Cuba and other left-wing governments with whom the US had been in conflict under previous administrations. With Cuba, a dialogue was opened and some concrete results were achieved fairly quickly. The US granted visas to a number of Cuban citizens, lifted the ban on Americans travelling to Cuba, negotiated the establishment of interest sections in Havana and Washington, sponsored talks between the respective coastguards to initiate co-operation in search and rescue operations and drug traffic control, modified the US trade embargo on Cuba to permit Cuban–US transactions through a third country, and helped work towards the release of a number of American and some Cuban political prisoners held in Havana. The prospect of a substantial normalisation of relations and thus the removal of a long-standing obstacle to the development of a more coherent policy for the whole of the hemisphere was heralded. With Jamaica, the conflict was not so entrenched, but relations had reached a very low ebb towards the end of 1976, when the Manley government had openly accused the United States of seeking to 'destabilise' its position. Aware that Jamaica was toying with the possibility of adopting a fully socialist strategy which could lead it to seek large-scale Soviet economic assistance, Carter moved to re-establish friendly relations and urged Jamaica to pursue a solution to its economic problems via the International Monetary Fund, on which he was prepared to lean to ease the terms upon which a loan would be provided.[16] By this means in good part, Jamaica was coaxed back into the Western camp.

A similar willingness to reassess previous policies was evident in the Carter administration's reaction to events in other parts of the Caribbean. When in 1978 in the Dominican Republic it seemed that members of the armed forces were about to rig elections to prevent the victory of the opposition Dominican Revolutionary Party (PRD), led by Antonio Guzman, the United States moved to dissuade them, thus ensuring that Guzman became President. He was more of a social democrat than a revolutionary and was looked to by Washington to reform a number of features of Dominican society which were thought to be archaic and obstructive of social and economic development. In Puerto

Rico, too, new consideration was given to the island's status in the face of the growing demand for independence, especially from forces outside the territory. This latter option was not taken up, but favourable noises were made about the possibility that Puerto Rico might become the fifty-first state of the union, an option favoured by a strong body of opinion in the island. In these various ways, therefore, the Carter people appeared in this first phase of their administration to be ready to look at Caribbean problems with a fresh and broadly liberal perspective.

The same outlook underlay Carter's economic strategy for the region. The centre-piece of this was the United States' initiative in forming, under the aegis of the World Bank, the so-called Caribbean Group for Co-operation in Economic Development. This was conceived as a sort of funnel for channelling increased aid to the Caribbean from willing donor countries and the various international lending agencies. Upon its establishment, in 1977, representatives from over thirty countries — including Venezuela, Japan, Brazil, Canada and several European countries — began to meet regularly to plan the flow of economic assistance to the region. Such a scheme particularly appealed to the Carter administration, since it could be said to embody several of the principles, such as support of regional co-operation, local involvement in decision-making and ideological tolerance, which had been earlier proclaimed as the basic tenets of its Caribbean policy. The Group was also highly successful in its immediate goal. By 1979, total economic assistance transmitted to the region through this agency had almost tripled, reaching a figure of US $612 million. To support this framework, Carter also gave a higher priority to US contributions to the major international financial institutions themselves, notably the Inter-American Development Bank and the World Bank, and increased direct US economic aid to Caribbean countries, both bilaterally and through the Caribbean Development Bank, the regional bank established in 1968 by the Commonwealth Caribbean states. To indicate the scale of increase, total US development assistance and food aid to the region nearly doubled between 1976 and 1979, rising from approximately US $70 million to US $130 million in the period. In fact, according to State Department figures, it made the countries of the Caribbean the highest recipients of US aid in per-capita terms in the developing world.[17]

All in all, the Carter government must be credited with the inauguration of a new liberal phase in US relations with the Caribbean. It was not that fundamental US interests were neglected, for the people that

Carter befriended, like Manley and Guzman, were more than prepared to work within the capitalist system, and many American businessmen saw rich pickings to be made from a *rapprochement* with the Cuban regime. Indeed, the whole of the economic strategy developed by the Carter administration for the Caribbean was conceived with a view to maximising the role that US private capital could play in the economy of the region — to its undoubted advantage, quite apart from such benefits that might accrue to the Caribbean. In short, US interests were defined less narrowly, but more sensitively and sensibly than before. From the point of view of the Caribbean governments, the situation seemed to hold in prospect the inauguration of an era of friendly co-operative relations with the United States.

Carter the Conservative

Such hopes were soon to be dashed. As the administration progressed, the liberal elements within Carter's foreign policy began gradually to be abandoned in favour of a more conservative approach. The administration displayed increasing concern about the Soviet threat, especially after the invasion of Afghanistan, and in doing so it steadily lost confidence in the revisionist perspective on which its foreign policy had initially been based. Many reasons have been put forward to explain the disintegration of this approach. In part, it was that it failed to transform public opinion in America, which was still deeply attached to cold-war ideology. Equally, it failed to convince powerful public and private interests of the necessity of the US to adjust its role to changing international realities. The Pentagon, the armed services, the intelligence services and other important government bureaucracies, as well as defence contractors in the private sector, all had a vested interest in the traditional tenets of the US policy. They were suspicious of revisionism from the outset and seized on such problems as Iran as evidence that it dangerously undermined US interests. Internal conflicts generated increasingly intense bureaucratic in-fighting within the administration, over which Carter was unable to assert himself. The Caribbean became caught up in these arguments and, indeed, contributed to the administration's retreat from its earlier goals and commitments.

The key issue in this connection was the role of Cuba. In retrospect, it is clear that, for all the conciliatory moves initiated by Carter, little was required to deflect the US–Cuban relationship back into the more familiar pattern of endemic suspicion and hostility. Concern had long existed in Washington about Cuba's military presence in Africa, but had generally been played down by Carter. It reached a new peak of intensity in January 1978, when Cuban combat troops were sent to Ethiopia to help the revolutionary government of that country repulse a Somali invasion of the Ogaden. The US government saw this as further evidence of Cuban 'intervention' overseas against American interests, despite the fact that it bore some responsibility for the situation that had developed by its decision the year before to supply the Somali government with arms.[18] At any rate, the despatch of Cuban forces to Ethiopia brought to an end the incipient process of normalisation which was developing in United States–Cuban relations. Instead, it resurrected US anxieties about 'Soviet–Cuban military activism in the Third World'.

As if newly alerted, the United States began to see signs of Cuban intervention closer to home, not only in places such as Nicaragua, where there was reason to believe that the Cubans were supplying small quantities of arms to the Sandinistas, but also where the evidence was distinctly more flimsy. In particular, it interpreted the revolution in Grenada, in March 1979, not as the victory of a frustrated people against a nasty and capricious regime, but as evidence of the growing influence of Cuba and the Communist system within the Caribbean itself. The US suddenly became alarmed that the gradual withdrawal of Britain from colonial responsibility in the Caribbean and the economic vulnerability of the tiny independent states it had left behind had created a vacuum which might be exploited by Cuba to bring about more leftward changes of government, as in Grenada. Seeking to prevent this, the administration responded in a particularly chilly manner to requests for help, especially of a military kind, from the new regime in Grenada.[19] According to the island's Prime Minister, Maurice Bishop, it also provided him within a week of the revolution with a typed statement of instructions containing the following warning: 'although my government recognises your concern over allegations of a possible counter-coup, it also believes that it would not be in Grenada's best interests to seek assistance from a country such as Cuba to forestall such an attack. We would view with displeasure any tendency on the part of Grenada to develop closer ties with Cuba.'[20] In fact, unable to obtain support from the US and other traditional allies like Britain, the Grenadian government was virtually forced to do precisely what the US sought to avoid and turn to Cuba for protection and assistance.

By mid-1979, Cuba had already begun to resume its traditional position within the demonology of US foreign policy. Administration officials talked more and more of the danger of Cuban adventurism and of the flaws within Cuba's domestic economic and political system. Its old *bête-noir* status was finally confirmed towards the end of the year in connection with the most sensitive of all US–Cuban issues, the presence of Soviet forces in Cuba. An incident of this sort had already occurred in 1978, when it was detected that the Soviet Union had supplied Cuba with a squadron of new MIG 23 attack aircraft which could conceivably carry nuclear weapons. Upon receiving assurance from the Soviet Union that the planes would not be used for nuclear purposes, Carter dropped the issue, but ordered the resumption of aerial-photo reconnaissance missions over the island. In September 1979, they 'discovered' the presence of a Soviet combat brigade conducting exercises in Cuba. Carter alleged that this violated the 1962 Soviet–US agreement and demanded that the brigade be withdrawn or its combat ability limited. For the domestic public, the issue was proclaimed as new evidence of Soviet–Cuban aggressiveness and as a test of US reactions. It was, though, only a 'pseudo-crisis'. The brigade had been in Cuba a long time and posed no real threat to the United States. The Soviet Union claimed that the number of Russian troops in Cuba had been reduced from the level at the time of the missile crisis, and that the mission of the brigade was unchanged, namely, the training of Cuban forces in Soviet military techniques. Carter was forced to back away from what had become a highly embarrassing situation diplomatically. As one former official of the administration recently admitted, 'virtually out of thin air the Carter administration had spun a public relations problem with which it then had to live'.[21]

Clumsy and unnecessary, the incident exacerbated the deterioration of US–Cuban relations and, more generally, further undermined the Carter administration's plan for the Caribbean. In a significant change of emphasis, the State Department began to talk of the Caribbean more as a 'trouble spot' than an underdeveloped region in desperate need of aid. Hoist by its own rhetoric, the US government had to respond to its identification of a Soviet and Cuban threat by announcing a number of measures designed to neutralise Communist influence in the hemisphere. Although steps were taken to strengthen US intelligence and diplomatic services in the Caribbean, including the establishment of a Voice of America radio station and the opening of a new US consulate in Antigua in the Eastern Caribbean, these measures were mostly military in kind. They included the decision to set up a new Caribbean Joint Task Force Headquarters in Key West, Florida, and to expand US naval exercises in the Caribbean. American warships were soon seen more frequently in the area — both on 'goodwill' cruises and engaged in military manoeuvres like 'Operation Solid Shield 80', which took place in May 1980 and involved some 20,000 men, 42 naval vessels and 350 plants. With the same aim of increasing the region's security against internal and external aggression. Carter also sought supplemental assistance to help the government of the Dominican Republic replace a variety of military equipment destroyed in a hurricane and to meet the requests of several Eastern Caribbean governments for funds to establish a regional coastguard capability. This was followed by the provision of further military aid to Barbados, St Lucia and St Vincent in 1981.

The fact that the security, rather than the social and economic, dimension of Caribbean underdevelopment was now uppermost in the administration's mind was not concealed by the announcement of further increases in economic assistance to the region and the continuing references made in public speeches to US acceptance of 'ideological pluralism' in the Caribbean. Whatever was said about support for progressive forces and respect for democratic processes, clearly it was still to be the Americans who determined what was progressive and democratic. Thus aid was given to certain states in an attempt to pull them back from the embrace of socialism (for example, St Lucia, where in US terms the Labour government elected in July 1979 was initially perceived to be a progressive government, and Guyana, where fear of an extreme left alternative persuaded the United States to ignore the existing government's many abuses of democracy), and refused to others states which were deemed to be uninterested in Western-style elections and to have moved too far in a socialist direction (for example, Grenada). Even then, over half of the US aid requested for the Caribbean for 1981 was destined for the Dominican Republic and Haiti, two of the staunchest allies of the USA in the region. The deployment of aid in a politically motivated fashion, the increased display of military force and the constant warnings about the dangers of Cuban influence combined to suggest that, at the end of its period in office, the Carter government had come to reject the practical implications of its proclaimed toleration of ideological pluralism. The brief flirtation with liberalism was at an end; the dominant security paradigm was again in the driving seat.

The New Right

Even as it tried to preside over events in the Caribbean and the hemisphere as a whole, the Carter government, as we have seen, was being
forced to react to a powerful critique of the new revisionist foreign
policy consensus advanced by what has been called the 'new right'.
This critique was developed within pressure groups, such as the Committee on the Present Danger, and right-wing 'think tanks', like the
American Enterprise Institute and Georgetown University's Center for
Strategic and International Studies. It asserted that the various problems and difficulties which US policy encountered in the Carter era
were more than the personal failure of a naive man unskilled in the
ways of diplomacy. They derived from more fundamental mispercep-
tions of the nature of international affairs — in the phrase of one critic,
destined to become US ambassador to the United Nations in the
Reagan administration, 'from an ideology rather than from tradition,
habit or improvisation'.[22] In fact, the novelty suggested by the phrase
the 'new right' is misleading, since the burden of this critique was to
call for a reversion to the traditional basis of US foreign policy. According to one academic account, the world-view of the new right embraced
at heart three fundamental postulates.[23]

The first was that the United States must accept responsibility for
the direction of international affairs on a global scale and must perma-
nently reject isolationism. The charge was not so much that Carter's
approach had been isolationist, but that too much emphasis had been
placed on the constraints and limits that bore upon American actions
in an interdependent world. Instead, there ought to be greater efforts to
project American power abroad in order to achieve a tighter grip on
global political developments. By implication, the propriety of the
missionary role in which the United States has long liked to cast itself
in international affairs, and which had fallen into disrepute in the wake
of Vietnam and Watergate, was to be questioned no more. For Latin
America and the Caribbean, all of this required a reassertion of hegemony as the secure base from which active US management of global
affairs could be conducted. The morality of human rights and the
commitment to universal values were to be set aside for traditional
considerations of national interest.

The second component of this world-view rested on the belief that
Communism was the principal danger facing the world and on its
corollary, that its spread should be resisted by the United States with
all means at its disposal. In the event, Carter did little to displace the

anti-Communist focus of US foreign policy, succumbing himself ultimately to the simplistic desire to see international politics almost solely
as the struggle between the forces of good and evil. But in the first
phase of his administration, he did challenge this particular American
obsession, observing in his Notre Dame address in 1977, that 'we are
now free of that inordinate fear of Communism which once led us to
embrace any dictator who joined us in our fear'.[24] Such rhetorical
disclaimers fuelled the anti-Communism of the new right, leading them
to see just about every event which disturbed the political *status quo* as
the consequence of the revolutionary activities of Communist conspira-
tors. An effort was made to give this form of analysis greater intellectual credibility by the claim that Communism was merely an abhorrent
phase of history already in decline. Of course, in the cause of hastening
that decline, it was held that help should once again be accepted from
oppressive regimes which opposed Communist movements, even if they
denied human rights to their own people. For the Caribbean, as for
other parts of the world, this mode of thinking meant that the causes of
movements of change were seen to lie less in the social and economic
conditions of underdevelopment and more in the subversive appeal of
the Communist ideology. No link was seen to exist between the two.

The third element was the simple belief that since the Soviet Union
was the spearhead of the Communist challenge, US foreign policy must
be dedicated, above all else, to containing the expansion of Soviet
influence. Again, it was not as if the Carter administration did not place
emphasis on this goal: the emphasis increased as time went on. But it
did briefly expand the foreign policy agenda to include a variety of
other issues – such as the North–South division, the energy shortage
and the general scarcity of resources, and the phenomenon of resurgent
nationalism in the Third World and elsewhere – none of which necessarily implied confrontation with the Soviet Union. Such issues were
viewed by the new right not only as secondary, but as potentially
diverting of US resources and energy to the detriment of the prior need
to contain Soviet expansionism. In this sphere, only the most resolute
and unswerving resistance could hope to succeed. The challenge was at
once a test of military might, but also of nerve and moral fibre. In
the context of the Caribbean, the Soviet Union could be taken to mean
Cuba, which was seen simply as a surrogate of Moscow performing at
all times to instructions from its master. As a result of Soviet–Cuban
subversion, it was suggested, Nicaragua and Grenada had already been
'lost', El Salvador and Guatemala were engaged in violent conflict with
Cuban-backed guerrillas, Mexico was already in danger and, ultimately,

the United States, 'the last domino', was itself threatened. A major priority was therefore attached to the destruction of Cuban influence in the Caribbean.

In summary, the ideology of the new right represented a crude reaction against the early revisionist thinking of the Carter period. It picked up and re-emphasised much that was traditional in US foreign policy, but it did so in a particularly strident fashion. In political terms, it was the more potent for being simplistic and emotional in appeal. It had an obvious impact on the policies of the Carter administration, but had to wait for the advent of the succeeding administration to assert itself fully over American foreign policy.

The Reagan Administration

Ronald Reagan shared all of the elements of the world-view of the new right. He campaigned very effectively upon foreign policy issues during the 1980 presidential election and won widespread support for his approach to international affairs from businessmen, members of the 'moral majority' and conservative Americans of all persuasions. In office, he set about placing several leading ideologues of the right in important positions in the foreign policy-making apparatus, from where they sought to give US policy something of the flavour of an anti-Communist crusade.

Perhaps more than in any other part of the world, in the early months of the Reagan administration this aspect of policy made itself felt in the Caribbean. In a significant adjustment of the practice of the Carter era, the new administration drew no distinction between the Caribbean and Central America. The differing social and economic traditions and different patterns of development of these two sub-regions were not viewed as significant compared to the common security problem they posed for the United States. As a result, both were treated by the Reagan administration as constituent parts of a new concept, the Caribbean Basin. The countries of the Basin had little in common beyond their geographical location in the USA's traditional backyard, but were forced together by the administration's determination to reassert US hegemony in the area and expunge Cuban influence for good.

Cuba has accordingly been under consistent attack ever since the Reagan administration took office. Inspired by the rhetoric of the campaign, the initial position was that the United States would not even talk to the Cubans until they ceased all interventionist activities in the Caribbean and Central America (by which was meant the provision of assistance to the Sandinistas in Nicaragua and the rebel forces in El Salvador) and withdrew their troops from Africa. If they refused to do so, the US could exclude no option, including the possibility of a naval blockade. The belief seemed to be that pressure could be brought to bear on Castro which would make him retreat from his interventionist policies and foresake his close alliance with the Soviet Union. There thus ensured a series of moves designed to contribute to this end: the abandonment of all day-to-day diplomatic contacts with Cuba such as the granting of visas to Cuban officials; the release of propagandist State Department papers such as the notorious document of February 1981, which claimed to provide detailed evidence of Cuban involvement in the insurgency in Central America, but was in fact largely a collection of forgeries, innuendoes and irrelevancies; the toleration of Cuban exiles training in paramilitary camps in Florida; the establishment of Radio Marti to broadcast anti-Communist propaganda to Cuba; and the use of US economic power in a variety of ways to prevent loans being made to Cuba and to make it harder for Cuba to sell its sugar on the world market. At the same time, the US sought to isolate Cuba diplomatically within the Caribbean and Central America by pressing Colombia, Costa Rica and Jamaica, following the defeat of Manley in October 1980, to break off relations with Havana. For all this, the policy of intimidation did not work. As Wayne Smith, the chief of the US interests section in Havana between 1979 and 1982, has explained in his account of this period, the Cubans in fact made three attempts in the first eighteen months of the Reagan administration to initiate talks with the United States with a view to reducing regional tensions and seeking an improvement in relations, all of which were rebuffed.[25] Having publicly linked talks with the ending of what it defined as Cuban interventionism and having failed to bring that about by its aggressively anti-Cuban policies, the Reagan administration drove itself into a corner from which it has found it difficult to move.

The Reagan administration also made similar efforts to undermine the revolutionary government in Grenada. Diplomatically, it lobbied to isolate Grenada in the Caribbean and succeeded in March 1981, in restricting the number of Caribbean states which sent representatives to the second anniversary celebrations of the revolution to Guyana, St Lucia, Belize, Suriname and Venezuela. Economically, it sought unsuccessfully to prevent the European Economic Community from providing aid for the island's new airport, which it feared might be used for military purposes by Cuban jet aircraft, and tried, again without success, to persuade the other Commonwealth Caribbean governments to exclude Grenada from sharing in a proposed US $4 million 'basic human needs' grant from the United States administered through the Caribbean Development Bank. Militarily, it sought to frighten Grenada by including within a huge NATO exercise held in the Caribbean in August 1981 a mock invasion of the island of Vieques off the coast of Puerto Rico. The objective was to take power in a fictitious country called 'Amber and the Amberines' (unavoidably suggestive of Grenada and the Grenadines, especially since there was a district called Amber in Grenada) until an election could be called and a pro-US government installed.

In marked contrast to the pressures deployed towards its perceived enemies in the region, the Reagan administration moved quickly to reward friends and allies in the Caribbean, especially with military assistance. Since the election of the right-wing Seaga government in October 1980, Jamaica has been particularly favoured. Indeed, Seaga was the first foreign leader to be entertained in the White House by President Reagan. He has been described as 'America's man in the Caribbean', offered substantial military aid and lauded for his efforts to revive free enterprise in Jamaica. The Dominican Republic and the Eastern Caribbean states also benefited from a general increase in security assistance given to Latin America for the fiscal year 1982, and Haiti has developed closer relations in defence matters with the United States since the ending of the constant criticisms of its human-rights record characteristic of the Carter presidency.

However, from the point of view of Reagan's anti-Cuban perspective, the problem was that the pro-Western leaders of the Caribbean were more interested in trade, aid and investment than they were in military assistance on its own. Several countries saw the chance to exchange their anti-Communist credentials for tangible measures of economic support. The Puerto Rican government was alert to this and so too was Seaga in Jamaica. He was concerned not just to secure substantial economic assistance for Jamaica (in which he has been very successful), but for the Caribbean as a whole. During his visit to Washington shortly after Reagan's inauguration, he made a speech calling upon the United States and its allies to put together a rescue programme for the region along the lines of the Marshall Plan prepared for Europe after 1945. The then West German Chancellor, Helmut Schmidt, urged the United States to consider the idea seriously and other congressional leaders concerned about the Caribbean gave it their support. The Reagan administration made no immediate response. It was committed to tax cuts, a substantial increase in defence expenditure and a balanced budget, all at the same time, and was in any case ideologically opposed to the whole notion of foreign aid. 'Charity' was best carried out in its view by private, rather than governmental, bodies.

The Caribbean Basin Initiative (CBI)

Nevertheless, the proposal of such a rescue plan did restore the state of the regional economy to a more central place in US government perceptions of the Caribbean. This bore fruit in the programme of special assistance to the countries of the Caribbean and Central America, announced by President Reagan on 24 February 1982 and subsequently labelled the Caribbean Basin Initiative. The idea of setting up some sort of 'Mini-Marshall Plan' for the Caribbean had been revived at a meeting of US Secretary of State, Alexander Haig, with the foreign ministers of Canada, Mexico and Venezuela in Nassau in the Bahamas in July 1981. Officially heralded as evidence that the US government was sincere in its attitude towards Latin America and was not obsessed, as its critics alleged, by the security implications of underdevelopment, the plan soon ran into difficulties. The Nassau meeting was followed by a period of consultation with the countries of the Caribbean, ostensibly to determine the best way to stimulate the social and economic development of the region. As this took place, it became gradually clearer that the US government viewed the supply of aid and the promotion of economic growth in the Caribbean primarily as another means of cutting the ground from underneath the feet of the leftist movements in the area and their alleged patron, Cuba. As the underlying political aims of the initiative became more overt, the effect was to cause the governments of Mexico, Canada and Venezuela to seek to distance themselves from the Reagan plan. Mexico made it clear that it was opposed to certain conditions that the US was trying to include in the aid package, notably the exclusion of Cuba, Nicaragua and Grenada from its provision. Canada was also disturbed by this aspect of the plan, and Venezuela steadily lost interest, preferring to return to its traditional policy of bilateral dealings with countries in the region. When the CBI was finally unveiled, therefore, it constituted a unilateral programme proposed by the United States for the Caribbean Basin and designed, according to Reagan, to 'help revitalise the economies of this strategically critical region by attacking the underlying causes of economic stagnation' and thus to 'make possible the achievement of a lasting political and social tranquillity based on freedom and justice'.[26] Underlying these grandiose claims were the following six measures.

Offer of One-way Free Trade

This was the centre-piece of the programme and represented something of a break from the United States' traditional attachment to a global trade policy. Although under existing arrangements some 87 per cent of Caribbean Basin exports already entered the US market duty-free, it was argued that the Generalised System of Preferences (GSP) had such a complex structure that small and relatively inexperienced traders, such as those in the Caribbean Basin countries, were limited in their ability to take advantage of the opportunities it offered. It was also felt that the conventional reasons for excluding certain products from the GSP were not relevant to the Caribbean and, in any case, some of the duties which remained in place were in sectors of special interest to Basin countries. The administration therefore sought legislative authority to grant beneficiaries of the CBI duty-free treatment for twelve years on the export of all products, excepting only textiles and apparel items which are subject to particular agreements. Sugar was to receive duty-free treatment, but the import fee was to be maintained in order to protect the US domestic sugar price-support programme. For any goods seeking duty-free entry, it was required that Basin countries supply a minimum of 25 per cent of local value added, although this could be achieved cumulatively via a number of countries. Finally, the President was to be given the discretion to designate countries as beneficiaries of the free-trade area, subject to the exclusion of Communist countries and those which expropriate without compensation or discriminate against US exports. It was also revealed ominously that the President would take into account 'economic criteria such as the attitude of the beneficiaries towards private enterprice and the policies recipient countries are pursuing to promote their own development'.[27]

Tax Incentives

In order to overcome the expected hesitancy of some US entrepreneurs to invest in the Caribbean area, the President asked Congress to provide to new equity investors in the Caribbean Basin an extension of the 10 per cent tax credit previously applicable only to domestic investment. He also indicated a readiness to negotiate bilateral investment treaties with interested Basin countries so as to provide an agreed legal framework for investment. Finally, reference was made to the existence of the Overseas Private Investment Corporation, which offers political risk insurance for US investors abroad, and a commitment was given to increase its activities in the Caribbean Basin.

Financial and Military Assistance

A considerable increase of US concessional assistance to the Caribbean Basin was planned. In particular, President Reagan asked Congress to provide an emergency supplemental appropriation of US $350 million for fiscal year 1982 to be allocated as follows: El Salvador US $128 million; Costa Rica US $70 million; Honduras US $35 million; Jamaica US $50 million; the Dominican Republic US $40 million; Eastern Caribbean US $10 million; Belize US $10 million; and Haiti US $5 million. These funds were to be used primarily to finance private-sector imports and, again according to Reagan, would 'help foster the spirit of enterprise'[28] necessary to take advantage of other parts of the initiative. Beyond this, the administration also gave notice of its intention to seek a total of US $664 million of economic assistance for the Basin for the fiscal year 1983, a sum less than the new request for 1982, but double that for 1980.

Military assistance was treated separately within the CBI, but was increased by an even greater amount. The initial appropriation requested for the fiscal year 1982 was US $112.1 million, more than double the US $50.5 million of the year before, but it was subsequently to be increased still further by US $60 million, largely for El Salvador, which in any case was designated to receive some 70 per cent of the original budget. The estimate for 1983 was given as the rather lower figure of US $101.3 million.

Technical Assistance and Training

The CBI promised technical assistance and training to assist the private sector in the Basin countries to benefit from the programme. Efforts were to be concentrated upon such areas as investment promotion, export marketing and technology transfer.

International Assistance

Despite its failure to enact the CBI as a multinational initiative, the United States still proclaimed its intention to work closely with Mexico, Canada and Venezuela, as well as Colombia, to assist the development of the region, and it further indicated its intention to seek to involve other European and Asian allies, as well as multilateral development institutions, in future Caribbean Basin programmes.

Puerto Rico and the US Virgin Islands

The Reagan administration recognised the need to ensure that the economic development of US possessions in the Caribbean was enhanced by US policy towards the region as a whole and accordingly proposed a number of specific measures for these territories. They included: the continuation of arrangements whereby excise taxes on imported rum were rebated to these two territories; the concession that Puerto Rican and Virgin Island inputs be considered as Caribbean inputs under the rules-of-origin requirement for the free-trade area; agreement that industries in these areas will have recourse to the same safeguard procedures as mainland industries, in the event that they are seriously injured from increased US imports from the Caribbean; and a request for congressional support for a series of development projects to be located in the islands.

These were the six main facets of the CBI which Reagan introduced to representatives of the Organisation of American States (OAS) when he addressed them in February 1982. Beyond these measures, there was subsequently expressed a willingness to help the Caribbean Basin countries modernise their agriculture sectors and a strong desire to have the private sector play a more central role in economic development. In this connection, the US committed itself to working with governments in the region 'to design private sector development strategies which combine private, public and voluntary organisations' resources in imaginative new programmes'.[29] It all added up, Reagan claimed, to an integrated set of proposals 'under which creativity, private entrepreneurship and self-help can flourish' in the Caribbean.[30] From the US point of view, it was 'a far-sighted act by our own people at a time of considerable economic difficulty at home', but one which was 'vital to the security interests' of both the United States and the whole hemisphere.[31]

CBI and Congress

However, from the moment it was introduced into the United States Congress, the CBI was caught in a series of domestic political battles preceding the mid-term legislative elections of November 1982. The Bill was subjected to intense lobbying from all sides. Although support came from the anti-immigration lobby, who hoped that a more prosperous Caribbean Basin would stem the flow of both legal and illegal immigrants into the United States, opposition was voiced, from one point of view, by liberals who were concerned that the whole package was a ploy to aid El Salvador in the face of widespread doubts about the human-rights record of its government and, from another in perhaps even more telling fashion, by protectionist opinion which feared that the free trade concessions would damage the US economy by causing the export of 'American jobs' to the Caribbean. Trapped between these various conflicting pressures, the CBI was amended and amended again in the committees of both houses of Congress during the course of the summer of 1982.[32] In the Senate, the Foreign Relations Committee recommended that the aid package be disbursed through an international fund to be overseen by the World Bank, only to reverse its decision a month later. The Ways and Means Committee responded to pressure from US industry and trade unions to remove leather and rubber footwear, luggage, gloves and handbags from the duty-free access list, and to pressure from Puerto Rico and the US Virgin Islands to limit rum imports. In the House, in turn, committees recommended that aid to any country should be limited to US $75 million (thus thwarting the intended US $128 million allocation to El Salvador) and proposed that 25 per cent of the fund should go for infrastructural and social service development. The Senate also suggested that the legislation be renamed the Caribbean and Central American Aid Bill.

The administration responded by reiterating the importance it attached to the problems of the Caribbean Basin and the merits of the CBI package as a means of ameliorating them. Following Haig's resignation, the new Secretary of State, George Shultz, appeared before the Senate Finance Committee at the beginning of August 1982 to argue that the domestic fears expressed about the Bill, although understandable in a time of recession, were exaggerated. In a revealing passage which placed the debate about the CBI in proper context, he declared:

We are such a big economy compared to those of the Caribbean Basin that what looms large in the Basin will still have a small impact here. The combined GNP of all the Caribbean Basin countries amounts to less than 2% of our GNP. Our imports from the Caribbean Basin account for less than 4% of our total imports world-wide. The imports that would be affected by our free trade proposal are at present less than ½% of our total imports − or 0.0002% of our GNP.[33]

Moreover, the long-term economic benefits for the US were notable: 'a stable, democratic and prosperous Caribbean Basin means a much larger and growing market for our exports, and consequently significantly greater job opportunities for our workers'.[34]

Responding to Shultz's pleas for urgency, the Bill was brought to the floor of the two Houses. In a move which pleased Reagan, the Senate passed a further amendment proposed by Senator Symms of Idaho, urging the US to use 'whatever means necessary including the use of arms' to contain 'Marxist–Leninist subversion' in the region. He was much less happy with a vote in the House of Representatives which tacked the CBI aid programme on to a huge supplemental appropriations Bill. A joint conference committee of the two legislative houses confirmed these two votes and agreed a final compromise basis for disbursement of the aid fund as follows: El Salvador (not more than US $75 million); Costa Rica (not less than US $70 million); Jamaica (not less than US $50 million); the Dominican Republic (not less than US $41 million); Honduras (not less than US $35 million); Eastern Caribbean (not less than US $20 million); Haiti (not less than US $10 million); and Guatemala (not more than US $10 million). The allocation was marginally more even-handed, in that, under the administration's original plan, the first three mentioned countries were to receive 70 per cent of the total and would now be given 56 per cent. In this form, Congress passed the CBI as part of an appropriations Bill on 19 August, and sent it to the White House for signature. In an ironic twist, Reagan proceeded to veto the whole piece of legislation on the grounds that it exceeded budgetary spending limits, only to see Congress override his veto in mid-September by securing the required two-thirds majority in favour of the Bill in both Houses.

In such circumstances, it is easy to lose track of who was the winner and who was the loser. The Reagan administration certainly recognised that many of the central provisions of the CBI had been pared away during the months of congressional consideration and was disappointed not to secure legislative passage of the entire initiative. Politically, the defeat was the greater since the United States at that time badly needed something to indicate a sense of commitment to the hemisphere, following the bad taste left in many Caribbean and Latin American mouths by its support for Britain against Argentina in the Falklands/ Malvinas war of April–June 1982. Indeed, Shultz had made this very point in his plea to the Senate Finance Committee in August. Accordingly, the administration hoped that the trade and investment parts of the Bill might be passed during the 'lame duck' congressional session in December 1982, following the elections of the previous month. It

brought what pressure to bear that it could: officials lobbied Congress-
men assiduously, Reagan delivered a radio speech to the American
people from Costa Rica urging the final passage of the legislation, and
Vice-President Bush spoke in a similar vein at a Caribbean conference
in Miami. Yet, despite a favourable vote in the House of Representatives at the end of the year, the Bill died in the Senate in the final days
of the session and was thus put off for the new Congress in 1983 where,
reintroduced, it would have to be reconsidered afresh.

In a sense, much of the argument and pressure was misplaced since,
from the moment the CBI was unveiled, the view had been strongly
advanced, both inside and outside the United States, that, even if
fully implemented, the package of measures was unlikely to have a
serious remedial effect on the deep-rooted problems of Caribbean
underdevelopment.[35] At the centre of such criticism was the proposed
free-trade area. One view held that the effect was likely to be at best
psychological, since by the US administration's own admission 87 per
cent of Basin goods already entered the US market duty-free. Of the
remaining 13 per cent about half was textiles and clothing, which were
totally excluded from duty-free treatment under the CBI, and sugar,
for which in May 1982 provision under the CBI was abandoned in
favour of a global quota system with no preferences for Basin countries, designed to maintain the legal support price of US domestic
growers, following the collapse of sugar prices on the world market.
Several Caribbean sugar producers are thus worse off than they were
before the CBI was announced. If, therefore, rum, leather and rubber
footwear and leather goods were also to be excluded, as recommended
by the Senate Ways and Means Committee in its first consideration of
the Bill, it would have meant that virtually no new trade for the Caribbean would result from these proposals. Even if these objections were to
be discounted, another critical view suggested that the various non-
tariff barriers remaining in existence would themselves constitute a
serious impediment to an expansion of regional exports to the United
States. Another viewpoint stressed that a duty-free market was meaningful only if a country had the productive capacity to take advantage of it.
The Eastern Caribbean states, for example, would need to develop their
physical infrastructure before they could significantly expand their
production and would not get much help to this end from the CBI. The
additional expenditure of US $350 million was intended primarily to
finance private-sector imports, and in any case only brought the proposed level of US aid to the region, including military aid, for 1982
to a notional US $20 per capita, compared to the estimated US $700

per capita supplied by the USA to Israel.[36] Without governmental action to correct infrastructural deficiencies, the emphasis on encouraging private capital inevitably meant that normal commercial criteria would dictate the location of new investment in territories already more advanced economically, such as Jamaica and Costa Rica, thereby exacerbating rather than lessening regional disparities in levels of development. In short, what these critics were saying was that the provision of markets was not going to be the crucial impetus to economic development in the Caribbean unless a range of difficult structural problems, which a free-enterprise model did not even address, were solved at the same time.

This type of analysis of the CBI exposed very clearly the political origins of the programme. As Abraham Lowenthal, one of the United States' leading Latin American scholars, put it: 'an east–west focus distorts every aspect of the CBI'.[37] The initial publicity surrounding the programme, with its association with the Marshall Plan of the 1940s, gave rise to some hopes that the Reagan administration had at last come to accept that the root causes of the growing instability of the Caribbean were to be found in the region's social and economic history, rather than some subversive Cuban or Soviet challenge to US interests. The concern to promote foreign capital investment in the region, the crude distinction devised to exclude such countries as Grenada and Nicaragua, the unwillingness to make the necessary political compromises to have drawn Mexico, Venezuela and Canada into a genuinely multilateral response to the Caribbean's problems – all of these factors demonstrated that the launching of the CBI did not represent any new thinking on the part of the Reagan team. It was but another mechanism by which more effectively to impose political loyalty on the majority of the states of the Caribbean in the cause of US national security and the reassertion of traditional regional hegemony.

Anyone who had forgotten this was amply reminded when, in April 1982, the US vetoed a UN Security Council resolution calling on all states to abstain from using force against any Central American or Caribbean country, and in May the US Atlantic fleet began another huge naval exercise in the Caribbean. There was no relief from the regime's outspoken hostility towards Cuba and Nicaragua or its persistent attempts to procure further military aid for El Salvador from a reluctant Congress. Suriname emerged more to the forefront of US disapproval, and allegations were made in Paramaribo that American embassy personnel had played a key role in generating anti-government disturbances in October 1982. For a while, tiny Grenada was spared Reagan's invective, but in March 1983 he returned to the attack, claiming that the island was housing Cuban and Soviet naval bases and other sophisticated military installations. He even released aerial surveillance photographs purporting to show not only Soviet MIG bases in Cuba, but the alleged military aspects of Grenada's new airport. This flurry of accusations came just a month after the *Washington Post* had published a detailed account of a covert operation prepared against Grenada by the CIA in the autumn of 1981, which had been cancelled only when a Senate Committee dismissed it as an absurdly inappropriate venture. Understandably alarmed, Bishop's government in Grenada attacked Reagan's statement as an 'open declaration of war' and put its armed forces on the alert. The tension produced in the Caribbean as a result of US policies thus reached a new height and showed no immediate signs of diminution, especially as another month-long naval exercise involving some 77 US and allied warships began on the day of Reagan's speech in March.

In the midst of this military posturing, the US administration had not forgotten the CBI. It was reintroduced into the Senate in April 1983, although it was not discussed in the House of Representatives until Committee consideration in the upper House was complete. The same political obstacles remained, in particular the opposition of the trade union movement, fearful of further loss of jobs. The chief lobbyist of the Council of the Americas, one of the major voices of the corporate investors who have such a large financial stake in the economies of Latin America and the Caribbean, argued, however, that the Bill had 'better than 50% chances because it is the only iron in the fire to address the region's economic problems'.[38] The White House itself took over responsibility for ushering the legislation through Congress from the Special Trade Representatives Office, which was a measure of its determination to secure its implementation, if at all possible. Eventually, the administration's efforts were successful: the CBI was approved by Congress in August 1983, broadly in the form in which it was reintroduced. Teams of officials have now been despatched to potential beneficiaries to discuss participation on a bilateral basis. However, many practical problems remain to be solved, and few believe that the CBI will put an end to the region's underlying economic crisis.

Notes

1. For a historical account of US policy towards the hemisphere, see G. Connell-Smith, *The Inter-American System* (Oxford University Press, New York, 1962).

2. See J. Pearce, *Under the Eagle: US Intervention in Central America and the Caribbean* (Latin America Bureau, London, 1982).

3. S. Shelton, 'US Interests and Policy toward the Caribbean', speech by US ambassador to Barbados to the Johns Hopkins School of Advanced International Studies, 15 October 1980, p. 11.

4. See the detailed analysis of this possibility contained in J.I. Domínguez, 'The United States and its Regional Security Interests: the Caribbean, Central, and South America', *Daedalus*, vol. 109, no. 4 (1980), pp. 119-24.

5. This scenario is raised in *The Caribbean Strategic Vacuum* (Institute for the Study of Conflict, London, 1980).

6. See J. Child, 'From "Color" to "Rainbow": US Strategic Planning for Latin America, 1919-1945', *Journal of Interamerican Studies and World Affairs*, vol. 21, no. 2 (1979), pp. 233-59.

7. L.B. Johnson, 'Text of a Nationwide Presidential Broadcast', 2 May 1965, cited in Pearce, *Under the Eagle*, p. 64.

8. See L.-D. Bender, *Cuba vs United States: The Politics of Hostility*, 2nd edn (Inter American University Press, San Juan, 1981), pp. 26-8.

9. M. Manley, *Jamaica: Struggle in the Periphery* (Third World Media, London, 1982), p. 116.

10. Ibid.

11. V.A. Lewis, 'The United States in the Caribbean: the Dominant Power and the New States', presidential address to the Caribbean Studies Association Annual Conference, St Thomas, US Virgin Islands, 27-30 May 1981, p. 13.

12. Z. Brzezinski, *Between Two Ages* (Viking, New York, 1970).

13. S. Linowitz *et al.*, *The Americas in a Changing World* (Commission on United States-Latin American Relations, Washington, 1974).

14. P.C. Habib, 'Address by the US Ambassador-at-large to the Miami Conference on the Caribbean, 28 November 1979' in United States Department of State, *US Relations with the Caribbean and Central America* (Bureau of Public Affairs, Washington, 1979), p. 2.

15. Shelton, 'US Interests and Policy', p. 16.

16. See N. Girvan, R. Bernal and W. Hughes, 'The IMF and the Third World: the Case of Jamaica, 1974-80', *Development Dialogue*, vol. 11, no. 2 (1980), p. 123.

17. Habib, in US Department of State, *US Relations with the Caribbean and Central America*, p. 4.

18. See W.S. Smith, 'Dateline Havana: Myopic Diplomacy', *Foreign Policy*, vol. 47 (1982), p. 172.

19. See D.S. Da Breo, *The Grenada Revolution* (Management Advertising and Publicity Services, Castries, 1979), pp. 301-10.

20. M. Bishop, 'One Month of the Grenadian Revolution', address by the Prime Minister, 13 April 1979, p. 4.

21. Smith, 'Dateline Havana', p. 158.

22. J. Kirkpatrick, 'US Security and Latin America', *Commentary*, vol. 71, no. 1 (1981), p. 29.

23. C.W. Kegley Jr and E.R. Wittkopf, 'The Reagan Administration's World View', *Orbis*, vol. 26, no. 1 (1982), pp. 225-31.

24. Cited in ibid., p. 227.

25. Smith, 'Dateline Havana', pp. 160-70.

66 *United States*

26. President Reagan, 'The Caribbean Basin Plan', speech to Congress, 17 March 1982, p. 2.

27. The White House, *Fact Sheet on President Reagan's Caribbean Basin Policy* (The White House, Washington, 1982), p. 11.

28. President Reagan, 'The US Caribbean Basin Initiative', speech to the Organisation of American States, St Lucia, 24 February 1982, p. 7.

29. White House, *Fact Sheet*, p. 23.

30. Reagan, 'US Caribbean Basin Initiative', p. 6.

31. Ibid., p. 8.

32. For the details, see L. Blackburn and F. Merry, 'EEC and US Policies towards the Caribbean Basin' in C. Stevens (ed.), *EEC and the Third World: A Survey 3. The Atlantic Rift* (Hodder and Stoughton, London, 1983), pp. 112–15.

33. G.P. Shultz, 'Statement by the Secretary of State to the Senate Finance Committee on the Caribbean Basin Initiative, 2 August 1982', p. 4.

34. Ibid.

35. For a debate on the likely impact of the CBI, see the articles by A.F. Lowenthal, P. Johnson, R. Hernández-Colón, B. Corrada, S. Weintraub, R.E. Feinberg and R.S. Newfarmer in *Foreign Policy*, vol. 47 (1982), pp. 114–38. See also R. Pastor, 'Sinking in the Caribbean Basin', *Foreign Affairs*, vol. 60, no. 5 (1982), pp. 1038–58, and R. Ramsaran, 'The US Caribbean Basin Initiative', *The World Today*, vol. 38, no. 11 (1982), pp. 430–6.

36. *The Economist*, 11 September 1982, cited in Blackburn and Merry's article in Stevens, *EEC and the Third World*, p. 117.

37. A.F. Lowenthal, 'The Caribbean Basin Initiative: Misplaced Emphasis', *Foreign Policy*, vol. 47 (1982), p. 115.

38. *Latin America Regional Report: Caribbean*, RC–83–03, 31 March 1983, p. 6.

4 CUBA: MENACE OR MODEL?

In many ways Cuba is the pivot around which the international crisis of the Caribbean revolves. The extent of its involvement in the politics of the region has grown enormously in recent years, arousing much comment. Interpretations of Cuba's role differ: although some see it as a development model which other Third World territories in the Caribbean and elsewhere ought to follow, the orthodox Western view sees Cuban foreign policy working in tandem with Soviet interests, with Cuba construed essentially as a satellite state. The surrogate thesis, as this might be called, rests essentially on Cuba's high level of dependency on the Soviet Union for both economic and military support. It effectively reduces Cuba's diverse interests in Europe, Africa, Latin America and the Caribbean to a global pattern which has, as its alleged dynamic, the promotion of revolutionary socialism and the subversion of the Western economic and political system on Moscow's behalf. From this ideological perspective, Cuban foreign policy is generally denounced before it has been analysed. In reality, it does not correspond at all closely to the popular myth. In the first place, it is a good deal more complex and diverse, sometimes to the point of contradiction; secondly, it possesses a sufficient degree of autonomy from Soviet interests to make it both a distinct and distinctive strand of diplomacy, especially in regional contexts such as the Caribbean.

Soviet Perceptions of Cuba and the Caribbean

Nevertheless, the centrality and longevity of the Soviet alliance within Cuban foreign policy necessitates a preliminary assessment of Soviet perceptions of Cuba and the Caribbean. Because of the region's proximity to the United States and its traditional geopolitical position as part of the Western sphere of influence, the Caribbean is unavoidably a challenge to the Soviet Union. From the Soviet point of view, it is part of the US 'strategic rear', where any weakening of US control inevitably shifts the international struggle between imperialism and Communism — which the Soviets term the 'correlation of forces' — to the advantage of the latter.[1] The Soviet Union is concerned, therefore, not with the particular fate of the Caribbean, but with the way in which its future political and economic development contributes to the expansion of the world socialist system. This gives its role in the international politics of the Caribbean a somewhat detached air, but it does not mean that it is not involved.

Prior to May 1960, when it formally established diplomatic relations with Cuba, the Soviet Union had few ties with the region. With the exception of Mexico, relations were limited to support for the small number of official Communist parties in the area. However, once Cuba began to move in a Marxist–Leninist direction, Moscow's relationship with Havana became one of the most significant features of a new interest in Latin America and the Third World. As Soviet scholars put it:

> The Cuban revolution was a shattering blow to the theory of 'geographical fatalism' that for a long time had determined the policy of most of the Latin American countries. According to this theory, the territorial proximity of the Latin American states to the USA doomed them to permanent dependence and to following in Washington's wake. Cuba's experience had demonstrated that a revolutionary people can shake off Imperialist oppression.[2]

Quite apart from its importance to the international struggle against imperialism, the Cuban revolution also gave the Caribbean region significance in Soviet ideological and national perceptions. Soviet attention turned towards an expansion of diplomatic activity in the region, which by 1980 had led to the establishment of embassies in Guyana, Jamaica and Grenada, and the appointment of non-resident ambassadors in Suriname and Trinidad and Tobago.[3] Over the years it has provided small amounts of assistance to these countries – perhaps rather more to Bishop's Grenada – and has taken an interest in the diplomacy surrounding the sale of raw materials produced in the Caribbean. Yet it has been determined not to become the patron of any of these states, preferring to allow Cuba to play the dominant role amongst Communist powers in the region.

The Soviet Union's relationship with the Castro regime has not always been easy. At the outset, it did not rush to aid the revolution, moving to fill the vacuum only when the United States cancelled Cuba's sugar quota in mid-1960.[4] After the Bay of Pigs invasion, more substantive steps were taken to build up the alliance, including the famous installation of Soviet intermediate-range ballistic missiles. However, the resulting missile crisis in 1962 nearly shattered the emerging partnership.

Castro felt betrayed by the Soviet decision to remove what he saw as the Cuban deterrent and was insulted at being utterly excluded from the negotiations which resolved the crisis. Soviet aid to Cuba continued and the alliance held, but not without sharp Soviet criticism of Cuba's economic strategy in the mid-1960s, especially the heavy reliance on moral incentives to promote development. Reflection upon the high risks at stake in the missile crisis also had a sobering impact on Soviet perceptions of the potential for renewed revolution in the Caribbean and Latin America, and led to persistent conflict with the Cubans on this issue throughout the 1960s. In the early part of the decade, the example of the Cuban revolution spawned similar guerrilla movements in many Latin American states which Cuba endorsed and sustained with material assistance. Much to the disappointment of the Cubans, the Soviet Union viewed this policy as romantic and refused to support it. It was concerned at the response such activity might provoke from the United States and, preoccupied in other parts of the world, was unwilling to sponsor Che Guevara's call for the creation of 'two or three' or even 'four or five more Vietnams' for the United States in Latin America and the Caribbean. To Cuba, this was nothing but an abdication of socialist internationalism.[5] By 1968, however, Cuban-Soviet relations had reached their nadir. Given the continuation of US hostility towards the Castro regime, the defeat of the guerrilla strategy, symbolised by the death of Guevara in the mountains of Bolivia in 1967, the growing diplomatic isolation of Cuba within the hemisphere and, not least, the economic pressure imposed by the Soviet Union through such measures as the delay of petroleum shipments, Havana was forced to draw closer to Moscow, regardless of ideological misgivings. Castro recognised the necessity of *rapprochement* in 1968 in giving qualified approval to the Brezhnev doctrine of 'limited sovereignty', as exercised in the invasion of Czechoslovakia. Mutual concessions were also subsequently made about revolutionary strategy in that the Soviet Union agreed to give some support to guerrilla insurgency in Latin American states with extremely pro-American and anti-Communist regimes, and the Cubans accepted the Soviet case for adopting peaceful and diplomatic methods in the first instance as the means to challenge US hegemony in the hemisphere.

During the course of this turbulent decade the Soviet Union built up an extensive programme of economic assistance to Cuba. Following the revolution, Cuban trade was very quickly re-oriented away from the United States to the socialist countries — exports to the US fell between 1958 and 1962 from 66.8 per cent of the total to 1.0 per cent, and increased to socialist countries from 2.6 per cent of the total to 86.7 per cent. Bilateral Cuban-Soviet trade perennially resulted in a Cuban deficit, which the Soviet Union absorbed through the 1960s and early 1970s by granting balance of payments credits on highly concessionary terms. By 1974, these subsidies amounted to about US $3.6 billion.[6] In exchange, the Soviet government insisted on a say in the way its aid was used and, in 1970, in reflection of the better relations that had come to exist between the two states, there was established a joint Soviet-Cuban Intergovernmental Economic, Scientific and Technological Co-operation Commission which has, over time, assumed more and more responsibility for the central planning of the Cuban economy. This was followed in 1972 by Cuba's acceptance into membership of the Council for Mutual Economic Assistance (Comecon). Yet these developments have not obviated the need for continuing Soviet subsidy of Cuba's economy, which has been provided since the early 1970s largely by the negotiation of preferential pricing arrangements. The Soviet Union has paid premium prices for Cuban sugar and nickel, while charging below-market prices for petroleum. Under this system, which merely transferred the financing of the trade imbalance from credits to grants, Soviet economic aid to Cuba has grown from some US $2 billion per year between 1975 and 1977 to over US $3 billion a year in the last years of the decade. This amounts to almost US $10 billion a day,[7] which sounds huge and has been the subject of much condemnation in Western political circles, and yet, according to Lynn-Darrell Bender, is less than the direct federal payments made by the United States to Puerto Rico.[8]

Even so, the sums are not negligible. For a long while, the sole advantage this expenditure brought to the Soviet Union was the political gain which derived from the existence of a socialist state in the US backyard. In the 1970s, however, Soviet sustenance of the Cuban regime has paid increasing dividends for Moscow. Whatever their motivation, a whole variety of policies pursued by Cuba in recent years — from its assertively Third World stance inside and outside the Non-Aligned Movement to its intervention in Angola in 1975-6 and Ethiopia in 1977-8 — have served Soviet interests very effectively. At the end of the decade the two states stood more firmly bound together than at any time since the revolution, especially in the military arena. From the outset, the Soviet Union had provided all the military equipment used by Cuba's armed forces, but following the Angolan civil war both the amount and the technological sophistication of Soviet military assistance was increased markedly. The Cuban ground forces, which are equipped with Soviet T-62 tanks, are now more formidable than those of any other power in the Caribbean Basin, including Mexico. Thanks to Soviet-supplied MIG 21s and MIG 23s, Cuba has the best-equipped airforce in Latin America and, thanks again to Soviet assistance, a small but very modern and efficient navy. In the last few years, the USSR has supplied the Cubans with several guided-missile attack boats, more than a dozen Turya-class patrol boats, several landing craft and two Foxtrot Whiskey-class submarines. In exchange, as it were, the Soviet Union has had use of a military base in the Caribbean for over two decades. In 1980, there were some 2,800 Soviet soldiers in Cuba as well as several thousand intelligence personnel, technicians and other specialists. In addition to protecting sophisticated communications facilities in Cuba, they are training the Cuban armed forces for overseas missions and for combined Soviet-Cuban military operations. In 1970, facilities for servicing visiting Soviet submarines were built in Cienfuegos – a potential submarine base, which allows the USSR the option of establishing a permanent naval presence in the Caribbean. Since 1978 Soviet pilots have also been flying patrols from Cuba, and Soviet reconnaissance planes have conducted regular missions monitoring US naval activity in the Atlantic. Beyond this there exists substantial co-ordination of activity in the intelligence field.[9] In short, the military establishments of the two states have become progressively more integrated with time. In logistical terms, Cuban military operations of recent years have only been made possible by Soviet support, and the Soviet Union's growing naval presence in the Caribbean, especially as indicated by regular visits of submarines and warships, relies heavily on the Cuban alliance. From the Soviet point of view, military co-operation is a very valuable feature of the alliance, since it enables the Soviet Union to demonstrate more tangibly than in any other way its ability to project its political power into the Western hemisphere.[10]

The bottom line of the Soviet-Cuban relationship is therefore fairly clear and should not be forgotten. Yet too much concentration upon this facet of Cuban dependence on the USSR can easily lead to a failure to appreciate the politics which go on well above the bottom line. Two points are worth stressing. First, there is the fact that, since Angola, Cuba's standing within the Soviet bloc and its political leverage upon the Soviet Union have been immeasurably strengthened. Castro's receipt of a long standing ovation, led by Brezhnev, at the Soviet party congress held at the conclusion of the Angolan war of independence was a mark of Cuba's new status in Soviet eyes. The reality is that Cuba has received high levels of Soviet support since 1976 in large part

because it is in a position to command such support. As some commentators have suggested, the role of paladin is a more appropriate analogy
than surrogate.[11] Second, there is the fact of Cuba's own national
interests. Such interests do not disappear even in a tight economic and
military alliance with a superpower. It is apparent that more often than
not in the 1970s Moscow's and Havana's perceived international
interests have seemed to converge and run in parallel, but that has not
been so in every instance or every emphasis, not excluding the situation in the Caribbean, and in any case does not mean that Cuban
foreign policy is made directly by the Soviet Union. Other factors
beyond the looming presence of the Soviet Union contribute to the
formation of Cuban foreign policy and need to be incorporated into the
analysis.

Political Elites and Cuban Foreign Policy

Cuba's abandonment around 1968 of the policy of 'exporting' revolution by giving support to other guerrilla movements did not lead
quickly to the formation of a new foreign policy. For three or four
years the Cuban government turned inward, preoccupied with the
ultimately unsuccessful drive to produce 10 million tons of sugar in the
1970 harvest. Its retreat from the extensive foreign involvements of
the previous decade was so striking that one writer was prompted to
talk of Cuba's pursuit of 'socialism in one island'.[12] In fact, in these
years important changes were taking place domestically within the
Cuban political system, as well as within the world at large, which by
the mid-1970s had come together to shape the development of a different Cuban approach to external relations.

At home, the Castro regime had recovered politically and economically from the damaging effects of its attempt to expand sugar production dramatically. What is generally referred to as the 'institutionalisation' of the revolution had taken place, producing a diversification of
political elites within Cuba's ruling coalition. The leadership circle was
widened as veteran *fidelistas* from the original July 26 movement which
made the revolution increasingly shared party and government posts,
with new elements drawn from the 'old Communists' associated with
the Popular Socialist Party (PSP), from a new technocratic and
managerial strata, and from military officers of the Revolutionary
Armed Forces (FAR) and the Ministry of the Revolutionary Armed
Forces (MINFAR) under the command of Raul Castro. Fidel and his

brother remained the dominant figures, monopolising the top leadership positions of party, state and armed forces, but the basis of their power was henceforth less the possession of charisma and more the construction and maintenance of elite coalitions. The administrative bureaucracy was reorganised to incorporate the creation of several deputy prime ministers sitting within a new executive committee, and the system of economic management was also brought under tighter control. Bolstered by Soviet assistance and profiting from the high world-market price of sugar in the mid-1970s, the Cuban economy regained momentum, growing according to official Cuban figures at a rate of 8 per cent per annum in the first years of the decade.

Internationally, too, Cuba's position was strengthened by a series of developments in the first half of the 1970s. As already indicated, relations with the Soviet Union improved, and within Latin America a number of states began to break away from the Organisation of American States policy of sanctions, imposed during the era of Cuban sponsorship of continental revolution, by re-establishing diplomatic and economic ties with Havana. Even the US government adopted a conciliatory posture, following the termination of the Nixon presidency and the inauguration of the Ford administration. Most importantly, though, the Cuban leadership claimed to detect a significant change in these years in the international correlation of forces. The US defeat in Vietnam, the increased strategic influence of the Soviet Union, the new international cohesion of the Third World, symbolised by the success of OPEC – all these factors were interpreted as signs that the balance of world power was tipping in favour of socialism. Castro himself averred in October 1974: 'Capitalism and imperialism are living in a crisis hour . . . for many, the capitalist world is on the brink of the most serious disaster it has confronted since the sombre periods of the great depression of the '30's.'[13]

Emboldened by this perception of world trends and strengthened domestically by the 'institutionalisation' process, the Castro regime embarked from about 1973 onwards upon a range of new foreign policy ventures. In the context of the romanticism of Cuban policy in the previous decade, the most telling characteristic of these new ventures was the greater recognition given to the essential role played by power in international politics and to the consequent need to frame policies to secure Cuba's own national interests. Like any other country, Cuba is concerned to preserve its security and political independence and to secure economic development. From such a realist perspective, its particular problem was that it had to relate to both of the world's superpowers. Given its location and the continuing US hostility to the Castro regime, Cuba's thinking could not but be dominated by an awareness of American power and the realisation that any weakening of that power conversely strengthened its position. If, as one writer put it, 'the Caribbean is located in Washington's strategic back yard, it is equally true that North America lies in Cuba's strategic front yard, a point Havana can never forget'.[14] At the same time, for all the ties of international proletarian solidarity, Cuba had no desire to exchange past dependence on the United States for a similar relationship with the Soviet Union. Although having no serious ideological grievance with the Soviet Union and knowing that the preservation of fraternal relations with the USSR was vital if Cuba's economy was to sustain a growing role in international politics, it was nevertheless concerned to acquire as much independence and freedom of action as was possible within the framework of its relationship with Moscow. Into these conventional perceptions of national interest, there had also to enter in Cuba's case the regime's ideological commitment to Marxism–Leninism. Obviously this provided the regime with a ready-made list of friends and enemies in the world community – friends were those pursuing anti-capitalist and anti-imperialist struggles, enemies those resisting them – thereby directing Cuba's attention towards the need to establish strong links with other radical Third World governments. Yet it did so in a way which served, above all, to reinforce the major geopolitical determinant of Cuban foreign policy, namely, sensitivity to the economic and political power of the United States, seen in Havana as the principal defender of Western capitalist interests and thus the principal advocate of anti-Communism all around the world.

In these broad terms, a basic consensus thus emerged amongst the Cuban leadership in the mid-1970s as to the overriding goals which the country's foreign policy should in future seek to attain. In practice, though, the very diversity of the post-1970 ruling coalition has contributed to a complex and sometimes apparently contradictory mix of foreign policy stances as they have emerged in different parts of the world and on different issues. In an important contribution to the analysis of contemporary Cuban foreign policy, Edward Gonzalez has suggested that this is because different elites in the government have either emphasised some goals over others or favoured a particular strategic line for the achievement of a particular goal.[15] He has identified the existence of three foreign policy 'tendencies' in Cuba in the 1970s, each of which reflected 'the basic policy interests, mentality, or organisational mission of the major elite actors within the new ruling coalition'.[16] These were the pragmatic, the revolutionary political and the military mission tendencies which are examined below.

The Pragmatic Tendency

The impulse towards greater pragmatism in foreign policy-making reflected the new influence of civilian, technocratic and managerial elites in agencies dealing with technical, financial and economic matters. They were led by Carlos Rafael Rodriguez, who assumed direction of Cuba's foreign economic affairs in 1970 and whose continued prominence was confirmed by his appointment as vice-president of both the Council of State and Council of Ministers in 1976. These pragmatists, as Gonzalez has called them, obtained support from many of the 'old Communists' from the PSP, who also rose in influence in the early 1970s, and were further reinforced within the leadership by the greater Soviet involvement in Cuban affairs and the resulting new concern for efficiency which followed the economic dislocation of the period up to 1970. They were aware that Cuba remained economically and technologically underdeveloped and relied for the continuing modernisation of its economy on the import of foreign technology — preferably from the Soviet Union, with whom economic ties were assiduously promoted, but if necessary from capitalist countries since, as Rodriguez admitted in early 1975, 'a whole range of technologies is not yet available in the socialist camp'.[17] Accordingly, he began to negotiate a series of trade agreements, long-term credits and investment contracts with non-socialist countries, especially during the years 1974 and 1975, when booming sugar prices gave him increased negotiating leverage. Rodriguez also appears to have been the driving force behind the several attempts made to seek a new opening with the United States, first in the Ford period and then during the Carter presidency, a prime motivation from the pragmatists' point of view being to secure badly needed US agricultural equipment and other technology, not to mention the lifting of the US embargo on trade with Cuba.

The Revolutionary Political Tendency

The second tendency reflected the return to more revolutionary and political postures in foreign policy. It was associated with Castro himself and was backed mainly by those veteran *fidelista* revolutionaries still in top leadership positions. The aim was, as ever, the promotion of anti-imperialism, principally in Third World settings, but tempered by the realisation of Cuba's own underdevelopment and dependence and a concern that excessively adventurist policies should not jeopardise Cuba's own basic interests. Thus the policy was not only applied more selectively than in the 1960s, but it was directed more at governments than guerrilla movements. The concept which the Cubans created to guide their choice of allies was that of the 'progressive' government, defined rather loosely as 'any government which sincerely adopts a policy of economic and social development and of liberating its country from the imperialist yoke'.[18] Relations with such governments were to be developed on the basis of solidarity, which went further for Cuba than the mere existence of a common understanding concerning the tasks and obstacles at hand to imply nothing less than unity in action in opposition to US imperialism.

This commitment manifested itself in several ways. In his self-appointed role as Third World spokesman, Castro called time and again after 1973 for the OPEC countries to unite with the less-developed world in order to ease dependency and further swing the global balance against imperialism. Within the Non-Aligned Movement, Cuba spent considerable effort trying to isolate and force out of the movement those countries not considered progressive, in order to establish a deeper internal solidarity. Its influence was recognised in September 1979, at the summit held in Havana, when Castro was elected chairman of the organisation for the next three years. Within Latin America, too, Cuba played an active part in regional organistions, joining the Latin American Economic System (SELA), set up in 1975 by the governments of Mexico and Venezuela, two 'progressive' administrations with whom Cuba established close relations in the mid-1970s. Indeed, to individual 'progressive' regimes all over the world – in Africa and the Middle East as well as Latin America – Cuba was ready and willing to extend military and economic assistance in an attempt to solidify Third World links. By all these means, of course, as Castro, a master practitioner of leverage politics, was no doubt only too well aware, Cuba acquired a measure of global influence in its own right and, in so doing, gained a valuable degree of autonomy *vis-à-vis* the Soviet Union.

The Military Mission Tendency

The third foreign policy tendency elaborated by Gonzalez was embodied by Raul Castro and other politically influential FAR/MINFAR officers and stressed the external role or mission of the Cuban armed forces. In large part, this derived from the success of the efforts undertaken after 1970 to strengthen the capacity of the civilian sector to carry out administrative and economic activities previously assigned to the army because of its high level of technical competence and organisational skills. The army, which was pared down as a consequence to a highly professional and increasingly well-equipped force of about 120,000 men, was thus able to devote itself to mainly military tasks. Given that fact that the degree of threat from the United States appeared to have diminished by the mid-1970s, it was also freed somewhat from the traditional military task of domestic defence to a point where it could be used overseas to support other Cuban foreign policy objectives. Indeed, there is a view that the army deliberately sought just such opportunities.[19]

Indicative of this strand of policy was the announcement made by Castro during military exercises in November 1974 that the Cuban armed forces were at the service of 'our sister peoples of Latin America in their struggle against imperialism and . . . on the side of the peoples who face up to imperialism in all parts of the world'.[20] As is well known, it was in Africa that Cuban troops were first used with a vengeance in a foreign territory. In September 1975, 1,000 troops embarked from Cuba *en route* to Angola, constituting even at that point the largest overseas mission ever mounted by the FAR. Subsequently expanded to some 12,000 men, the Cuban presence became the decisive factor in the victory and accession to power of the Marxist Popular Movement for the Liberation of Angola (MPLA). Soviet support was an essential part of the operation, but there is every reason to believe that the original inspiration behind the decision to intervene in the Angolan struggle in so positive a way was Cuban.[21] The Angolan affair hugely increased Cuba's standing in the Third World, entrenching at the same time the influence of the FAR/MINFAR elite at home. So much so that, three years later, in 1978, Cuban troops were again in action on the African continent – in Ethiopia this time, helping a Marxist government defend the Ogaden region against Western-backed Somali aggression.

Gonzalez's identification of these three foreign policy tendencies goes a long way towards explaining the practical contradictions of Cuban foreign policy in the 1970s. Conflicts appeared in a variety of instances, most fundamentally perhaps between the desire to re-establish some limited ties with the United States and the decision to intervene militarily in Angola. The latter effectively brought to a halt high-level secret talks which had been taking place between Havana and Washington. In that particular situation the revolutionary and military mission tendencies were in the ascendancy, but that was not so in every area of policy. The relative influence of the different elites fluctuated both according to the issue and the moment. Within the complex pattern thereby weaved, one consistent threat emerges which reveals the sophisticated political game which Cuba was playing throughout the period, namely, the assertion of as much autonomy as possible within a relationship of very considerable dependency on the Soviet Union.

Cuban Policies in the Caribbean

In Cuba's policies towards the Caribbean the same mix of elite influences can be seen at work as already identified in the formation of foreign policy generally, but with the difference that over the last decade they have nearly always cohered very effectively. The Caribbean is a region to which in recent years the Cuban leadership has given high priority. It is an area where countries are beginning to experiment with socialist models of change, which appeases Cuba's ideological predilections; it is sufficiently distanced from the immediate concerns of the Soviet Union for Cuba to be able to demonstrate its independence in foreign policy; and, above all, it is identified by the United States as part of its sphere of influence. This last factor supplies the common theme to Cuba's Caribbean policies during the 1970s.

The most direct form which Cuban opposition to US interests has taken has been its long-standing support for the granting of independence to Puerto Rico. This was viewed by Washington as a relatively minor irritant in the gamut of US–Cuban animosities until, in 1972, Cuba successfully internationalised the issue by placing the question of Puerto Rico's political status before the UN Committee of Decolonisation, where it branded the territory's existing relationship with the United States as 'colonial' and called for recognition of Puerto Rico's miniscule 'liberation' movement as the legitimate representative of the people of the island. To add insult to injury, Cuba then promoted and sponsored an international conference of solidarity with the Puerto Rican independence movement in Havana in September 1975. Angrily, Kissinger, who was then US Secretary of State, condemned the meeting as an 'unfriendly' and 'totally unjustified' act of interference in the domestic affairs of the United States.[22] During the 1970s, Cuba also gave considerable diplomatic support to the movement to bring about independence for Belize and called upon Britain to hasten the granting of independence to the remaining Associated States amongst the tiny territories of the Leeward and Windward Islands. However, these policies generated no controversy since they coincided with the general direction of Western policy. Cuba spoke too of the need to free Guadeloupe and Martinique from French control but, although the French government has on occasion denounced Cuban interference in the small nationalist movement in these islands, there is no evidence to suggest serious Cuban support for this particular cause.

As in the rest of Latin America, Cuba has lately been much more concerned to establish good relations with the existing governments of the Caribbean than it has to promote revolutionary change. The closest inter-governmental links it has effected have been, rather surprisingly, not with the Latin countries of the region, but with some of the Commonwealth Caribbean countries. For a long while the Commonwealth Caribbean did not figure at all prominently in Cuban concern. Scant attention was paid to this area in the 1960s, because most of the territories were still colonies and those that were independent were still largely under British influence. Even in the early 1970s, when the Cuban government began a diplomatic offensive aimed at re-establishing relations with many of its neighbours in the hemisphere, following the bitter arguments of the previous decade, the Commonwealth Caribbean nations were not included.[23] The initiative was taken within the Commonwealth Caribbean itself when, in October 1972, well before the OAS could bring itself to lift its ban on such relations, the four independent states of the region — Jamaica, Trinidad and Tobago, Guyana and Barbados — issued a joint declaration affirming their intention of working towards the rapid establishment of diplomatic relations with Cuba. Castro hailed this 'challenge to Imperialism', which he said indicated that 'the English-speaking nations of the Caribbean did not acquire the bad habit — as did the Latin American governments — of being dreadfully afraid of Yankee Imperialism',[24] and moved promptly to establish ties.

Although the original decision to approach Cuba was made collectively by the four Commonwealth Caribbean states, a uniform relationship with Cuba has not developed. Barbados has not built up many ties with Havana, and indeed at times relations have been distinctly cool, notably after Barbados refused to allow Cuban aircraft to continue to refuel in Bridgetown *en route* to Angola. Trinidad has traditionally had a closer relationship, but one forged rather more on the basis of the personality and reputation of its eminent first Prime Minister, Dr Williams, than the accumulation of functional or diplomatic relations, which have never become extensive. In his history of the

Caribbean, *From Columbus to Castro*, written in 1969, Williams, although critical of Cuba's dependence on an external prop, praised Castro's programme as 'pure nationalist, comprehensible and acceptable by any other Caribbean nationalist'.[25] He called as early as 1970 for the reabsorption of Cuba into the OAS, and in June 1975 visited the island to receive an honorary degree from the University of Havana. Cuba was always part of Williams's vision of a united Caribbean, even though the essential conservatism of his foreign policy prevented him from forging too intimate a relationship with Havana. Indeed, as Cuba's influence in hemispheric politics grew during the 1970s, relations with conservative governments in all parts of the Commonwealth Caribbean worsened. The most serious set-back came in May 1980, when Cuban fighter planes attacked and sank a Bahamian naval vessel in its home waters. Although Cuba eventually apologised and paid compensation for the mistake, the incident shocked many of the more pro-Western Caribbean governments into a new wariness of Cuban military power. In marked contrast over the same period, close diplomatic links and active working relationships were established between Cuba and the socialist governments of the Commonwealth Caribbean in Guyana, in Jamaica (until Manley's defeat) and latterly in Grenada.

Admittedly, Cuba's relationship with Guyana has been somewhat ambivalent. The Cuban government applauded the radical phase of Burnham's foreign policy in the early 1970s and particularly stressed this when awarding him the prestigious Jose Martí National Order in 1975. This is only given, according to the citation, to 'heads of state and government and leaders of political parties and movements who have distinguished themselves for their international solidarity with the struggle against imperialism, colonialism and neo-colonialism and for their friendship with the Socialist Revolution of Cuba'.[26] From Cuba's point of view, Burnham again demonstrated these qualities when, in December 1975, in the face of a strong US protest, he permitted Cuban transport planes to refuel in Guyana on their way to Africa. Trade and technical assistance agreements were subsequently signed in a number of areas, but without the relationship being pushed too far by the Cubans. This hesitancy probably reflected the existence of well-founded doubts about the depth of the Burnham government's commitment to socialism, especially in domestic matters, but also undoubtedly stemmed from the fact that the official opposition in Guyana, the People's Progressive Party, is a Communist Party with whom the Cuban Communist Party has fraternal relations. Inevitably, this checked the development of too intense a relationship between Havana and the

Burnham regime, and by the end of the decade it was not at all close.

No such reservations existed in the friendship which grew up between Cuba and the Manley government in Jamaica. Unlike its assistance to Guyana, which consisted mostly of exchanges of technical personnel and information, Cuban aid to Jamaica was highly visible, widely publicised and aimed directly at the problems of the poor. The construction of a secondary school in Spanish Town by a joint Cuban–Jamaican workforce, the assignment of Cuban doctors to the Jamaican health service and the provision of condensed milk from Cuba for sale in Jamaica to low-income groups are just a few examples. There also developed collaboration in the fields of fisheries, agriculture, tourism, transportation and public health, to name only some of the more prominent areas; wider commercial relations between the two countries; exchanges of personnel, including the training of young Jamaicans in Cuba in aspects of the construction business; and a considerable degree of co-operation and joint endeavour in foreign policy matters, especially in connection with North–South issues. Moreover, on the great test case of Cuban involvement in Angola, Manley was unequivocal in his support: 'we regard Cuban assistance to Angola as honourable and in the best interests of all those who care for African freedom'.[27] In return, Castro enthusiastically praised Manley's qualities of leadership on a number of occasions and bestowed on him not only the Jose Martí National Order, but the favour of a personal visit to Kingston in October 1977. Although Manley's democratic socialism differed considerably from Cuban Marxist–Leninism, there clearly emerged something of an ideological bond between the two regimes. In fact, the Manley government was ideally suited to the broad thrust of Cuban policy towards the Third World in the 1970s. As Castro himself put it, 'in a nutshell, we like the government of Jamaica because we believe it is a progressive government'.[28] Jamaica's special link with Cuba was, however, swiftly brought to an end by the right-wing Jamaican Labour Party government under Edward Seaga, which ousted Manley from office in 1980.

The closest relationship which Cuba developed with a Commonwealth Caribbean state was with Grenada,[29] to whose revolutionary government it supplied light arms and some military advisers in the immediate aftermath of the assumption of power in 1979, when the threat of an armed counter-attack by the deposed Gairy was real. From that moment close friendship blossomed, involving Cuban political support and provision of technical assistance in a number of areas. These included the loan of doctors and dentists, the training of Grenadian fishermen and, most notably, the provision of machinery and labour as well as finance for the building of the controversial new airport. Bishop was frequently invited to Cuba and was well regarded by Castro.

It should be stressed that, in respect of its relations with Caribbean states, Cuba was perhaps more wooed than wooing, at least in the first instance. The initial *rapprochement* was a Commonwealth Caribbean initiative and, although the Cuban government has undoubtedly taken a greater interest in the region since then, much of the impetus behind the relationship still comes from the Caribbean states. This side of the story is particularly important, given the widespread tendency in the West to condemn Cuban behaviour in such regions as the Caribbean as imperialist. The Caribbean states that have sought Cuban friendship view Cuba in a variety of ways. They see, first, a neighbour they cannot ignore. Cuba cannot be wiped off the map simply because of American disapproval. Secondly, they recognise that Cuba, courtesy of Soviet support, is a source of technical expertise in the region in all manner of fields, and they are aware of the problems of excessive techno-logical dependence on the West. Thirdly, they appreciate that the Cuban connection can be a valuable weapon in the domestic political arena. It gives an air of revolutionary legitimacy to the most reformist of regimes and thus helps to undermine opposition from left-wing forces at home. Fourthly, they share many of Cuba's foreign policy goals, especially in the wider world in connection with the ending of apartheid and the negotiation of a new international economic order. Finally, they undoubtedly hold Cuba in high regard as a model of social and economic development. Whether this is deserved or not is a matter of debate, for Cuba's own economy has had its ups and downs and, as we have seen, has for two decades been heavily supported by the Soviet Union. Even so, there is no denying the political fact that in many parts of the Caribbean Cuba is viewed favourably as a development model. This derives partly from an emotional sympathy with the break it has made from the Western world, but also reflects the unquestionable successes of the Castro regime in reducing inequality, eliminating open unemployment, virtually eradicating illiteracy, improving public health and building up the housing stock. These achievements are con-trasted with the low levels of social welfare in most other Caribbean societies.

In sum, Cuba's new involvement with the Caribbean in the 1970s was not motivated by altruism, but equally it was not based, as has often been alleged, upon a determination, simply and crudely, to promote Communism within the region. There was no Cuban grand design to create such an axis in the Caribbean, stretching from Jamaica to Puerto Rico and on through the little islands via Grenada to Guyana. It befriended governments representing a broad range of ideological positions and did not seek to bring down regimes which it regarded as friends of imperialism. Nor was there an oppressive Soviet hand guiding the Cubans in all that they did. The fact is that Cuban policies towards the Caribbean derived their impetus in the last few years largely from anti-Americanism and the accompanying realisation that this could most effectively be pursued in alliance with other similar-minded 'progressive' states in the region. Havana was, without doubt, more influential in Caribbean affairs at the end of the decade than at the beginning, but it was as a result of the interplay of a variety of recent global trends which worked to Cuban advantage, rather than a concerted effort at ideological or political subversion.

Cuba, Reagan and the CBI

Just as Cuban influence in the Caribbean and the Third World reached a new peak around 1978-9, it began unexpectedly to decline. Several factors contributed to the weakening of Cuba's international standing, but three stand out as of particular importance. The first reflected the beginnings of a reaction against Cuba's close alliance with the Soviet Union. Whereas intervention in Angola had generated widespread admiration amongst Third World governments, Cuba's Ethiopian involvement was less well received. For many non-aligned states, it looked rather too much like a favour dutifully performed for a powerful patron, and voices began to be heard warning of the dangers of a new colonial presence in Africa in the form of the Cubans. The Non-Aligned Summit held in Havana in September 1979 also brought problems for Cuba, even though Castro was elected chairman for the next three-year period. The Cuban position was thought by many members to be too close to that of the Soviet Union on two critical issues: the question of the movement's traditional neutrality between the power blocs of East and West, in respect of which Cuba argued the case for the acceptance of a 'natural alliance' between the underdeveloped world and the socialist camp, and the problem of giving recognition to the new Cambodian regime of Heng Samrin, which Cuba favoured despite the fact, deeply upsetting to more moderate governments attending the summit, that it had been installed by Vietnamese troops with Soviet backing. Largely for this reason, the Cuban position did not win majority support in either case.[30]

For many Third World governments, the suspicions raised about the potentially harmful effects of Cuba's relationship with the Soviet Union were confirmed in full just a few months later by the Soviet invasion of Afghanistan. According to one American foreign-affairs analyst, the implications of this event for Cuba were 'devastating'.[31] It was an unequivocal illustration of the Soviet Union intervening in a nominally non-aligned state in defence of its own national security and was, not surprisingly, condemned throughout the Third World. The UN General Assembly resolution calling for the withdrawal of Soviet troops was supported, amongst Caribbean countries, by the Bahamas, Barbados, the Dominican Republic, Guyana, Haiti, Jamaica, St Lucia and Trinidad and Tobago; only Cuba and Grenada voted against it. Cuba tried to minimise the loss of face it was to suffer in the Third World by making no effort to defend the Soviet intervention, but the damage was done. Proof of this came with the withdrawal of support by non-aligned nations for the election of Cuba, and the subsequent selection of Mexico, as Latin America's representative on the UN Security Council later in 1980. For Cuba, the incident amply illustrated that it had yet to devise effective means for managing the tension inherent in its dual identity as a member of the Third World and a close ally of the Soviet Union. Forced to choose between these two roles in the case of Afghanistan, it could not avoid losing respect with one of its two constituencies, in this case, the nations of the non-aligned Third World, many of which, including some in the Caribbean, had genuinely looked to Cuba for leadership in the previous decade.

The second factor which brought about a fall in Cuba's standing, especially in the Caribbean, was the election of Ronald Reagan to the US presidency. Reagan's views about Cuba's role in the politics of the hemisphere were well advertised before he won office, and so the many measures taken by the United States with a view to damaging Cuba's economic and political position since his inauguration at the beginning of 1981 have come as no surprise to those in power in Havana. For all that, they have not been easy to resist. The US propaganda machine is highly experienced and the weight of US economic influence in the hemisphere still very considerable. Moreover, American charges of Cuban subversion, especially in Central America, had something to bite on. Although never intending to return to the policies of the 1960s, Cuba had been sufficiently impressed by the prospects for revolutionary change in Central America that it had provided material support, including arms, to the Sandinistas in Nicaragua in late 1978 and early 1979, and to left-wing guerrillas in El Salvador in 1980. The level of assistance given was carefully circumscribed and cannot be said to have been critical to the success or failure of either enterprise. Nevertheless, there is no doubt that Cuba's renewed sponsorship of such movements, even though only to a limited degree, did damage its efforts to maintain friendly state-to-state relations with Caribbean and Latin American countries. In 1981, as we have seen, Costa Rica, Colombia and Jamaica, with US encouragement, all broke off diplomatic ties with Cuba, and relations with other countries such as Venezuela, Panama and Peru deteriorated. Only Mexico was prepared to risk Reagan's wrath by offering open support for Cuba in this period. The US offensive against Cuba has far from broken the resolve of the Castro regime and has not isolated Cuba, but it has undeniably reduced its influence in the politics of the hemisphere.

The final factor contributing to the recent fall in Cuban prestige has been the difficulties into which its own economy ran at the end of the 1970s. Despite some expansion of the industrial sector, the Cuban economy remains heavily dependent on sugar production after more than twenty years of revolutionary government. Crop diseases in sugar and tobacco led to a sharp fall in foreign-exchange earnings in 1980, and a consequent decline in domestic consumption and economic growth. Many of the refugees who fled the island in 1980, after seeking asylum in the Peruvian embassy in Havana, reported food rationing, shortages of consumer goods and high prices. Since then the world recession has badly affected sugar producers, with prices plunging from US $0.28 per pound in 1980 to a mere US $0.07 per pound in 1982. Thus, in spite of achieving the second biggest sugar harvest ever in 1981/2 and other increases in export production, Cuba experienced a further fall in export earnings. To make the situation worse, US economic pressure succeeded in blocking Cuba's access to several lines of credit, including a large loan arranged by Credit Lyonnais, until, in August 1982, the regime was forced to announce that it intended to seek the rescheduling of part of its foreign debt. Cuba's total debt was not huge by the standards of some Latin American countries. It amounted to US $3.5 billion, of which the Banco Nacional de Cuba sought a ten-year postponement of repayment of some US $1.2 billion, falling due before the end of 1985. On the whole, Western banks were impressed with Cuba's response to the situation, particularly its plans to balance its budget and its firmly expressed intention to meet debt-service repayments as a matter of international obligation; thus reasonably satisfactory terms were quickly agreed for a rescheduling of the most imminent part of the debt. The price which Cuba has had to pay is the promise of tight financial management, involving a considerable degree of austerity, for the next two or three years at least. This means that Cuban economic dependence on the Soviet Union will be further intensified and that spare resources will scarcely be available, even if they were desired, to finance subversion or military activity in the Caribbean or anywhere else in the near future. The Cuban economy is not about to collapse, but it is hardly in a position to spread largesse around the Third World, and it no longer looks quite the model of economic development which it once appeared to be to so many.

All in all, it is not easy to say where Cuban foreign policy stands at present. One point which is clear is that the Cuban relationship with the Soviet Union is as close as at any time since 1959. The Reagan administration's hard line, including threats of a blockade, has pushed Cuba in this direction: for, if Cuba is to be seen in Washington, however incorrectly, as a Soviet puppet, then it must seem in Havana that Cuban security can best be guaranteed by placing itself unequivocally under the protective umbrella of Soviet power. It was significant that in December 1980, in a report to the Second Congress of the Cuban Communist Party, Castro endorsed for the first time Soviet intervention in Afghanistan — the very issue over which Reagan, in his election campaign, had threatened to blockade the island. The Soviet Union responded appropriately, President Brezhnev warning the United States in a speech on the Polish crisis in April 1981 that Cuba was 'an inseparable member of the Socialist camp'.[32] The closeness of this connection will continue to make Cuban relations with non-aligned states rather uneasy and will thus place an obvious limit on Cuba's ability to restore its prestige in the Third World as a whole. Its own economic difficulties further hamper the attainment of this objective.

To reduce its dependence on Moscow and indeed to help with the revival of the economy, Cuba needs to establish some sort of *modus vivendi* with the United States. Indeed, as indicated earlier, the Cubans made no less than three such attempts in the first eighteen months of the Reagan administration, all unsuccessful. However, they will not sacrifice their pride or their revolutionary commitment for such a goal. As Castro put it in July 1982, 'no Imperialist threat or aggression will make us step back as much as half an inch. Not even half an inch.'[33] In fact, Cuba seems to have resigned itself to continuing US aggression as long as Reagan remains President and it took the opportunity of US support for Britain's position in the Falklands/Malvinas conflict to regain some of its standing in Latin America. Cuba firmly backed Argentina, inviting the Foreign Minister, Costa Mendez, to Havana — the first visit by such a minister since 1959 — and condemning the American stance as 'anti-Latin American'. Its stand on this issue provided the opportunity for the beginnings of a *rapprochement* with Venezuela, which, like Cuba, strongly opposed the Anglo-US position. Within the Caribbean so too did the Dominican Republic, Haiti, Grenada and Suriname, although the majority of the Commonwealth Caribbean governments remained, to a greater or lesser degree, pro-British.

In respect of the Caribbean, Cuba has also lately come out with scathing criticisms of the US Caribbean Basin Initiative. According to an editorial in *Granma*, Reagan's speech on the subject to the OAS in February 1982 was 'a confirmation of the political sclerosis of the ultra right now ruling the United States, an indication of how that government attempts to replace reality at whim with primitive and false formulas while arrogantly ignoring the facts'.[34] More substantively, according to the Cubans, the CBI erred because it failed to make provision for structural change in the economies of the Caribbean, offered only crumbs in the amount of aid provided, aimed basically to provide guarantees for US private investment in the region and, finally, overemphasised military support at the expense of genuine development assistance. All these were questions which have been widely raised in comment and discussion of the CBI. To the extent that the United States' much-vaunted plan for reviving the Caribbean economy ultimately fails, Cuba would be better placed to rebuild its standing in the region.

Notes

1. See S. Mishin, 'Latin America: Two Trends of Development', *International Affairs* (Moscow), no. 6 (1976), p. 54 and L. Gouré and M. Rothenberg, *Soviet Penetration of Latin America* (Miami Centre for Advanced International Studies, Miami, 1975).

2. V.I. Popov, I.D. Ovsyany and V.P. Nikhamin (eds.), *A Study of Soviet Foreign Policy* (n.p., Moscow, 1975), p. 151.

3. See W.R. Duncan, 'Moscow, the Caribbean, and Central America' in R. Wesson (ed.), *Communism in Central America and the Caribbean* (Hoover Institution Press, Stanford, 1982), p. 8, Table 1.1.

4. See J. Levesque, *The USSR and the Cuban Revolution* (Praeger, New York, 1978), pp. 115–25.

5. See H.S. Dinerstein, *Soviet Policy in Latin America* (Rand, Santa Monica, 1966), pp. 28–30.

6. The figures quoted for Soviet aid to Cuba vary considerably. For a clear

and reliable discussion, see J.I. Domínguez, 'Cuban Foreign Policy', *Foreign Affairs*, vol. 57, no. 1 (1978), pp. 83–108.

7. Ibid.

8. L.-D. Bender, *Cuba vs United States: The Politics of Hostility*, 2nd edn (Inter American University Press, San Juan, 1981), p. 50.

9. See J. Valenta, 'Soviet and Cuban Responses to New Opportunities in Central America' in R.E. Feinberg (ed.), *Central America: International Dimensions of the Crisis* (Holmes and Meier, New York, 1982), pp. 137–8 and 144.

10. See J.D. Theberge (ed.), *Soviet Seapower in the Caribbean: Political and Strategic Implications* (Praeger, New York, 1972).

11. E. Gonzalez, 'Complexities of Cuban Foreign Policy', *Problems of Communism*, vol. 26, no. 6 (1977), p. 10.

12. J. Petras, 'Socialism in One Island: A Decade of Cuban Revolutionary Government', *Politics and Society*, vol. 1, no. 3 (1971), pp. 203–24.

13. *Granma Weekly Review*, 27 October 1974.

14. W.R. Duncan, 'Soviet and Cuban Interests in the Caribbean' in R. Millett and W.M. Will (eds.), *The Restless Caribbean* (Praeger, New York, 1979), pp. 141–2.

15. E. Gonzalez, 'Institutionalization, Political Elites, and Foreign Policies' in C. Blasier and C. Mesa-Lago (eds.), *Cuba in the World* (University of Pittsburgh Press, Pittsburgh, 1979), pp. 3–36.

16. Ibid., p. 17.

17. *Le Monde*, 16 January 1975, cited in ibid., p. 18.

18. Cited in R. Espindola, 'Cuba: Centre of Peace or Conflict', *South* (August 1982), p. 20.

19. See J.I. Domínguez, 'Institutionalization and Civil-Military Relations', *Cuban Studies*, vol. 6, no. 1 (1976), pp. 47–55 and 61–2.

20. *Granma Weekly Review*, 1 December 1974.

21. See W.M. LeoGrande, 'Cuban–Soviet Relations and Cuban Policy in Africa', *Cuban Studies*, vol. 10, no. 1 (1980), pp. 1–48.

22. See A. Linsley, 'US–Cuban Relations: The Role of Puerto Rico' in Blasier and Mesa-Lago, *Cuba in the World*, pp. 119–30.

23. See R.E. Jones, 'Cuba and the English-speaking Caribbean' in ibid., p. 131.

24. *Granma Weekly Review*, 20 April 1974.

25. E. Williams, *From Colombus to Castro: The History of the Caribbean 1492-1969* (André Deutsch, London, 1970), p. 486.

26. *Granma Weekly Review*, 20 April 1975.

27. *Caribbean Contact*, January 1976.

28. *Granma Weekly Review*, 30 July 1975.

29. For a discussion of this relationship, see A.P. Maingot, 'Cuba and the Commonwealth Caribbean', *Caribbean Review*, vol. 9, no. 1 (1980), pp. 44–5.

30. See W.M. LeoGrande, 'The Evolution of the Nonaligned Movement', *Problems of Communism*, vol. 29, no. 1 (1980), pp. 35–52.

31. W.M. LeoGrande, 'Foreign Policy: The Limits of Success' in J.I. Domínguez (ed.), *Cuba: Internal and International Affairs* (Sage, Beverley Hills, 1982), p. 176.

32. *The Times*, 8 April 1981.

33. *Granma Weekly Review*, 5 September 1982.

34. Ibid., 6 March 1982.

5 THE OLD EUROPEAN POWERS: BRITAIN, FRANCE AND THE NETHERLANDS

In the present era, the traditional imperial powers of Western Europe are no longer the dominant forces in Caribbean affairs that historically they have been. Forced by economic necessity to restrict their global commitments in the post-war period, they have generally found their interests in other parts of the world to be more pressing than those in the Caribbean. As a result, their involvement in the contemporary international crisis of the Caribbean pales by comparison with that of the United States and Cuba, the major protagonists in the struggle for influence.

Yet the old European powers still cannot be ignored. In relative terms, their role in Caribbean politics may have diminished, but it has not yet disappeared. Britain's policy over the last few years has been to withdraw from individual commitments, but it has continued to give loyal support to the position of the United States. France is still directly responsible for possessions in the area and seeks to consolidate its position as a middle power interested in the Caribbean. Under President Mitterrand, it also takes a different view of political trends in the region from that of the United States. The Netherlands concerns itself primarily with its own territories and ex-territories in the area and finds them still a significant preoccupation of foreign policy. By comparison, Spain, the first imperial power to discover the region, can almost be said to have given up its Caribbean destiny. In recent years, it has not sought to assert itself in the region, although that statement must immediately be qualified by reference to the growing international visibility of the socialist government of Felipe Gonzalez, which came to office at the end of 1982. Spain's new left-wing Prime Minister embarked on a Caribbean and Latin American tour in June 1983, visiting amongst other places the Dominican Republic, and several times uttered sharp criticisms of current US policy towards the area, especially in Central America. Spanish involvement in regional politics may therefore grow again in the future.

The actions of each of these powers are also affected by the fact that the European Economic Community (EEC) must these days be viewed as an additional European actor in Caribbean affairs. By virtue of its trade and aid policies, and lately by more political means, the

Community has come to stand as an important source of external support for the developing states of the region and a potential counter weight to excessive US influence. Some assessment of the role assumed by the EEC in the international politics of the Caribbean is therefore needed to complete the discussion of European involvement.

Britain

British interests in the Caribbean are less today than at any time during the last three centuries. From being one of the dominant imperial powers in the region, Britain has retreated to the point where it possesses very few remaining political commitments in the area, which is generally thought of in Britain simply as the Commonwealth Caribbean. There is Belize, which, although independent, is an awkward diplomatic problem to which the Foreign Office still has to devote attention; there are the colonies of Montserrat and now Anguilla; and there are the other tiny dependencies, the British Virgin Islands, the Cayman Islands and the Turks and Caicos Islands, which are not part of the mainstream of Caribbean politics. These territories are all that is left of Britain's former West Indian empire, and themselves scarcely constitute compelling reasons for Britain to maintain a close interest in Caribbean affairs. The reality is that Britain's main interests in the region have now been effectively reduced to three considerations: trade, investment and aid.

Apart from the United States, Britain is still the Commonwealth Caribbean's most important trading partner. Until 1965, the value of Britain's imports from the Caribbean exceeded the value of its exports to the region. Since then, with exports rising and imports fluctuating, the balance of trade has swung increasingly in Britain's favour. In 1978, for example, Britain's surplus in its trade with the Commonwealth Caribbean was £59.4 million; in 1979, it was £64.0 million; and even in 1980, despite the general depression of the international economy, it was over £29.0 million.[1] British exports to the region consist mainly of manufactured goods, machinery and transport equipment, and imports from it are almost exclusively primary agricultural products. For Britain, trade with the Caribbean constitutes only a tiny share of the country's total trade — imports in 1979 amounted to 0.3 per cent, exports to 0.5 per cent — but for the Caribbean, Britain is still the main market for its major export crops, taking the bulk of the region's sugar exports, almost the entire banana crop and most of the citrus. None of these products are very competitive on the world market, and in the past they have relied heavily on the help Britain has given in providing guaranteed markets. The most important agreement in this context was the Commonwealth Sugar Agreement, first implemented in 1951, under which Britain provided a long-term guarantee of access and price for more than two-thirds of the Commonwealth Caribbean's sugar exports.

The future of this and other similar preferential agreements became highly controversial during the course of Britain's negotiations to join the European Community, but various promises of safeguards were extracted from the EEC and the long-standing system of Commonwealth trading preferences was eventually dismantled. The Caribbean's agricultural trading arrangements with Britain have now been subsumed within a wider EEC framework and are conducted according to the terms of the Lomé Convention, signed in 1975 and renewed in 1979. The end of Britain's special trading relationship with the Caribbean brought considerable relief to British policy-makers, who found their residual responsibilities to former colonies in the Caribbean increasingly hard to reconcile with the reality of Britain's perceived new future with Europe. This attitude no more than reflects the extent to which trade with the Commonwealth Caribbean is of minimal importance to Britain's overall economic performance.

Britain has also traditionally been one of the main sources of outside private investment entering the Caribbean. Agriculture was the focus of this investment, but in the last decade more money has gone into tourism, real estate, engineering, communications and other modern sectors of the economy. As this has occurred, British private investment has been overtaken by American and Canadian finance and now plays a much less significant role in the Caribbean economy. From the British point of view, the rewards from this are fairly low in the context of the economy as a whole. According to the official *Business Monitor*, net earnings of British companies in the whole of the Caribbean, Central and Southern America in 1978 amounted to only £143.5 million, which represented just over 6 per cent of the economy's total earnings from direct investment overseas.[2] Earnings from the Commonwealth Caribbean alone would have been very much less.

Finally, in respect of aid too, Britain has lately reduced its commitment to the Caribbean. Ever since the Moyne Commission visited the region in 1938 and revealed the extent of the deprivation suffered in the West Indies, Britain has recognised the need to deploy aid to the Caribbean in order to help reduce the incidence of poverty. To this end, in 1966, there was established in Barbados the office of the British

Development Division, charged with advising the British government of the aid requirements of the area and providing advice to the regional governments on the implementation of their development programmes.[3] However, in regard to the Caribbean, as elsewhere, the recent problems of the British economy have brought pressure to bear on the supply of aid. In respect of the Caribbean, this has meant that in 1979 British bilateral aid totalled only £28.9 million at 1970 prices, a marginal increase only upon the figure of £26.2 million supplied in 1971, eight years earlier, whereas in 1980, under Conservative control, the figure fell to a mere £23.7 million.[4]

It cannot, then, be said that the Caribbean is a part of the world in which any major British interests are at stake. Whether it be in the matter of political responsibilities, trade, investment or aid, Britain's commitment to the Caribbean is now minimal. However, such a statement disguises one very important consideration which arguably ought to be the central touchstone of British policy towards the region, namely, the not insignificant element of the British population which is of Caribbean extraction. West Indians, especially Jamaicans, constitute one of the major non-European minorities in Britain and have been a major focus of racial conflict in British society. One might have thought that the makers of British foreign policy towards the Caribbean would have incorporated this fact into their thinking. Yet the reality is that it has not been permitted to become a relevant consideration. The artificial barrier between domestic and foreign policy has been rigidly maintained on this issue, and the West Indian 'problem' officially consigned to the spheres of immigration and race relations. Paradoxically, therefore, the fact that Britain is a society with a Caribbean element does not have a recognisable influence on the formulation of British foreign policy towards the Caribbean. Nobody in Whitehall has dared to apply their minds to an exploration of what might be the implications of such a connection.

This narrow view of the extent of Britain's interests in the Caribbean has been accepted by governments of both major parties in Britain since the 1960s. Indeed, the main theme of policy in these years has been to reduce commitments in the area, especially political ones, as fast as possible, a goal firmly emphasised by British entry into the EEC. The four leading British territories in the region — Jamaica, Trinidad and Tobago, Barbados and Guyana — were given independence between 1962 and 1966, and the concept of Associated Statehood was only created in 1967 because the islands of the Leewards and Windwards were at the time thought to be too small to be viable as independent entities. However, by the early 1970s the myth that there was some equation relating size and sovereignty had been exposed by sundry political developments in other parts of the world: independence had come to be perceived much more as a formal status in international society and less as a reward for the achievement of viability in some practical sense. As a result, the little Eastern Caribbean islands gradually began to consider the possibility of cashing the 'independence cheque' which the notion of Associated Statehood had given them from the outset. According to the terms of the West Indies Act, which established these particular constitutions, all the island governments had to demonstrate was that they had the support of the people in wanting to move to independence, a condition which it had been intended should be met by the achievement of a two-thirds majority in a referendum. Yet in 1970, when Eric Gairy began to examine the possibility of independence for Grenada and drew attention to the difficulties of attaining such a large majority in the highly partisan political climate existing in the small islands, it seems that the British government, in the form of Joseph Godber, the minister of state with responsibility for the region in the Conservative administration of Edward Heath, gave him to believe that Britain might itself use its powers under another section of the Act to abrogate the association if he, Gairy, won a general election in which independence was an issue.[5] In February 1972, Gairy won the necessary electoral victory and constitutional talks were announced. Despite evidence of bitter opposition in Grenada to the prospect of independence under Gairy, culminating in a general strike and violent disturbances, the British government adhered to its commitment and introduced the necessary legislation into Parliament. It was formally explained that metropolitan abrogation of the constitution was the appropriate method of decolonisation, if there was mutual agreement between Britain and the respective island government; a referendum was only needed to enable an Associated State to move to independence 'in spite of the opposition of this country'.[6] Although somewhat embarrassed by allegations of unseemly haste in withdrawal from its responsibilities in the area, the Heath government had clearly decided that accelerated decolonisation for the semi-dependencies was the most economic option for Britain and determined to override objections from wherever they came.

These events set the pattern for the other Associated States. The Labour government that came to power in Britain in 1974 did not demur from the new policy and presided over the independence of Dominica and St Lucia without requiring a referendum to be held in either case. Indeed, Labour's minister of state at the Foreign Office, Ted Rowlands, was happy to style himself 'Minister for Decolonisation'. For all the willingness of successive British governments to shed these responsibilities, the particular negotiations were long drawn out and complicated on each occasion, consuming considerable amounts of diplomatic effort. British policy towards the Caribbean in these years was thus dominated by the process of decolonisation. The flow of aid continued at modest levels, the Labour goverment trying hard to spare the Ministry of Overseas Development from public-expenditure cuts without being fully able to do so. Only occasionally did British policy show any awareness of the broader developmental and geopolitical problems which were brewing in the region. Towards the end of the decade, the government found some extra money to help the fellow social democratic regime of Michael Manley in Jamaica, and on one occasion the Prime Minister, James Callaghan, successfully used Britain's influence at the International Monetary Fund to ease the terms on which financial assistance was given to that country's ailing economy.[7] But these were *ad hoc* gestures: although Rowlands tried manfully to alert his own colleagues, and indeed also members of the US administration, to the political dangers of the economic difficulties facing the region, the Labour government never succeeded in developing the basis of a coherent post-imperial policy towards the Caribbean, and in truth never accorded the region a sufficiently high priority.

The Thatcher government which came to office in 1979 has, in fact, been drawn more fully into Caribbean affairs – not by desire, but as a consequence of the quickening pace of the regional crisis. Its policy towards the Caribbean has, however, been set in an unimaginative and distinctly conservative mould. It is founded upon the assumption that the best prospect for the economic development of the Commonwealth Caribbean lies in the region's whole-hearted integration into the world economy as currently organised. It seeks to encourage the inflow of foreign private investment, sees little need for extensive aid programmes and believes that traditional free enterprise policies pursued by Caribbean governments can still lead to the achievement of economic development. Regimes which reject these premises, like that in Jamaica between 1972 and 1980, and that in Grenada after 1979, are regarded as dangerously radical and treated accordingly.

Indeed, under pressure from the United States, Grenada became a target for British censure. Among Washington's Atlantic partners, the British government has been the most responsive to requests for support in bringing economic and political sanctions to bear on Grenada. It has continued to meet existing aid obligations to Grenada, but after the revolution deliberately excluded the island from further assistance, even including aid extended to the other Windward Islands to rehabilitate the banana industry following hurricane damage. This was justified on the grounds that Grenada suffered much less damage and is less dependent on the banana crop than the other islands. In fact, the reason was political. Former minister of state at the Foreign Office, Nicholas Ridley, was quoted as saying: 'Grenada is in the process of establishing a kind of society of which the British government disapproves, irrespective of whether the people of Grenada want it or not.'[8] Britain also supported US pressure on the EEC governments to abandon a scheme to help build the new airport on Grenada. This was not totally successful, since a loan was made, but it very probably caused a reduction in the amount of money made available. Finally, Britain joined with the United States in repeatedly bringing diplomatic pressure to bear on the Grenadian government to hold 'free and fair' elections and release or bring to trial those who had been detained since March 1979.

Indeed, in all matters pertaining to the geopolitics of the area, the British Conservative government of the early 1980s has given virtually uncritical support to the Reagan administration's view of the Caribbean. In particular, it seems entirely to endorse American fears about Cuba's role. At a press conference on a visit to Venezuela in August 1980, the former Foreign Secretary, Lord Carrington, described Cuba as 'a destabilising force in the area' and accused the Castro regime of 'exporting its system of government, or seeking to export it, by subversion to other countries'.[9] Ridley's successor as minister of state, Richard Luce, spoke also of Cuban policy in the Caribbean as the actions of 'those who are solely interested in exploitation as opposed to sustaining peaceful evolution and reform and democratic development'.[10] Unlike the United States, Britain does maintain diplomatic relations with Cuba and has done so ever since Castro came to power in 1959, but in every other respect it follows the line of the United States. Minister never seem to show any awareness of Cuba's positive role as a model of development in the region, or even of its potential as a source of technical assistance to some of the smaller and more underdeveloped ex-British territories.

On the issue of Belize too, there is some reason to believe that the British government sees its faithful support for the United States as a means, perhaps the only means, of ending an expensive military commitment which it cannot otherwise terminate because of the continuing Guatemalan threat. Since Belizean independence, talks have taken place between the United States and the Belize government on the issue of establishing a US airbase in the territory and permitting US troops to engage in what is described as 'jungle training'. The US government is obviously attracted by the idea of securing another military base in Central America and might well be prepared in due course to take over Britain's formal defence responsibilities to Belize, even at the cost of angering its Guatemalan ally. Left-wing elements within the Belizean government would be bitterly opposed to such an arrangement, but if Britain was to insist upon withdrawal following a deal with the United States, there would be no realistic defence alternative.

Finally, a word should be said about the Thatcher government's attitude towards Guyana. Britain no longer recognises a specific involvement in the border dispute with Venezuela and has formally correct relations with the Guyanese government. The significance of the policy lies in what it omits. The government has uttered no particular condemnation of the many by now well-documented abuses of human rights committed by the present Guyanese government. Aid continues to be supplied: indeed, in 1980 Guyana was the fourth largest recipient of British aid within the Commonwealth Caribbean countries. Suffice to say that all of this contrasts strikingly with the policy pursued towards Grenada.

These policies brought forth a considerable amount of domestic criticism from Labour and Liberal politicians, academics concerned with the area, informed journalists, voluntary aid agencies such as Oxfam, and even some businessmen and bankers with interests in the Caribbean. Opposition crystallised around the investigation of British policy towards the region undertaken by the House of Commons Select Committee for Foreign Affairs during the course of 1981 and 1982. Following the hearing of evidence from many expert witnesses, the committee eventually produced a lengthy report highly critical of the approach of the Thatcher government. Taking the view that Britain had perhaps withdrawn too abruptly from its long-standing commitment to the area, it argued that in the present circumstances there was 'ample justification for making an active British contribution to the achievement of stability, security, and development in the Caribbean', albeit on the basis of 'a sympathetic assessment and support of the legitimate aspirations of the individual nations' of the region.[11] It further identified economic problems as the key to the instability of the Caribbean and criticised the Foreign Office for generally taking an unjustifiably optimistic view of the economic prospects of the area. In this connection, it applauded the considerable degree of success achieved by the economic and social policies of the revolutionary government in Grenada and noted, by comparison, the bleak development prospects of the other small territories of the Eastern Caribbean.

On the international questions which relate to the Caribbean, the committee firmly expressed its opinion that the view of the region as a theatre of East-West confrontation was 'an unsatisfactory and insufficient policy framework'.[12] It noted the present US government's 'paranoid antagonism towards any government in the area which may be remotely described as left wing, let alone Marxist'[13] and judged that President Reagan's Caribbean Basin Initiative 'will not remotely match up to the basic needs of the area'.[14] Cuba, in turn, was not seen simply as a proxy of the Soviet Union. Its ideological commitment to revolutionary change was recognised, but so were its achievement in housing, education and health, and its assertion of Cuban independence against outside domination.

Cuba also came up for further discussion in the conclusions and recommendations of the report, for the committee's central demand was that Britain should do all in its power to urge the United States to pursue 'an imaginative initiative . . . which would . . . recognise the legitimacy of Cuba's place in the region's affairs, and help remove a major stumbling block to peace and stability'.[15] The presence of the United States as the strongest and most immediately interested external power was recognised, but it was nonetheless felt that in this and other ways Britain could perhaps help the United States reach an accommodation with the fundamental changes that have taken place in the Caribbean over the last decade. To do this, Britain would have to improve the quality and breadth of its representation and be prepared to reaffirm its commitment to the area by embarking upon such specific moves as the negotiation of a new bilateral aid programme with Grenada, the cultivation of greater international awareness of the concept of a Caribbean zone of peace, and the promotion of a greater emphasis upon infrastructural development in the support programmes of multilateral aid bodies.

Under the procedures of the Select Committee system at Westminster, the British government is bound to make a formal reply to the recommendations of a parliamentary report within three months of its publication. The government's response, tabled by the Secretary of State, Francis Pym, in March 1983, therefore constitutes the most recent statement of official British policy towards the Caribbean. It was a long document, very detailed, describing at length the minutiae of British aid and technical assistance programmes to the area, and yet utterly irrelevant to the broad geopolitical thrust of the committee's recommendations and its critique of present government policy. There was no discussion of US policy towards the region, no mention of the Caribbean Basin Initiative. There was no reply to the committee's major proposal concerning the promotion of *rapprochement* between Cuba and the US. Indeed, unbelievably the word Cuba does not appear once in the government's reply; it was apparently not allowed to sully the document. In other words, there was literally no discussion of the broad strategy which a country like Britain should adopt towards a part of the world like the Caribbean. The best the government could come up with was the bland assertion that its 'continuing commitment to long-term development in the region is already clear'.[16]

Very little of the rest of the government's reply is worthy of further attention. One of the few occasions when it came near to the bone politically was in the discussion of Grenada. In this connection, it restated the Thatcher government's policy, first announced in February 1980, that 'greater weight should be given in the allocation of British aid to political, industrial and commercial considerations alongside our basic development objectives'.[17] In Grenada's case, the island was receiving substantial aid from other sources − a fact which it said had to be taken into account − whilst there was still the hoary question of human rights to consider. In short, the government would not agree to begin informal negotiations to draw up a new bilateral agreement, although the minister promised − in that famous phrase − to keep the situation under continuous review. For the rest, there was extensive discussion of banana support programmes, links with parliamentary bodies in the Caribbean, the provision of legal resources to the region, the dangers of arms sales, diplomatic representation in the area, the role of volunteer aid agencies and so on. None of these issues are unimportant in themselves, but what the Select Committee was urging was that each should have a place within a coherent approach to the region that was sensitive more to the question of development than security. In the Secretary of State's reply they stood only as a series of piecemeal measures, advanced in a self-justificatory manner.

In conclusion, it must be said that the Select Committee's report has failed to change the direction of the Thatcher government's approach to the Caribbean. By stepping outside the ideological parameters of government thought, it rendered itself automatically unacceptable.

Indeed, there is some evidence in the last year that the British government has been prepared to come out even more fully in support of the Reagan administration's view of the situation in the Caribbean. British warships were about to take part in a NATO exercise in the region when they were called away to the Falkland Islands, but have since participated in the 1983 manoeuvres. Although Britain under the Thatcher government has not shown much concern for regional economic development, even as conceived by the CBI, it has clearly demonstrated its willingness to contribute to the defence of Western security interests in the area, albeit in a relatively minor way.

France

French perceptions of the Caribbean are determined above all by the fact that the region includes three territories which are *départements* of metropolitan France. With the establishment of the Fourth Republic in 1946, the decision was taken that some form of decolonisation was necessary for French possessions in the Western hemisphere. In keeping with the assimilationist philosophy which underlay French colonial administration, it was proposed that they should become integral parts of France with their citizens having the same rights as any other French person. Referenda were held in Martinique, Guadeloupe and French Guiana to assess the local reaction to the idea; in each case, these produced large majorities in favour of departmentalisation, which was then quickly effected. Unconcerned by the growth of independence movements in other parts of the colonial world, the French thus believed that they had successfully fulfilled their commitment to decolonisation in what they called the Antilles.[18]

From this moment onwards, the policy of all succeeding French governments has been to maintain this arrangement as a permanent feature of the political structure of France itself. The subsequent emergence of discontent in the Caribbean territories was generally met by the provision of financial resources to build schools and houses and institute welfare services, rather than by the granting of political concessions on the road to independence. In the French view, there were no concessions which could constitutionally be made. In June 1967, in response to growing agitation for autonomy or independence in Martinique and Guadeloupe, the French Minister of State for Overseas Departments and Territories, Pierre Billotte, declared that the people of the French West Indies were bound by a contract to France: it was legitimate for them to seek to be free, but 'useless to demand to be independent' since departmentalisation served to assimilate them to their compatriots of the metropolis.[19] Neither the events of 1968 in France nor the acquisition of independence by other territories in the Caribbean changed this view. When President Giscard D'Estaing visited Martinique in December 1974, he made just the same point. No adjustments were necessary to the political status of the French Caribbean, although there was still room for progress in the social and economic fields. French governments have long accepted prime responsibility for promoting the economic development of their Caribbean territories and have engendered a much higher standard of living for their people than that generally achieved in other comparable parts of the region, but they have all without hesitation regarded the question of political status as closed.

This aspect of French policy has had important implications not only for the people of the *départements* themselves, but also for the rest of the Caribbean, which has had similarly to accept the permanence of France's involvement in the region's affairs. It is not that France has sought to take up a dominant position in the Caribbean, as it once did in South-East Asia and as it still does in parts of Africa; rather, that it has been consistently involved in the geopolitical conflicts which have divided the region, acting generally as a firm defender of French national interests first and those of the West as a whole second. Relations with Cuba are a case in point. The French government maintained a dialogue with the Castro regime after the revolution, but came to believe in the late 1960s that Cuban machinations were primarily responsible for the outbreak of unrest which briefly disturbed the *status quo* in the Caribbean *départements*, particularly in Guadeloupe. Yet, in the early 1970s, when France decided to promote a more active role in Latin America, Cuban co-operation was sought and closer trading relations promoted, so much so that by 1975 a mixed French–Cuban commission had been created to foster the relationship. The growing friendship was suddenly shattered later the same year by the so-called 'Carlos Affair', in which a Venezuelan terrorist by that codename killed two policemen and a civilian in Paris allegedly with the assistance of two Cuban diplomats whom the French authorities expelled. Cuba's involvement in Africa threatened French economic and political interests more directly and caused the two countries to grow further apart. As Cuban influence in the Caribbean also became more marked in the latter part of the decade and threatened to influence politics in the *départements*, so France was prepared to assert itself more openly to help the United States check the threat to French and Western interests, which was perceived to be emanating from Havana. This was made clear in a statement made by Paul Dijoud, the French Secretary of State for Overseas Territories in the Giscard administration, in March 1980, in which he denounced Cuban influence on the nationalist movement in Martinique and openly stated that France was prepared to co-operate with other Western countries to contain Cuban activity in the region. The French garrison in the Caribbean was already 3,000 strong, but this did not stop Dijoud declaring ominously that 'France is one of the rare countries in the world which is capable of transporting to the Antilles and Guiana, in 10 hours, a division and a half of crack troops'.[20]

Beyond the security of its own possessions, which unquestionably lay at the centre of French thinking, what worried the Giscard government at this time was the vulnerability of some of the small Commonwealth Caribbean states, especially those which had been historically influenced by French possession for certain periods in their history. The island of Dominica has been a particular concern, since it is also situated between the French islands of Guadeloupe and Martinique and thus commands two of the sea approaches into the Caribbean which would otherwise be completely under French control. Considerable sums of French aid were provided for Dominica, especially after it was devastated by a severe hurricane in late 1979. During 1979 and 1980, several senior French political figures toured the Commonwealth Caribbean with a view to extending French influence to this part of the region. The most important was Oliver Stirn, Minister of State in the French Foreign Ministry, who visited Grenada, Barbados and Trinidad in February 1980. He surprised even those in the area most willing to accept France's advances by floating the idea of France being granted observer status at meetings of the Caribbean Community (CARICOM) Council of Ministers. Even though this proposal did not meet with a ready response, warm receptions were accorded to him in Trinidad, where France was engaged in a government-to-government arrangement providing aid in housing and health development, and Barbados, which according to Stirn was admired in France for its stability and balance and with whose government he arranged to hold annual meetings to discuss areas of co-operation. In revolutionary Grenada, the minister offered some help in the spheres of agriculture and education, but he also made it clear that the provision of assistance would be made easier if, as he put it, Grenada was 'truly non-aligned', as opposed to being under the wing of the Cubans.[21] This reaction was typical: for more than three decades French governments had pursued consistently conservative policies towards the Caribbean, both in respect of the *départements* in particular and the region in general. French national pride had prevented the emergence of a close alliance with the United States, either in the Caribbean or anywhere else, but that should not conceal the fact that the overall impact of French policy was broadly supportive of US hegemonic designs over the region.

The election of President Mitterrand in May 1981 seemed initially as if it might presage a fundamental change of approach in the form of the adoption of a radically different socialist foreign policy. In the event, it has produced less a change in the ends to which French policy has long been oriented than the means by which it has recently been conducted. Like his immediate predecessors as president, Mitterrand considers foreign policy to be the exclusive domain of the head of state, and has thus sought to bring to bear upon traditional French concerns some of his own particular moral and ideological preoccupations. He sees a political and economic crisis facing both the West and the East — in the former, recession, unemployment, the rejection of collective effort and the possible gradual disintegration of the social fabric; in the latter, economic stagnation combined with an assertion of diverse forms of socialist experimentation in different countries within the bloc as a whole. He is, moreover, particularly concerned that escape should not be sought from these problems via an escalation of competition between the superpowers, which would not only be dangerous in itself, but would impose an East-West straight-jacket upon the interpretation and possible resolution of all North–South problems. In an attempt to undermine this sort of thinking, Mitterrand has deliberately aligned France with Third World interests on several major international issues.[22]

This can be seen in a number of areas of policy. At the global economic level, there is the support France has given to the pursuit of a more equitable international economic order. At various summit meetings, Mitterrand has insisted that a start should be made on the negotiations called for by the 'Group of 77' and resisted by the United States and other Western countries such as Britain and West Germany. For itself, France has newly given a commitment to reach an aid provision of 0.7 per cent of GNP by 1988 and has subtracted grants made to its overseas possessions from the calculated figure to make this target more meaningful. An effort has also been made to design a philosophy of co-development, according to which economic relations with developing countries can be organised. At the political level, France's 'Third Worldism' has brought it into conflict with the United States. Whereas the Reagan administration sees in every conflict an attempt at destabilisation by the Soviet Union, France under Mitterrand rejects this line of analysis. As Marie-Claude Smouts put it in a recent assessment, not only does France 'consider that non-alignment is not contrary to western interests, but it considers that it is poverty, oppression and injustice which clear a path for the Soviet Union'. Rather than letting people 'struggle alone against oligarchical and repressive regimes, and find support only in the pro-Soviet camp', the new government's view is that 'it is better to help them find other alternatives'.[23] This thinking lay behind the celebrated Franco-Mexican declaration of 28 August 1981, made during Mitterrand's visit to Mexico, formally recognising the rebels leading the guerrilla war in El Salvador as a 'representative political force'. It also underlay the contract for the sale of arms signed with Nicaragua in December 1981 and inspired the friendly relationship which France established with Grenada.

In the context of the Caribbean, this last move was the most striking illustration of the new emphasis of French foreign policy. The French Foreign Minister, Claude Cheysson, visited Grenada several times in the months following the revolution in his former role as EEC Commissioner for Development and admitted to being impressed by the energetic way the new regime was tackling the island's long-standing underdevelopment. Mitterrand accordingly welcomed Bishop to Paris in September 1983 as the first Commonwealth Caribbean head of government ever officially to visit France. Bishop persuaded the French to extend their aid and co-operation fund — which until that moment had disbursed funds almost exclusively to France's former African colonies — to all the ex-British Eastern Caribbean states. During his visit, proposals for co-operation in health, education and agriculture were agreed upon, as was the possibility of establishing Air France flights to Grenada once the new international airport was open. Responding to criticism of the talks, Cheysson described objections to France helping countries like Grenada as simply 'preposterous'.[24] The Mitterrand regime is manifestly not shy about using the provision of aid as a political weapon to demonstrate its views about the way to handle radical social and political change. Rather than push countries such as Grenada and Nicaragua irreversibly towards the Soviet camp, it prefers to seek to accommodate such governments and channel them as much as possible in a pro-Western direction. Mitterrand is not necessarily any less anti-Communist than Reagan; he simply uses different and rather more subtle methods to contain it.

For all this important change of mood in respect of French Third World policy, the Mitterrand regime has remained true to tradition in its handling of the overseas *départements* in the Caribbean. No attempt has been made to tamper with 'the ties of national solidarity' which officially bind the peoples of France and the French West Indies over a distance of some 3,500 miles. However, even before it was elected, the government had proclaimed its intention of decentralising the administration throughout metropolitan and overseas France. Despite having to amend some of its proposals in the face of opposition, it has pressed ahead in the overseas *départements* with plans to institute new *conseils régionaux*, elected by proportional representation, with a view to checking some of the powers of the local administration. These elections took place in 1983, amidst charges by Gaullist politicians in France that Mitterrand had a secret plan to give the French Caribbean territories independence. There is no evidence for such a charge. Indeed, the truth is the reverse: by appeasing the demand for autonomy which has existed to some degree in the *départements* for more than a decade, the French government expects to have undercut the small pro-independence movements and to have ensured the continuity of the whole arrangement. Under Mitterrand, as firmly as under any of his modern predecessors, France intends to retain a Caribbean presence for a long time to come.

The Netherlands

The Netherlands is the other European power with possessions in the Caribbean, but unlike France it has tried its best over the last decade to divest itself of its historical responsibilities in the region. Initially, in the post-Second World War period, the Dutch did not favour independence for their Caribbean colonies, preferring — rather like the French — to incorporate them into the metropolitan political system. The Netherlands Antilles and Suriname were first granted internal self-government in 1950 and then, four years later, formally linked with Holland within what was called the Tripartite Kingdom of the Netherlands. In this political structure, their autonomy was constitutionally guaranteed and they were given the right to participate in the formulation of policies for the kingdom as a whole.[25] The UN General Assembly accepted this as evidence of decolonisation and so too, it seems, did the majority of the inhabitants of the two semi-independent territories. The main opponents were members of the Dutch Labour Party and other socialist groupings in the metropolitan Netherlands, who were aware that the arrangement was still viewed as neo-colonial by many leading Third World figures.

Furthermore, the Tripartite scheme did not succeed in insulating the government and people of the Netherlands from Caribbean problems. High unemployment, low wage levels and the absence of effective welfare provision produced a steady flow of immigrants from Suriname to Holland, attracted by the prospect of greater economic opportunities. From the late 1960s onwards, the numbers seeking to settle in Europe increased sharply, reaching a total of nearly 150,000 by 1975, and included not only members of the Surinamese elite, but people of all races and from all levels of society, including the working class. Such arrivals were greeted with less and less enthusiasm by the Dutch people, partly because they put pressure upon jobs, more generally because they threatened the traditional fabric of the country's social structure.[26] The Netherland Antilles generated many fewer immigrants, but could no more be forgotten by the Dutch government. In 1969, the Antilles government was forced to ask for Dutch military assistance to quell the riots which broke out in Curaçao, as workers protested against the employment practices of the Shell company. The government in the Hague was obliged to comply by the terms of the charter of the Tripartite Kingdom, but did so with great reluctance, aware that intervention was unpopular at home and in the Third World, where it was widely reported as imperialist intervention.[27] Independence for the two overseas parts of the kingdom seemed to be the only way to avoid these sorts of semi-colonial problems. It would remove both the right of free migration to the Netherlands and the necessity of having to come to the defence of governments many miles away in the Caribbean.

From the early 1970s onwards, therefore, the policy adopted by the Dutch Labour government of Joop Den Uyl was to grant full independence to Suriname and the Netherlands Antilles. The Surinamese government was responsive to the pressure to move in this direction emanating from the Hague and agreement upon independence was achieved quite easily, the final dissolution of the constitutional link with the Netherlands coming in 1975. The government of the Netherlands Antilles, on the other hand, was rather more reluctant to have independence forced upon it. Obviously, greater difficulties existed — the small size of the territory, its unusual geographic structure (the three larger islands of Aruba, Curaçao and Bonaire situated off the

Venezuelan coast and over 500 miles away from the other group of tiny Windward Islands to the south-east of Puerto Rico), its diverse ethnic composition and linguistic division, and its weak internal economic integration. All these factors made Antillean leaders hesitate about the wisdom of breaking away from the protection of the Netherlands. There was also the prior need to agree maritime boundaries with Venezuela, but this was achieved in 1978 and the prospect of independence for a while seemed closer at hand. Of late, though, a further obstacle has arisen — Aruban separatism. Arubans, who are generally not of African descent but are mostly Mestizos and whites, have long felt that the central government of the territory in Willemstadt, Curaçao, did not satisfactorily serve their interests; they have now come openly to oppose Aruban participation in an independent Antillean Federation. The Netherlands has declared itself willing to grant independence only to all six islands together, which means that the others fear that Aruban ambitions will force them to remain tied indefinitely to the mother country. The present, more conservative Dutch government presided over talks in early 1983 to try to resolve the issue and came up with proposals which allow Aruba 'separate status' within the territory and the option of independence on its own by 1996. It is far from clear whether this will solve the problem. Even if the formula works, it will mean that the Dutch will have to wait some time yet before being able to effect their final retreat from colonial power in the Caribbean.

Indeed, as a European power seeking to put its imperialist past behind it as much as possible, the Netherlands has not had much luck. For some eight years after granting independence to Suriname, it still finds itself embroiled in the violence and vicissitudes of that country's politics following the military coup of 1980. At independence, the Dutch government instituted a large US $1.8 billion aid programme for Suriname, to be disbursed over the next fifteen years, no doubt assuming that this would boost development sufficiently to stave off trouble and in any case would be spent largely within the metropolitan economy. Dutch business still has considerable financial interests in Suriname. Instead, the government of the Netherlands has repeatedly found it necessary to use the threat of suspension of the programme in an attempt to control the excesses of the Bouterse government and prevent it from moving too sharply to the left. The United States has more than once expressed its alarm at recent developments in Suriname and will certainly have sought to stiffen the resolve of the Dutch. The executions at the end of 1982 finally persuaded the Hague to act and break off the supply of aid. In these circumstances, the Netherlands cannot avoid continued involvement in the tense internal situation in Suriname, no matter how embarrassing it finds it, but generally it has no taste for geopolitical action in the Caribbean. Beyond its association with the Netherlands Antilles and its enforced role in Surinamese affairs, it does not seek to play a major part in the resolution of the general international crisis affecting the region.

The European Economic Community (EEC)

The historical links which have grown up between the Caribbean and Britain, France and the Netherlands have also had a secondary effect that has already become more important for some parts of the region than the continuation of bilateral ties with the former colonial powers. Because the three European powers in question are all members of the European Economic Community, that organisation has had to involve itself in Caribbean affairs. Although the organic links between the EEC and the Caribbean date back to the time of the Yaoundé Conventions of the 1960s, at that time they only involved the Dutch and French territories in the area. It was with Britain's entry into the EEC in 1973 that the Caribbean came to be accorded a higher priority in Brussels, since the relationship had then to be extended to include the large number of former and existing British colonies in the region. This constituted an important part of the background to the signing in 1975 of the Lomé Convention, which broadened the EEC's relationship with its former associates into a highly complex arrangement with a diverse grouping of African, Caribbean and Pacific (ACP) states. By means of this and the tentative links which the EEC has lately developed with some of the non-associated states in the Caribbean, the Community is able to claim that Europe, which for so long contributed to the division of the region, is now in the process of reuniting it. In their more lyrical moments, spokesmen for the EEC Commission have even been known to assert that the Congress of Berlin is at last being reversed!

Nevertheless the EEC can justifiably point to the extensive range of differing political and economic relationships it has established with the various states of the Caribbean. These fall into four categories, described briefly below.

ACP States

Twelve states in the Caribbean — Antigua–Barbuda, the Bahamas,

Barbados, Belize, Dominica, Grenada, Guyana, Jamaica, St Lucia, St Vincent, Trinidad and Tobago, and Suriname — are full signatories to the Lomé Convention, as renewed in 1979. St Kitts-Nevis, having only just gained independence, will accede to the Convention as quickly as possible.

Overseas Countries and Territories (OCTs)

Six non-independent overseas countries and territories — Anguilla, the Netherlands Antilles, the Cayman Islands, Montserrat, the Turks and Caicos Islands, and the British Virgin Islands — are also formally associated with the Community by virtue of their ties with their respective mother countries. Although OCT status is sometimes seen as inferior, all the states in these first two categories enjoy virtually the same relationship with the EEC. They receive financial and technical assistance from the European Development Fund (EDF), are eligible for loans from the European Investment Bank (EIB), can benefit from the system for the stabilisation of export earnings (STABEX), and have the right to practically tariff-free access to the EEC market for most of their goods. For some, the sugar protocol is of particular importance, since it provides them with guaranteed prices and export quotas to the community market.

Overseas Départements

Although the status of the three French overseas *départements* within the Community was discussed in the Treaty of Rome, it took a decision of the European Court of Justice in 1978 to put an end to all the ambiguities concerning their place in the EEC. The decision was that the terms of the treaty should apply automatically to them as integral parts of France, although the proviso was expressed that this did not rule out special measures being adopted at a later date to meet their specific needs. Thus the *départements* are not entitled to funds from the EDF, but they are eligible for assistance from the EEC's Regional Fund, which is a good deal more generous, as well as the EIB and emergency aid. In short, they receive treatment which is analogous to that of other economically depressed areas within the Community proper.

Non-Associated States

No formal relationship exists between the EEC and countries like Haiti and the Dominican Republic, but since 1978 the Community has pursued a policy of providing limited financial and technical assistance to non-associated states and both have benefited.

Beyond the arrangements represented by these different categories, the EEC also has a scheme to provide exceptional aid for disaster victims, an important provision for the Caribbean because of the region's propensity to volcanic disturbances, hurricanes and floods. In 1980, for example, following the devastation caused by Hurricane Allen, the EEC provided some US $16.35 million of emergency assistance, which went to St Lucia, Jamaica, Dominica, St Vincent, Grenada, Barbados, Haiti, Montserrat, Martinique and Guadeloupe, thereby assisting in one programme all of the four different types of state in the Caribbean with which it has relations.

In the light of the attempts so often made by other external powers to divide Caribbean states, special mention should perhaps be made of the EEC's commitment to support for regional projects. During the period covered by the fourth European Development Fund (1975-9), the amount allocated for this purpose was approximately 25 per cent of the total made available; in the fifth EDF (1981-5) it will be nearer 50 per cent. Under this provision, such regional organisations as the University of the West Indies, the Leeward Islands Air Transport Company and the West Indies Shipping Corporation have all received considerable support. A further dimension of regional co-operation in the Caribbean with which the European Community is concerned is that between the French overseas *départements* and the ACP states and the OCTs. A major meeting under the title Europe–Caribbean Contacts took place in Pointe-à-Pitre in Guadeloupe in February 1981, at which the hosts were the combined Chambers of Commerce of the French territories and the major invitees representatives of the governments and private sectors of most of the ACP and OCT states in the Caribbean. It was the first such contact for nearly forty years and produced a series of recommendations urging closer commercial and financial co-operation between all the Caribbean territories, regardless of their different relationships with Europe.

Described in this way, the contribution of the EEC to the development of the Caribbean seems very positive and so it is important to note that the Community's role is not necessarily as beneficent in practice as its carefully cultivated image would suggest. Analyses of the operation of Lomé have identified many flaws in the provisions of the Convention when viewed from the perspective of the ACP countries.[28] One study which examines the particular relationship of the Commonwealth Caribbean with the EEC under Lomé concluded as follows:

> Lomé is very much a second best. It is the product of an historical
> relationship with Britain that has been multilateralised by British
> entry into the EEC but not changed in essence by that fact . . .
> Lomé appears more to preserve the past within a new set of arrange-
> ments than to prefigure the future.[29]

Yet, even if the arrangement does not step outside the parameters of
economic dependency, there cannot be any doubt that the EEC
connection assists Caribbean governments in the day-to-day task of
managing their economic affairs. Between 1975 and 1979, approximately US $190 million was provided in EDF funds to the ACP states
and the OCTs; a further US $48 million by exceptional aid, food aid
and STABEX; US $28 million through the European Investment Bank,
largely to Commonwealth Caribbean states; and some US $22 million
in financial and technical aid to Haiti and the Dominican Republic. A
total of almost US $294 million of EEC assistance over the period is
not negligible. The overall position was accurately summed up by
Trinidad's experienced ambassador to the EEC, Dr O'Neil Lewis. As
he put it, 'the provisions of the Lomé Convention provide . . valuable
assistance, because no other assistance of that nature is available. But it
is no more than a step in the right direction.'[30]

Whatever its member states may do, the EEC also has a policy
of keeping 'political' considerations out of its aid decision-making
process. In other words, it seeks neither to favour nor to discriminate against particular states. In respect of the Caribbean, this
stance brought the EEC into conflict with US policy towards Grenada.
As we have seen, the Community did not bow to US pressure to
refuse funding for the airport project and it agreed to provide modest
assistance. In so doing, it unavoidably took up a position on one of
the more controversial issues in international politics in the Caribbean. The EEC further upset the United States by considering in
1982 an initiative to extend its real aid programme to the countries of
Central America as well as the two other Caribbean non-associates,
Haiti and the Dominican Republic. France was strongly in favour,
Britain obstinate and the Dutch pragmatic. In the event, the initiative
was considerably scaled down, but that did not stop it attracting
favourable comparison with the CBI in at least two respects: its non-
discriminatory approach to recipients and its concentration upon
balance of payments support to governments, rather than assistance to
the private sector.[31] The situation in the Caribbean has therefore been
but one more contributory factor in the growth over the last two or

three years of a discernible 'Atlantic rift' between the EEC and the United States.

Notes

1. Derived from *Overseas Trade Statistics of the United Kingdom* (HMSO, London, 1980).

2. *MA4 Business Monitor* (HMSO, London, 1979), p. 31.

3. See W.L. Bell, 'A Piece of Unrepeatable History? The British Development Division in the Caribbean 1966–72', *The Round Table*, no. 267 (1977), pp. 268–76.

4. Figures supplied by the Overseas Development Administration, London.

5. A.E. Thorndike, 'The Concept of Associated Statehood with Special Reference to the Eastern Caribbean', unpublished PhD thesis, University of London, 1979, p. 292.

6. Lord Balniel, Minister of State at the Foreign Office, in *House of Commons Debates*, vol. 886, col. 347 (11 December 1973), cited in ibid., p. 306.

7. See M. Manley, *Jamaica: Struggle in the Periphery* (Third World Media, London, 1982), p. 156.

8. *Caribbean Contact*, March 1981.

9. Lord Carrington at a press conference in Caracas (Foreign and Commonwealth Office, London, 1980).

10. R. Luce in evidence to the House of Commons Foreign Affairs Committee, 14 December 1981, printed in *Fifth Report of the Foreign Affairs Committee of the House of Commons: Caribbean and Central America*, together with an Appendix; part of the Proceedings of the Committee relating to the Report; and the Minutes of Evidence taken before the Committee with Appendices (HMSO, London, 1982), p. 54.

11. Ibid., p. xi.

12. Ibid., p. liii.

13. Ibid., p. lii.

14. Ibid., p. liv.

15. Ibid., p. lxiv.

16. *Observations by the Secretary of State for Foreign and Commonwealth Affairs* on Fifth Report from the Foreign Affairs Committee of the House of Commons: Caribbean and Central America, Cmnd 8819 (HMSO, London, 1983), p. 13.

17. Ibid., p. 15.

18. See G. Lasserre and A. Mabileau, 'The French Antilles and their Status as Overseas Departments', in E. de Kadt (ed.), *Patterns of Foreign Influence in the Caribbean* (Oxford University Press, London, 1972), p. 82.

19. 'Speech on 26th June 1967 by Pierre Billotte' in R. Preiswerk (ed.), *Documents on International Relations in the Caribbean* (Institute of Caribbean Studies, University of Puerto Rico, Rio Piedras, 1970), p. 579.

20. Cited in J. Pearce, *Under the Eagle: US Intervention in Central America and the Caribbean* (Latin America Bureau, London, 1981), pp. 146–7.

21. *Caribbean Insight* (London), vol. 3, no. 3 (1980), p. 7.

22. See Y. Berthelot with D. Besnaiou, 'France's New Third World Policy: Problems of Change' in C. Stevens (ed.), *EEC and the Third World: A Survey 3. The Atlantic Rift* (Hodder and Stoughton, London, 1983), pp. 28–41.

23. M.-C. Smouts, 'The External Policy of François Mitterrand', *International*

112   *The Old European Powers*

Affairs, vol. 59, no. 2 (1983), p. 166.

24. *Caribbean Contact*, November 1982.

25. For the background to this relationship, see H. Hoetink, 'The Dutch Caribbean and its Metropolis' in de Kadt, *Patterns of Foreign Influence*, pp. 103-20.

26. See F. Bovenkerk, 'Caribbean Migration to the Netherlands: From the Elite to the Working Class', *Caribbean Review*, vol. 11, no. 1 (1982), pp. 34-7.

27. See P. Verton, 'Emancipation and Decolonization: The May Revolt and its Aftermath in Curaçao', *Revista/Review Interamericana*, vol. 6, no. 15 (1976), pp. 88-101.

28. See, amongst a huge literature, C. Cosgrove Twitchett, *A Framework for Development: The EEC and the ACP* (George Allen and Unwin, London, 1981); F. Long (ed.), *The Political Economy of EEC Relations with African, Caribbean and Pacific States* (Pergamon Press, Oxford, 1980); and C. Stevens (ed.), *EEC and the Third World: A Survey 1* (Hodder and Stoughton, London, 1981).

29. P.K. Sutton, 'From Neo-colonialism to Neo-colonialism: Britain and the EEC in the Commonwealth Caribbean' in A.J. Payne and P.K. Sutton (eds.), *Dependency under Challenge: The Political Economy of the Commonwealth Caribbean* (Manchester University Press, Manchester, 1984), p. 231.

30. J. O'Neil Lewis, 'The Road to Lomé: Some Thoughts on the Development of ACP-EEC Relations', a memorandum prepared by Trinidad and Tobago's Ambassador to the EEC, Brussels, 9 September 1981, cited in ibid.

31. See L. Blackburn and F. Merry, 'EEC and US Policies towards the Caribbean Basin' in Stevens, *EEC and the Third World: A Survey 3*, pp. 120-1.

6 THE NEW LATIN AMERICAN POWERS: VENEZUELA, MEXICO, COLOMBIA AND BRAZIL

A full account of all the states currently competing for political and economic influence in the Caribbean must also include discussion of the new powers of Latin America. Four such powers stand out — Venezuela, Mexico, Colombia and Brazil. The first three all adjoin the Caribbean Sea, and the latter borders the southern boundaries of the mainland Caribbean territories of Guyana, Suriname and French Guiana. Although predominantly concerned with their geopolitical position within continental Latin America, each has a direct and legitimate additional concern with the affairs of the Caribbean, which has been much in evidence over the last few years.

Yet, historically, something of a gap has always seemed to separate the states of the Caribbean from these Latin American powers. For the former English and French territories, if not for those of Spanish descent, the problem has been one of tradition.[1] The differences of linguistic, historical, cultural, economic and institutional heritage have generally been perceived to be too great to overcome, although it should be added that this has not prevented large migrations of people from such Commonwealth Caribbean countries as Jamaica to continental locations requiring surplus labour such as Panama during the building of the canal and Costa Rica during the establishment of banana plantations. Of late, the cultural gulf has been narrowed and more frequently crossed, exposing the other main distinguishing feature between the two sets of states, the existence of substantial material differences, of which the most apparent is sheer land area. The total surface area of the entire Caribbean is only 282,248 square miles (and that of the islands is less than a third of that), which is smaller by far even than Venezuela, the least large of the four Latin American powers, and less than a tenth of the huge expanse of Brazil. Population figures reiterate the disparities involved and so does the measurement of gross national product. The economic development of Venezuela, Mexico, Brazil and Colombia is still constrained in many ways by dependence upon the industrial world of North America and Europe, but compared with the territories of the Caribbean they are economic powers with which to be reckoned. Notwithstanding present financial difficulties, they are considerably better endowed economically than any Caribbean state, especially in the case of the first two since the sharp rise in the price of oil at the beginning of the 1970s.

Conceived as 'middle powers'[2] within the contemporary international system, the freedom of operation of each of the four Latin American states in Caribbean affairs has, however, also been determined by their relationship with the dominant hemispheric power, the United States. Within the framework of US policy, Venezuela, Mexico, Colombia and Brazil have, at various times and in different ways, all been given special responsibilities for maintaining security and bringing about development in the Caribbean. For their part, they have been wary of the danger of being identified by Caribbean states as 'proxies' of the United States and have increasingly sought to assert their separate identities. They have done so in part by adopting independent policies towards Cuba — always the prime test of loyalty in Caribbean affairs as far as the United States is concerned — but more generally by seeking to develop recognised spheres of influence of their own within the region.

Venezuela

The Latin American power which has lately taken the most interest in the Caribbean has been Venezuela. This reflects a significant change of perspective. Despite the existence of historic ties with the region, well illustrated by the fact that Bolívar's celebrated letter of 1815 drawing up plans for the liberation and confederation of all Latin America was written in Jamaica, Venezuela subsequently concerned itself for fully a century and a half more with the mainland Spanish-speaking republics than with the predominantly non-Hispanic islands of the Caribbean.[3] Since the beginning of the 1970s, however, it has claimed a new diplomatic and strategic interest in the evolution of relationships between the countries of the Caribbean. Government spokesmen have frequently pointed out that Venezuela has 1,750 miles of Caribbean coastline, more than any other country in the region, stressing also that the most important commercial and industrial centres of the country are located on or near that coastline. The Caribbean Sea has always constituted Venezuela's geographic link with Europe and the United States, and is now the main avenue through which the country's vital exports of oil and oil-related products flow to the outside world. Contemporary Venezuelan interests in the Caribbean are thus perceived in Caracas to be substantial.

Several factors impelled Venezuela to advance these interests with a greater vigour and coherence after 1970 than previously. First was the easing of relations with the government of nearby Trinidad.[4] Disagreement had arisen in the 1960s over two issues: the retention of a 30 per cent Venezuelan surtax on imports emanating from Trinidad and the demarcation of territorial waters between the two states in the Gulf of Paria. On several occasions, Trinidadian fishermen were taken prisoner for being in Venezuelan waters, further complaining on release that they had been treated with unnecessary brutality. Although the fishing dispute dragged on, the surtax was removed in 1965 and a number of positive contacts established in the areas of economic, technical and cultural co-operation. In 1967, Venezuela successfully sponsored Trinidad's entry into the Organisation of American States (OAS), and three years later was ready to come to the rescue of the Trinidad government when the latter faced a succession of serious disturbances in Port of Spain and apparently made an appeal to its neighbour for military assistance. Action was unnecessary, but the request alone afforded Venezuela a new sense of legitimacy in its dealings with the Caribbean.

Secondly, by 1970 Venezuela's other long-standing dispute with a Caribbean country was approaching temporary abeyance, if not resolution. In a dispute relating back to the era of British colonial expansion in the nineteenth century, Venezuela had long claimed that the Essequibo region of Guyana, which constitutes about two-thirds of the territory of that country, was rightfully Venezuelan. It lost an arbitration award in 1899, but publicly revived the claim in 1962, seeing that Britain was proceeding towards the decolonisation of what was then still British Guiana. Talks were held between the respective foreign ministers of Britain and Venezuela and the premier of British Guiana, and eventually in Geneva, in 1966, a mixed commission was established, charged with the task of finding a peaceful solution to the territorial dispute within four years. During this period, the newly independent government of Guyana engaged in intense diplomatic activity on the international stage, seeking support for its position not only from other Caribbean countries, but at the United Nations and throughout the Third World. Venezuela found itself on the defensive and in 1970 signed with Guyana the Protocol of Port of Spain which agreed to 'freeze' the dispute for twelve years, during which time new solutions could be sought in 'an atmosphere of concord'. The signature of the Protocol immediately gave Venezuela a more acceptable image in the eyes of other governments in the Caribbean.

Lastly, Venezuelan relations with Cuba were also in the process of being re-established on more equitable lines. During the 1960s, the Castro regime gave support to various revolutionary groups within Venezuela, and on occasion sent both men and arms to assist opposition guerrilla movements. Since diplomatic relations between the two countries had been formally severed in 1961, the conflict was pursued with unconcealed bitterness, especially within the OAS, where Venezuela led the call for the adoption of collective sanctions against Cuba.[5] However, the level of hostility lessened from 1968 onwards, when the Cubans began to retreat from active encouragement of revolutionary movements throughout Latin America, and left-wing groups within Venezuela demonstrated a growing willingness to return to legal political action. This reduced the sense of beleaguerment felt by the Venezuelan government and further encouraged it to think in terms of the development of a more positive policy towards the Caribbean.

Freed of these constraints, Venezuela began to assume a more active role in regional and international affairs. Under the Christian Democrat (COPEI) government of Dr Rafael Caldera, elected in 1969, the country's foreign policy acquired a new economic emphasis. Venezuela spoke out against US trade policy, speeded up plans for the nationalisation of foreign-owned oil installations, and increasingly came to act as spokesman for the whole developing world on global economic issues. By this time the phase of national import-substitution industrialisation was coming to an end, creating an urgent need to sell Venezuela's growing output of manufactured goods overseas. The Caribbean was an obvious market to explore, a fact which prompted the Foreign Minister, Aristides Calvani (who was himself born in Trinidad), to embark upon a series of visits to both old and new states in the region with the aim of setting up a variety of economic and technical exchange projects. The Dominican Republic, Haiti, Jamaica, Barbados, Trinidad, the Netherland Antilles, several of the Leeward and Windward Islands — all were included in his itinerary. With Cuba, too, a process of *détente* was initiated and much welcomed in Havana, where the government was beginning to feel uneasy about its isolation within the Caribbean. In retrospect, the Caldera government can be seen to have laid the basis for Venezuela's current leading role in Caribbean politics, but it was not itself in a position fully to exploit the openings it had generated. During the 1960s and early 1970s the price of imports of industrial goods increased as inexorably as the export price of Venezuelan oil declined — from US $2.09 a barrel of crude in 1950 to a mere US $1.86 in 1970. Such adverse terms of trade created balance of payments problems and scarcely promoted a very expansive diplomacy. From 1973 onwards, of course, the situation changed dramatically, as oil prices suddenly quadrupled and massive new opportunities, both economic and political, were created for producer countries.

In Venezuela, the fortunate beneficiary was the social democratic *Acción Democrática* government of Carlos Andrés Pérez, which came into office in succession to the Caldera regime in March 1974. In that year government revenues, 85 per cent of which derived from oil exports, jumped to about US $10 billion, compared with US $3.82 billion in 1973 and US $2.9 billion in 1972. Even though the bulk of these 'petro-dollars' were devoted to an ambitious five-year development plan, the windfall was too great to inject wholly in the domestic economy without producing acute inflationary pressures. This prompted the government to invest a substantial amount of the money abroad as a means of extending Venezuela's international influence. It established a special bank called the Venezuelan Investment Fund, which was charged, *inter alia*, with 'developing a policy of international financial co-operation with the developing countries, particularly with those of Latin America, in order to accelerate their economic development, to rescue their natural resources, to stimulate their economic integration and to promote a more equitable new international economic order'.[6] Through this fund, Venezuela contributed considerable sums, amounting in total to nearly 10 per cent of its GNP, to OPEC's Special Fund for Non-Oil Producing Third World Countries, to the World Bank, to the Inter-American Development Bank and, in a variety of ways, to countries in the Caribbean.

Indeed, as far as Pérez was concerned, the Caribbean was the logical place to begin, containing, as it did, a large number of small territories hard-hit by the rise in oil prices. He was aware, too, that the gradual withdrawal of British influence had created something of a vacuum, especially in the Eastern Caribbean, which could easily lead to instability, unless some other power was willing to step in and provide developmental assistance. Accordingly, some Venezuelan money was channelled towards the Caribbean Development Bank, of which Venezuela had become the first non-English-speaking member in 1973; some was given to the Leeward Islands Air Transport Company (LIAT) to keep it flying when the British firm that owned it suddenly went into liquidation; but the largest amount was distributed directly to governments. During 1974 and 1975 a procession of Commonwealth Caribbean leaders, including Forbes Burnham of Guyana, visited Venezuela with a view to negotiating aid agreements, and none returned home empty-handed. An especially close relationship developed with Jamaica during the era of Michael Manley, with whom Pérez established a warm personal relationship. Venezuela made loans to the Bank of Jamaica, pledged to sell Jamaica oil at less than the world price, and negotiated a series of deals involving the construction of an aluminium smelter and the purchase by Venezuela of large quantities of Jamaican alumina and bauxite. Beyond the Commonwealth Caribbean, the Pérez government also signed economic co-operation agreements with the Dominican Republic and Suriname.

Such measures were more than manifestations of Venezuelan philanthropy. They reflected the amibition of the Pérez government to assume a position of leadership in Caribbean, Latin American and, by extension, Third World affairs. Venezuelan economic largesse was integral to its wider political goal of bringing about radical change in the organisation of the world economy. Venezuela was a founder member of OPEC, and for a decade and a half before 1973 had experienced the frustrations of trying to secure a better deal from the United States for the sale of its oil. It retained an obvious interest in other Third World economic demands and, under Pérez, threw itself energetically into the promotion of North–South bargaining. In doing so, it came to develop a closer relationship with Cuba, in effect leading that country's reincorporation into the Latin American community, and a rather more distant one with the United States. Washington was annoyed by Venezuela's recourse to measures of nationalisation at home and by its participation in such international initiatives as the creation in 1975 of the Latin American Economic System (SELA), a means to Latin American economic co-operation which specifically excluded the United States. By the same account, Venezuela's standing within Latin America and the Third World was increased by every such move.

In the Caribbean, too, Venezuela came almost universally to be regarded as a valuable friend and ally. The one significant exception was Dr Williams, the Prime Minister of Trinidad and Tobago, which was another oil-producing country and beneficiary of the new high price of energy. In 1975, he launched a lengthy and vitriolic attack on what he saw as Venezuela's improper ambitions towards the Commonwealth Caribbean territories. Two speeches indicated the nature of his concerns. In the first, delivered to a public meeting in Trinidad in April 1975, Williams attacked the notion that Venezuela was a Caribbean country, observing cynically: 'I expect next to hear that Tierra Del Fuego is', and warned that 'the recolonisation of the Caribbean is in full swing today'.[7] In the second speech, delivered to a special convention of his party in June, he described in detail Venezuela's penetration of the economy of the Commonwealth Caribbean and denounced his regional colleagues for encouraging this by going on a series of what he contemptuously termed 'pilgrimages to Caracas'.[8] He attacked with particular bitterness the economic co-operation agreement signed with Jamaica, which, he alleged, threatened the economic viability of an aluminium smelter to be built under the auspices of the Caribbean Community (CARICOM) and further committed Jamaica to full acquiescence in the so-called 'Declaration of Guyana', within which Venezuela had enshrined the oil-rebate arrangement accepted by the Manley regime. One of the provisions of this Declaration, he pointed out, was unreserved support for Guatemala's claim upon the territory of Belize, something which the Commonwealth Caribbean was pledged to resist. A further unspoken cause of Williams's hostility to Venezuela was perhaps a fear that Venezuelan policy would serve to undermine Trinidad's long-standing position as the major supplier of refined oil products within the Commonwealth Caribbean.[9] Other Caribbean leaders disassociated themselves from this analysis, revealing Williams to be a lone voice, and Venezuela naturally denied any 'imperial' ambitions towards the region. Yet, if his language was over-emotive, Williams was entitled to draw attention to the influence which Venezuela had quickly acquired over several Caribbean countries. He was also right to stress the unprecedented assertiveness of Venezuelan policy under the Pérez government.

However, in March 1979, the Pérez administration was succeeded by a COPEI government, led by Luis Herrera Campins, which set about the conduct of Venezuelan foreign policy in a distinctly more conservative, less flamboyant style than that of its predecessor. Domestically, Herrera was faced with the necessity of carrying out a programme of economic retrenchment. For several years, despite huge oil incomes, government expenditure had exceeded income, forcing Venezuela's external debt to rise to dangerously high levels. This meant that Venezuela could no longer afford to cut such a dash in foreign affairs. The new government determined accordingly to concern itself less with issues of global economic management and has given only limited support to collective Latin American organisations such as SELA. In the Caribbean, too, it sought to develop a less aggressive image. In his first message to the Venezuelan Congress in 1980, President Herrera declared that he rejected 'any attempt to transfer into the Caribbean the frictions and confrontations between the big powers or to transform it into an area of ideological or political influences'.[10] This did not imply a diminution of interest in the Caribbean: indeed, in retreating from the vision of Third World leadership, Venezuela has come to concentrate more upon its immediate geopolitical environment. New bilateral aid arrangements were established with Caribbean countries, including those with radical regimes such as Grenada, and in August 1980 a major new multilateral initiative was launched in conjunction with Mexico, the so-called San José Agreement. Under this agreement, the two states agreed to supply the net oil consumption of nine Caribbean and Central American countries, including Barbados, Jamaica and the Dominican Republic, and to make available to them over the next five years low-interest loans amounting to 30 per cent of their respective oil-importing bills. Belize has subsequently also been included. The cost of the scheme was high, but Venezuela saw it as a major contribution to the economic stability of the region.

On the ideological issues which confronted the Caribbean, Venezuela's position initially moved to the right under the Herrera administration. In particular, the government enunciated a much stronger commitment to the promotion of the ideology of Christian democracy, which had the effect of bringing it more into conflict with the socialist cause. Under Herrera, Venezuela has taken the view that, whatever the initial causes of the growth of political instability in the Caribbean and Central America were, Cuban policy has not been helpful and has added to the turbulence. In addition, two particular issues have caused further deterioration in Cuban–Venezuelan relations. One was the treatment, dating back to 1975, of Cubans who sought asylum by taking refuge in the Venezuelan embassy in Havana. The Cuban government argued that such persons were common criminals who lacked the right to seek asylum; the Venezuelan government maintained that they were political dissidents and should be treated accordingly. By April 1980, the controversy had escalated to such a point that both countries recalled their ambassadors. The second issue was the decision of a Venezuelan military tribunal in September 1980 to acquit four anti-Castro Cuban terrorists believed to have been responsible for the sabotage four years earlier of a Cuban airliner that crashed off Barbados with the loss of 73 lives. The Venezuelan government claimed that it was powerless to reverse the decision, but this was greeted sceptically in Havana and further diplomatic personnel were withdrawn from Caracas. More widely within the region, a degree of ideological and diplomatic competition grew up between the two states on a variety of issues and relations became, in Herrera's own words, 'very cold'.[11]

The new Christian Democratic orientation of the Herrera adminis-tration also had the consequence of bringing Venezuela into closer alignment with US policies in the Caribbean Basin. When a fellow Christian Democrat, Napoléon Duarte, emerged as the new head of the ruling junta in El Salvador at the end of 1980, Herrera immediately expressed his support. He thereafter maintained it as the conflict in El Salvador intensified and the pro-US Duarte government came under intense attack from seemingly all sides. In conjunction with its opposi-tion to Cuban policy in the Caribbean, this prompted accusations, inside and outside the country, that Venezuela under Campins was acting as a 'stalking horse' for the United States in regional matters. The Venezuelan government fervently denied the charge: it saw itself as supporting and sustaining moderate, centrist regimes in the national, rather than the American, interest and believed, with reference to the United States, that its responsibility was to persuade the Reagan administration that the problems of the region ran deeper than mere Communist subversion. It also strongly opposed any suggestion of direct US intervention in the Caribbean or Central America. Although for a while Venezuelan policy towards the Caribbean region did come close to that of the United States, it was always a 'coincidence of interests' which disturbed some members of the Venezuelan govern-ment. By early 1982, even before Duarte was removed from office in El Salvador, attempts were being made to distance Venezuela from US positions. The chance to make this clear came with the Falklands/ Malvinas conflict. Venezuela took a passionately pro-Latin American position, condemning US support of Britain and renewing contact with Cuba in the course of its attack upon Washington's stand. The tensions aroused have yet to disappear, leaving the implications of the episode for the development of Venezuelan policy towards the United States and the Caribbean still unclear.

The other recent preoccupation of the Herrera government on the international scene has been the renewal of Venezuela's territorial dispute with Guyana. The general expectation had been that the Port of Spain Protocol, which expired on 18 June 1982, would be renewed, thereby putting the dispute 'on ice' for several more years. However, following a visit to Caracas by Burnham in 1981, the conflict began again to take on a threatening character. The Venezuelan government expressed an intention to pursue its claim actively once more and some minor border incursions took place. Both sides raised the temperature of their verbal exchanges and hinted at military preparation. Under the terms of the Protocol, non-renewal brought the 1960 Geneva Agreement back into force, the relevant part of which was Article IV, committing the two parties to choose one of the means of peaceful settlement of disputes provided for in the United Nations charter. Failing that, they were to refer the problem of determining the most appropriate means of solution to an international organisation of their choice or, failing that, to the UN Secretary-General. Both sides profess a desire to resolve matters peacefully, and certainly it is hard to see Venezuelan troops actually invading Guyana, since such a move would ruin years of effort to appear a responsible participant in international affairs and an enlightened leader of the Third World. Venezuela's precise thinking is hard to discern: it may be that its aim is to exert sufficient pressure on Guyana to force agreement upon a number of joint development projects in the Essequibo, or it may be seeking a partial change of frontier which would give it greater access to the Atlantic, with obvious implications for the exploitation of offshore oil. Either way, its real desiderata are likely to be less than the full formal claim.

In recent months, however, the Venezuelan government has been more preoccupied with the management of the domestic economy than any international issue. The fall in the price of oil, which completely dominates the country's exports, created a current-account deficit in 1982 and brought pressure upon the Venezuelan bolivar.[12] The scale of the country's foreign debt is moderate by the standards of some Latin American countries, but problems have been encountered in the rescheduling of some short-term loans and, in December 1982, the government had to step in to rescue the country's largest bank. It also imposed exchange controls and a two-tier market for currency sales in an attempt to restore economic stability. The economy will certainly remain the main priority of the government for the rest of the Herrera administration's term of office. Elections are due in December 1983, which means that a coherent reformulation of the diverse elements of Venezuelan foreign policy will have to wait until at least 1984. In the interim the oil will not have run dry. Venezuela has proven reserves of 18 billion barrels of conventional oil and the expectation of further discoveries. There also exists an additional 700 or 800 billion barrels of heavy crude in the Orinoco oil belt, which the government is beginning to develop. These facts alone ensure that Venezuela will remain a considerable force in Caribbean politics.

Mexico

Although the extent of Mexico's involvement in the international politics of the Caribbean over the last two decades has been less than Venezuela's, it has still been considerable, growing significantly during the 1970s to the situation at present, where Mexico is one of the major regional powers. Contrary to some interpretations, the development of a more active presence in Caribbean affairs has not altered the traditional basis of Mexican foreign policy towards this part of the world. This has been founded since the Mexican revolution on the achievement of a balance between two potentially contradictory objectives: support for the principles of self-determination and non-intervention in international affairs, and the maintenance of good relations with the United States. The former commitment pays respect to the historical evolution of the Mexican state itself and contributes to the internal political stability of the country by affirming the continuing legitimacy of 'the revolution'. The latter indicates the importance and complexity of Mexico's bilateral relationship with the United States and the high degree of penetration of US interests in the Mexican economy. Effective reconciliation of these two principles has not always been achieved, but it has been facilitated by a long-standing US willingness to maintain a clear distinction between hemispheric politics and bilateral relations in its dealings with Mexico. Mexico, in effect, has a dispensation to dissent from US policy towards Latin America and the hemisphere which is tolerated with generally good grace by Washington out of deference to Mexico's need to appease the revolutionary tradition in its history and in exchange for Mexican co-operation on important global political issues.[13] In this critical respect, the nature of Mexico's current policy towards the Caribbean is far from new.

The origins of the policy were apparent even in the 1960s, when Mexico's interest in the Caribbean was relatively limited. Its main concern at that time was with Cuba, which points geographically into the mouth of the Gulf of Mexico and so sits at the entrance to Mexico's gateway into the Atlantic. During the course of the many attempts to isolate Castro's Cuba within the hemisphere during this period, Mexico stood firmly by the principles of self-determination and non-intervention. In 1962, at the OAS meeting in Punta Del Este, Mexico opposed the exclusion of Cuba from the organisation and in 1964, in Washington, it voted against a mandatory resolution calling upon all OAS members to break off relations with Cuba and subsequently refused to honour it. A year later, in 1965, at another OAS meeting, this time in connection with US intervention in the Dominican Republic, Mexico voted against the creation of an inter-American peace force and introduced a resolution urging US forces to leave the island. Another year later, in 1966, on a visit to Guatemala President Díaz Ordaz again spoke out against US policy by affirming the right of the people of Belize to self-determination. In each of these cases, the Mexican position was radical in the context of international politics at the time, but not as the result of a considered view of Mexican foreign policy interests. In this period, reactions to external events, especially those occurring in the region, were mainly still the product of the demands of the country's domestic political system, in particular the need to tie the Mexican left into conventional forms of politics.

After 1970, under the leadership of President Luis Echeverría Alvarez, Mexico did began to take a more intensive interest in the nations of Central America and the Caribbean, but again in part for domestic reasons. Echeverría had been Minister of the Interior during the major disturbances which had taken place in Mexico City in 1968, when a combination of political alienation and social and economic frustration had brought thousands of students and other citizens on to the streets in a confrontation with the security forces. He had borne the brunt of the criticism of the regime's repressive response to the crisis and determined on becoming president two years later to build a new liberal and progressive image for himself. The difficulties of introducing meaningful democratic reforms at home led him to seek to project a radical image in foreign affairs as the best available means of legitimising his rule in the eyes of the Mexican left. Accordingly, he began to present himself as an anti-imperialist leader, championing the cause of revolutionary and progressive regimes in Latin America and other parts of the Third World, and actively promoting the case for fundamental reform of the existing international economic order. A major part of this drive was the creation of new links with neighbouring countries in the Caribbean, especially those with apparently progressive regimes such as Cuba, Venezuela under Peréz, Jamaica under Manley, and Guyana under Burnham.

Between 1974 and 1976, these countries became the objects of a variety of ambitious Mexican initiatives. Increased contact with Cuba was symbolised by a visit to Havana by Echeverría himself in August 1974, the first time a Mexican president had gone to Cuba since 1959. Economic co-operation with Venezuela was inaugurated in 1975 with the establishment of SELA, and further extended by the formation in the same year of the Caribbean Multinational Shipping Company

(NAMUCAR), the reactivation of the Latin American Energy Organisation (OLADE), and the organisation of a variety of regional and international producer associations for bananas and sugar. All were designed to strengthen the collective bargaining position of the region in economic matters *vis-à-vis* the United States. With the states of the Commonwealth Caribbean as a group, a joint Mexico–Caribbean Community Joint Commission was established, whilst with Jamaica an agreement was signed in November 1974 envisaging the construction of a large alumina plant in Jamaica and an aluminium smelter in Mexico. Each government was to have had 51 per cent shares in the enterprise located in its territory, with 29 per cent of the remainder going to the other partner, and the rest being divided between privately owned companies, other governments or foreign investors. It was also anticipated that new joint manufacturing industries would be set up as a consequence of the establishment of these enterprises. With Guyana, too, extensive co-operative ventures were arranged: in August 1975, a deal was struck whereby Mexico would buy bauxite and lumber from Guyana and in turn supply cement, salt, trawlers and technical assistance, and a month later a joint agreement for co-operation in agriculture was signed. Mexico had traditionally demonstrated little concern for the territories of the Commonwealth Caribbean and so these latter initiatives were important extensions of its international relations.

Unlike Venezuela, the entry of Mexico on to the Commonwealth Caribbean scene did not arouse any hostility from governments such as that of Trinidad and Tobago. An important reason for this was that Mexico demonstrated a preference for dealing with the sub-region as a unit, as in the establishment of the Joint Commission with the Caribbean Community Secretariat. Bilateral deals were made with the larger states, but not with the very small territories of the Eastern Caribbean, with whom the possibility of domination more obviously arose. Mexico also won respect amongst many of the governments of the Commonwealth Caribbean in this period for its consistent and long-standing pro-Cuban stance and, of course, gained by not being an active party to any unresolved territorial dispute with a Commonwealth Caribbean country. Mexico does, in fact, have a historical claim to the northern part of Belize, but has long opposed Guatemala's much more substantial claim, refusing, for example, to sign the 1974 Guayana Declaration which so aroused Dr Williams's ire by its pledge of support for Guatemala. Mexican support for Belize on the self-determination issue has been much appreciated and undoubtedly helped to win it friends in the Commonwealth Caribbean region.

When Echeverría came to the end of his six-year term of office in 1976, Mexico's standing in the Caribbean and the world as a whole was undoubtedly greater than at any time in its history. Although, as one foreign-affairs analyst in the Caribbean has pointed out, 'this bid for Third World leadership did not produce tangible economic results for Mexico, or increase its leverage with the US, it did substantiate its position as a regional leader'.[14] This was no mean achievement, but it could not wholly offset the failure of Echeverría's domestic reform programme or the economic legacy which he passed on to his successor. By 1976, growth in the Mexican economy was slowing down, external debts had increased considerably, as had the balance of payments deficit, and private investment was stagnant. The new President, López Portillo, saw as his initial priority the solution of the country's financial problems and finally felt no need to develop a radical foreign policy image to sustain his domestic political credibility. Indeed, in response to the economic situation in Mexico, he announced Mexico's withdrawal from the various industrial projects agreed by his predecessor with the government of Jamaica. This decision fed speculation that Mexico intended to abandon its Third World orientation under its new government and certainly aroused some genuine bitterness in the Commonwealth Caribbean, which felt that it had been deceived by Mexican rhetoric. One comment wryly noted that 'relations between countries of unbalanced financial/political weight can only result in hegemonic behaviour and decision making by the stronger'.[15]

In the event, Mexico's retreat from Caribbean and Latin American leadership proved only to be temporary and, when renewed, was all the more credible and effective because of the emerging impact of Mexico's new discoveries of oil. It seems that major finds of oil were first made by the national energy company, PEMEX, as early as 1972. The government adopted a policy of secrecy and even when an exclusive report in the *New York Times* in October 1974 suggested that huge reserves, possibly as much as 19 billion barrels, had been discovered in Mexico, it determined to publicise the matter as little as possible.[16] Even so, oil production did increase, from some 525,000 barrels a day in 1973 to 896,000 barrels a day in 1976, and the government did embark upon a number of large refining and petrochemical ventures. Knowledge of the existence of the oil must have also given confidence to the enactment of an active Mexican foreign policy during the Echeverría period. It was, however, not until the economic crisis of 1976 and the inauguration of López Portillo that there was a change of policy and the decision was taken to exploit fully the potential of the oil in order to generate external financial support for the ailing economy in the short term and give Mexico new weight in regional and international affairs in the long term. To this end, oil-production levels were pushed up dramatically — to a daily average of 1.6 million barrels in 1979, just about 2 million barrels in 1980 and up to 2.6 million in 1981. This made Mexico a major oil producer by any standard and added immeasurably to the significance of its foreign policy.

López Portillo's approach to international politics was founded upon the traditional Mexican notion of a balance between the competing objectives of self-determination for Third World states and the maintenance of friendly relations with the United States, with the one difference that Mexico was in a more powerful position than ever before, courtesy of oil, to establish that balance at a point closer to its perception of its own national needs and interests. Under US pressure Mexico decided not to join OPEC, but it has naturally been keen to limit its dependence on the US by attracting consumers for its oil from as many countries as possible and has officially declared its intention eventually to place up to 40 per cent of its oil exports outside the US market. It supported the US position on the important issue of Afghanistan, but then endeavoured to distinguish itself from the United States on several other international questions, refusing to allow the Shah of Iran to return to Mexico, neglecting to follow Washington's boycott of the Moscow Olympics, and criticising the economic sanctions used by the US against Iran during the hostage crisis. Most importantly, under López Portillo, Mexico developed a line of policy towards Central America and the Caribbean which diverged significantly from that of the United States, especially after it altered during the latter part of the Carter administration and since the inauguration of Reagan at the beginning of 1981.

The Mexican view of the growing instability of the region differed from the familiar geopolitical perspective of the United States by placing social and economic questions at the centre of its thinking. It rejected the argument that Cuban and Soviet expansionism was the prime cause of the troubles and firmly maintained that the struggles of nations such as Nicaragua and El Salvador in Central America and Cuba, Jamaica and Grenada in the Caribbean constituted legitimate attempts to transform obsolete social, economic and political structures. It was alarmed at the way the region had been turned into an arena of superpower politics and was fearful that a Vietnam could be created in its own backyard by US determination to reassert hegemonic power in its own hemisphere. Such a conflict would, in the eyes of the Mexican government, utterly destroy the possibility of creating

an economically strong and political stable Mexico.[17] Initially, therefore, López Portillo did not hesitate to show support for the process of
change taking place in the region. In May 1979, his government formally
severed diplomatic relations with the dictatorial Somoza regime in Nicaragua and subsequently gave open support to the new Sandinista government. It also began to criticise the US-supported civilian-military junta
in El Salvador. Relations with Cuba were given a new vitality; López
Portillo visited Havana in 1980 at the height of the Cuban-US refugee dispute and made a strong statement supporting Cuban self-determination
and criticising US harassment of the Castro regime. 'We shall not tolerate
anything being done to Cuba,' he said, 'because we shall feel as if it
were being done to ourselves.'[18] In this last instance, one might feel
that Mexico was pushing its traditional right to dissent from US policy
in the Caribbean to its very limit, and perhaps beyond.

However, since the limits of dissent in Mexican-US relations have
never been precisely defined, confrontation can and does co-exist with
co-operation. Following the militant phase of 1978-80, López Portillo's
policy towards the region settled down into one of conciliation between
the contending forces, backed up where possible by positive measures,
such as the San José Agreement, signed with Venezuela in 1980, to
appease some of the social tensions and financial difficulties deriving
from the continuing world economic crisis. Mexico's moderating role
was especially important in the period immediately after the Reagan administration came to power, when talk of blockades and destabilisation
was rife. At his first meeting with the new US President in January 1981,
López Portillo reiterated Mexico's firm opposition to any US intervention
in Caribbean and Latin American affairs. At a subsequent meeting at
Camp David in June, a negotiation process involving two high-level
permanent committees was set up to work out major policy differences
between the two countries. The stage was also set at this meeting for
the much-publicised Nassau Conference between the foreign ministers
of the United States, Canada, Venezuela and Mexico to discuss the
preparation of a multilateral aid plan for the Caribbean Basin. At
Nassau, important differences of opinion about the nature of the
regional crisis were expressed. Mexico, supported by Canada and
Venezuela, argued strongly that an aid plan should not be conceived
as a political instrument directed against perceived Soviet and Cuban
influence in the area, but rather as a genuine attempt to address the
social and economic problems of the region, excluding no country on
purely political grounds. The United States was seemingly unmoved.
In the event, as has already been made clear, the plan emerged as a

unilateral US initiative, the other powers indicating that they would continue to provide aid to the region as they thought best. At least some recognition had been made in Washington that the problems of the Caribbean were best tackled via socio-economic means, for which López Portillo's diplomacy can perhaps take some credit. Moreover, right to the end of his term of office in 1982, he continued to make proposals for renewed negotiation and dialogue between the United States, Cuba and the other states at the centre of the ideological argument in the region. They were often ignored in their specific suggestions, but *in toto* they kept open the possibility of a negotiated settlement of the conflicts dividing the region. It was not Mexico's fault that they were not taken up more enthusiastically.

At present, Mexico's policy towards the Caribbean, as elsewhere, is surrounded by question marks. During 1981 and 1982 the Mexican economy began to develop a growing balance of payments deficit. On the basis of its discoveries of oil, Mexico borrowed vast sums of money from Western banks to promote industrialisation and sustain the spending of both state and people. Total external debt at the beginning of 1982 was in the order of US \$70 billion, the highest in the developing world. When oil revenues fell because of the world-wide glut and rises in international interest rates pushed up payments on the loans, the country found itself facing a financial crisis.[19] In February 1982, the government devalued the peso and allowed it to float downwards on the international exchange markets. This produced no immediate relief and the government was forced to eliminate subsidies on a wide range of fuels and basic foodstuffs and allow the peso to be still further devalued. In August 1982, López Portillo announced the imposition of exchange controls in order to halt a run on the country's reserves, and he subsequently nationalised the banks. Some of Mexico's debt was rescheduled and a further austerity package hastily assembled. The result was that the peso traded at the end of 1982 at about 150 to the US dollar, approximately one-fifth of the rate a year earlier.

López Portillo's successor as president, Miguel de la Madrid Hurtado, who took up office in 1982, thus inherited an even more serious economic situation than that which the country had faced in 1976. Unlike then, Mexico cannot pump its way out of difficulty by increasing oil exports. De la Madrid entered into negotiations with the International Monetary Fund and several of the world's major central banks in an attempt to stabilise Mexico's financial position and measures have been adopted to bring the country's economy back into balance. The requisite deflation has already aggravated social and political tensions in the country and will continue to do so. This means that de la Madrid's main priority in government will be to maintain the stability of the Mexican political system in the face of the serious problems of the economy – a task which will not make it easy for his administration also to play a major diplomatic role in Caribbean affairs. The first sign of this appeared in May 1983, when he displayed the greatest reluctance to renew the San José Agreement, which by then was costing Mexico approximately US $750 million a year; in the end he agreed only to a much weakened version of the original scheme. Yet, for all its present financial difficulties, Mexico's proven reserves of oil are vast and so its long-term standing in regional and international relations can be expected to stay high. For the immediate future, though, its influence and activity will be much less than in the recent past.

Colombia

Although Venezuela and Mexico are undoubtedly the most important Latin American powers playing a role in the international politics of the Caribbean, they are not alone. Another country with a growing, though perhaps ephemeral, interest in the region's affairs is Colombia. One of the continent's largest countries, with a population of about 26 million, Colombia has only recently woken up to the fact that it is a Caribbean power. It has done so largely at the behest of the United States, as Vice-President Bush issued the following invitation to the Colombia government on a visit to Bogotá in October 1981: 'I extend the hand of friendship to a natural ally with a long Caribbean coastline, and invite President Turbay Ayala to join in the efforts of other countries of the region to try and stabilise the political and economic situation.'[20] Prompted in this way, the Turbay government responded and quickly emerged as a staunch ally of the United States in regional affairs.

As Bush indicated, Colombia does have Caribbean interests. It has a number of tiny island possessions in the Caribbean Sea and has an unresolved dispute with Nicaragua about sovereignty over two islands, San Andrés and Providencia, and a few offshore cays which lie off the eastern coast of Nicaragua. In fact, it is particularly concerned with maritime issues, claiming a 200-mile territorial zone off its Caribbean coast and recently signing agreements with a number of Central American and Caribbean countries, including Haiti and the Dominican Republic, with which this claim would otherwise conflict. Economically,

Colombian industry would also greatly benefit from freer access to Caribbean markets, whilst politically the government faces a domestic threat from left-wing guerrillas, which it believes are supported by hostile governments in the region, such as Cuba.

Colombia was thus a relatively easy target for the United States to mobilise. The Turbay government's view of the geopolitics of the region corresponded closely to that of the Reagan administration and naturally disposed it to give support to US policies. In addition, it was aware that the United States was in a position to offer help on several specific issues of concern to Colombia. For example, after the Sandinistas took power in Nicaragua in 1979, they revived their country's claim to the disputed islands, arguing that the treaty recognising Colombian sovereignty was signed under duress and was therefore invalid; to the delight of the Colombian government, the US quickly demonstrated its support for its position by publicly ratifying the very same treaty. Colombia also became one of the main recipients of US military aid in Latin America, with an allocation of US $12.7 million in equipment in the 1982 fiscal year and a similar sum authorised for 1983. In return, the Colombian government supported US Caribbean policy up to the hilt. It joined in the orchestrated US effort to isolate Cuba from the rest of the region by breaking diplomatic relations with Havana in March 1981 under the pretext, subsequently invalidated, that a group of guerrillas who took part in an unsuccessful landing on Colombia's Pacific coast had been trained and supplied by Cuba. The Colombian Foreign Minister, Carlos Lemor Simmonds, toured the Caribbean during 1981 and 1982, denouncing the insidious influence of the Cubans wherever he went and declaring Colombian determination to resist its spread. Colombia also agreed to become a fifth member of the Nassau group, along with the United States, Canada, Mexico and Venezuela, set up to prepare a multilateral aid initiative for the Caribbean. It hosted one group meeting in San Andrés and subsequently offered a contribution of US $50 million to the Caribbean Basin Initiative which eventually emerged from the discussions. Finally, in a unilateral move, the government sought to negotiate economic openings with some of the Commonwealth Caribbean countries along lines previously adopted by Venezuela. It felt that this would not only bring it direct influence and some economic advantage, but could also help to ensure the future stability of the region. A stream of official visitors from Caribbean governments were thus invited to Bogotá, the Guyanese being made particularly welcome.

With the US assistance mentioned, Colombia was also quickly

established as a military power of some significance in Caribbean terms. It embarked upon an armaments programme quite out of proportion to any domestic need to replace equipment or counter guerrillas. Twelve Kfir ground attack fighters were supplied by Israel, twelve helicopter gunships by the US, four missile-carrying corvettes were ordered from West Germany, and transport aircraft were supplied by both Britain and the United States. A powerful new base was also built on San Andrés from which the Colombian navy stepped up its patrols in the Western Caribbean. This marked a definite shift in Colombian naval strategy from a traditional concentration on the mainland base of Cartagena and the pursuit of disputes with Venezuela about the precise demarcation of coastal waters, and caused observers to comment on Colombia's potential to assist the US in any attempted blockade of Nicaragua or, for that matter, of Cuba itself.[21]

The development of Colombia's Caribbean policy has, however, been thrown into reverse by the unexpected result of the election in May 1982. Reaction against eight years of Liberal Party rule in close associa-tion with the military and the candidacy of a dissident Liberal com-bined to give the presidency to the Conservative Party candidate, Belisario Betancur. His administration has already produced a number of changes of policy. At home, he has initiated a programme of austerity and conciliation, offering guerrilla groups an amnesty and a legitimate place in the political system. In foreign affairs, he has broken from the previous government's stance as a client state of the US. The new regime has talked disapprovingly of the 'scornful attitude' the US frequently adopted to Colombia and has announced its intention of joining the Non-Aligned Movement. It has offered some financial support to the revolutionary government in Suriname and would like to re-establish diplomatic relations with Cuba. In short, its aim, as expressed by the new Foreign Minister, Rodrigo Lloeda, is to 'shake off the image of being a satellite and play a clearly Colombian role'[22] in international and regional politics. It remains to be seen to what extent the government will carry through this commitment.

Brazil

Lastly, in consideration of Latin American powers that concern them-selves with the Caribbean mention should be made of Brazil. Its interest in the region is not particularly well developed, but it has played a role in the past and continues within limits to do so in the present. Brazil has generally taken a traditional geopolitical view of international relations which has often led it to adopt a lofty and commanding stance towards smaller powers. It has also traditionally been concerned to develop friendly and untroubled relations with the United States as the major power in the hemisphere. The vital interests of the two countries have only rarely clashed sharply and Brazil has usually been the best friend of the United States in Latin America. According to Robert Wesson, the reasons for this are twofold.[23] The first is size. Brazil, which encompasses 3,287,000 square miles and is the fourth largest country in the world, has long regarded itself as something of a counterpart of the United States in the southern continent, a perception which has been widely shared in Washington. It has felt more secure than other smaller Latin American countries and, as a result, has been largely immune to their sensitivity over questions of US intervention in Latin America. The second reason is that Portuguese Brazil has always — although to a much lesser extent in recent years — felt itself at odds with Spanish America. It has been prepared to support US policy in the hemisphere in the expectation of being backed by the United States in its relations with its Spanish-speaking neighbours, especially Argentina. Brazil perceives Argentina to be its most serious rival for influence within Latin American affairs and has long engaged in a competitive relationship with that country, regarding other neighbouring states such as Bolivia, Paraguay and Uruguay primarily as factors in that particular equation. Venezuela's assertion of a higher profile in the international politics of the hemisphere, in particular its claims upon Guyana, with whom Brazil shares a long border, has induced a second continental zone of competition in which Brazil has become involved, but one which has generally been secondary in the hierarchy of Brazilian concerns. In sum, Brazil's orientation to foreign policy questions has been largely strategic, concerned much more with the establishment of spheres of influence than the ideological thrust of political and economic developments within the continent and the hemisphere.[24]

In this context, the Caribbean has entered Brazilian geopolitical concerns only at second hand. It has not attracted attention unless it has been drawn into the articulation of a relationship with another power which Brazil considers to be important. In these circumstances, Brazil has been prepared to take up positions on Caribbean matters. As indicated, Brazil has given general support to US policies in Latin America for the bulk of this century, but at times has used the Caribbean as a means to adjust its relationship with Washington. For example, between 1961 and 1964, under Presidents Quadros and Goulart, Brazil began to develop a more neutralist and anti-US posture in foreign affairs, which it signalled, in part, by making friendly gestures towards Cuba. Following the military coup which brought the phase to an end, the new government of Castelo Branco determined to lead Brazil into a firm alliance with the United States. Brazil became the most pro-American of Latin American countries, a fact which it demonstrated in unequivocal fashion in the Caribbean in 1965 by sending troops and providing the nominal commander of the expeditionary force which intervened in the Dominican Republic to prevent the installation of Bosch as President. Since this high-point of collaboration, Brazil has steadily sought to acquire a greater degree of independence within its alliance with the United States. Disputes with the Carter administration over human rights and nuclear proliferation reduced Brazilian deference to Washington, with the result that Brazil has remained studiously aloof from recent US policies in the Caribbean Basin. It remains implacably opposed to Cuba's politics, but has not been prepared to involve itself in the US cause either by providing arms or covert assistance to US allies or by participating in development programmes directed towards the region. Indeed, so far from supporting the position of the Reagan administration, President Figueiredo, during a visit to Mexico in April 1983, seemed almost to endorse the Mexican view over the crisis. 'The region,' he said, 'cannot be considered only from the perspective of ideological confrontation or by resorting to solutions of force.'[25] He went on to imply that US security was a problem for Washington, not the rest of the hemisphere.

The one country in the Caribbean with which Brazil has had consistent dealings in recent years is Guyana, and here too its relationship has been developed more by reference to the position of Venezuela than to common points of contact with Guyana. In effect, a triangular system of diplomacy has grown up between these states. Venezuela has long been alert to the possibility of Brazilian influence being deployed northwards towards the Caribbean into its preferred sphere of influence. Brazil has been concerned lest a country adjoining its borders should come under the control of a continental rival, whereas Guyana has been keen to develop close relations with Brazil as one means of countering the influence of Venezuela in the boundary dispute. Since 1968, when a Guyanese mission visited Brazil and signed a cultural agreement and Brazil first established an embassy in Georgetown, a number of political, technical, academic and military exchanges have taken place between the two countries. In 1971, the establishment of a joint commission on economic co-operation was agreed and plans prepared for the building of a highway to link the Brazilian and Guyanese road networks. The most recent contacts have been concerned mainly with the development of Guyana's oil potential. Brazil has also consistently given Guyana diplomatic support in its efforts to resist the Venezuelan claim. Indeed, for Guyana in the long run, it may even be that the Brazilian connection will represent a greater opportunity for political and economic development than active participation within Caribbean regional institutions.

For the moment, from Brazil's point of view, the Caribbean is still only a political arena to be entered for limited and specific purposes. It has lately felt it necessary to involve itself in the troubled affairs of Suriname, which also borders its northern frontier. According to reports, Brazil has offered quite extensive aid and military assistance to the government, but only on the condition that it distances itself politically from Cuba. The Surinamese government is keen to promote the link, seeing it as an alternative to renewed Dutch aid. For its part, the US administration will have been relieved to see the ideological strings attached to the approach, but should not assume that Brazil is concerned about anything more than preserving the security of its own political system. Brazil's intervention in Suriname is an important one, but it does not presage the assumption of a wider-ranging role in regional politics.

Notes

1. For a discussion of this point, see R. Preiswerk, 'The Relevance of Latin America to the Foreign Policy of Commonwealth Caribbean States', *Journal of Interamerican Studies and World Affairs*, vol. 11, no. 2 (1969), pp. 245–71.

2. V.A. Lewis, 'Commonwealth Caribbean Relations with Hemispheric Middle Powers' in A.J. Payne and P.K. Sutton (eds.), *Dependency under Challenge: The Political Economy of the Commonwealth Caribbean* (Manchester University Press, Manchester, 1984), p. 238.

3. See D. Boersner, 'The Policy of Venezuela towards the Caribbean' in L.F. Manigat (ed.), *The Caribbean Yearbook of International Relations 1975* (A.W. Sijthoff, Leyden, 1976), pp. 435–64.

4. For the evolution of these relations, see H.S. Gill, 'Conflict in Trinidad and Tobago's Relations with Venezuela' in ibid., pp. 469–75.

5. See Boersner in ibid., pp. 454–5.

6. Fondo de Inversiones de Venezuela, *Memoria 1977* (Editorial Genesis, Caracas, 1978), p. 57, cited in J.J. Guy, 'Venezuela: Foreign Policy and Oil', *The World Today*, vol. 35, no. 12 (1979), p. 508.

7. *Trinidad Guardian*, 27 April 1975.

8. Ibid., 16 June 1975.

9. For a discussion of Williams's reactions, see Gill, in Manigat, *Caribbean Yearbook 1975*, pp. 481–7.

10. L. Herrera Campins, *First Message to Congress* (Government of Venezuela, Caracas, 1980), pp. 11–12.

11. Cited in R.D. Bond, 'Venezuelan Policy in the Caribbean Basin' in R.E. Feinberg (ed.), *Central America: International Dimensions of the Crisis* (Holmes and Meier, New York, 1982), p. 195.

12. See L. Kaffman, 'How they Stampeded the Innocent Bolivar', *South* (December 1982), p. 63.

13. For a discussion of this apparent dispensation, see R.H. Zúñiga and M. Ojeda, 'Mexican Foreign Policy and Central America' in Feinberg, *Central America*, pp. 180–2.

14. A.T. Bryan, 'Mexico and the Caribbean: New Ventures into the Region', *Caribbean Review*, vol. 10, no. 3 (1981), p. 7.

15. V.A. Lewis, 'Focus on Major Tasks facing CARICOM in 80s', *Caribbean Contact* (January 1980), p. 6.

16. See G. Philip, 'Mexican Oil and Gas: The Politics of a New Resource', *International Affairs*, vol. 56, no. 3 (1980), p. 478.

17. For a fuller discussion of these views, see Zúñiga and Ojeda in Feinberg, *Central America*, pp. 165–70.

18. Cited in Bryan, 'Mexico and the Caribbean', p. 35.

19. For discussion of this, see D.J. Newton, 'Mexico's Uneasy Progress', *The World Today*, vol. 38, no. 10 (1982), pp. 395–401; A. Singh, 'How the Bankers' Darling Fell on Hard Times', *South* (November 1982), pp. 25–7; and T. Heyman, 'Chronicle of a Financial Crisis: Mexico, 1976–1982', *Caribbean Review*, vol. 12, no. 1 (1983), pp. 9–11 and 35–9.

20. *Latin America Regional Report: Caribbean*, RC–82–01, 15 January 1982, p. 8.

21. R. Espindola, 'US Lynchpin cuts Loose', *South* (January 1983), p. 17.

22. Cited in ibid.

23. R. Wesson, 'Brazil: Independence Asserted' in R. Wesson (ed.), *US Influence in Latin America in the 1980s* (Praeger with Hoover Institution Press, Stanford, 1982), p. 59.

24. See W. Perry, *Contemporary Brazilian Foreign Policy: The International Strategy of an Emerging Power* (Sage, Beverley Hills, 1976).

25. *Guardian*, 29 April 1983.

7 THE CARIBBEAN VOICE: FOREIGN POLICY WITHIN THE REGION

The analysis of the preceding chapters has shown that a very wide range of political actors are currently vying for influence in the Caribbean region. Between the contending pressures of the United States and Cuba, the European powers and the Latin American powers, one may well ask: what has been the response of the objects of all this activity, the Caribbean territories themselves? How have they reacted to the international crisis in which they find themselves engulfed? For the most part, they remain only minor actors in the drama, reacting to events, rather than initiating them. One immediate limitation upon their freedom of manoeuvre is that some still do not possess control of their foreign policy. Puerto Rico and the US Virgin Islands, French Guiana, Martinique and Guadeloupe and the Netherlands Antilles all fall into this category. This leaves the Commonwealth Caribbean territories, Suriname, Haiti, and the Dominican Republic as the only regional states, apart from Cuba, able to conduct their own external relations. Nevertheless, the region, led in this respect by the Commonwealth territories, is now more active in international affairs than it has ever been. Indeed, of late, a Caribbean voice has begun to make itself heard in what was hitherto been an externally-dominated argument about the future of the region.

The paradox of intense geopolitical activity by major powers is that it can create economic and political opportunities for the small states at the receiving end. Because they are the focus of competition, the territories concerned have a measure of bargaining power with the outside forces that seek to assert influence over them. Clearly, the countries of the Caribbean do not compare in strength with any of the powers discussed. In global terms, they are all small, impoverished, dependent states. Yet that does not mean that they are powerless to act in international relations. All the powers active in the region look on it with different perspectives. They are not all simply 'imperialists' of the same type, which means that there are differences between them that, with sufficient skill, can be exploited. The Caribbean has perhaps been a little slow to realise this, but it has grasped it now. In the last few years, foreign policy-making in the region has been characterised by a conscious effort to diversify relationships with the rest of the world in order to avoid falling within the sphere of influence of any one major power. Jamaica sought during the 1970s to develop close relations with Cuba and Venezuela, so as to escape as much as possible from the consequences of US hegemony. Haiti has tried to use its connection with France to the same end. Grenada now solicits aid from a variety of sources as a means of lessening its reliance on Cuba. As has already been shown, extensive links of this sort now connect all the independent Caribbean states with a range of regional and extra-regional powers. Their significance is that they have enabled the Caribbean to avoid falling prey to a single avenue of dependence and have thus helped it maintain a certain degree of independence in the midst of the big-power conflicts surrounding it.

However, even this is essentially a reactive posture, a defensive kind of independence. It does not, of itself, enable the Caribbean to play a full and leading part in the unfolding of the international crisis in which it is enmeshed. Within the Commonwealth Caribbean sub-region, in particular, a good deal of thought and some effort has been put into the elaboration of a joint regional foreign policy which would enable the collective interest of the Caribbean to be articulated with one voice. As William Demas put it, 'to deal with giants a lot of pygmies have to get together'.[1] To their credit, the pygmies have tried to do precisely this. Although their achievements have been partial and halting, they have not been completely unsuccessful. Some discussion of the embryonic emergence of the Caribbean regional community as an additional actor in the situation is thus necessary to complete this portrait of the major protagonists in the crisis.

The Origins of Foreign Policy Co-ordination

The Commonwealth Caribbean has a long record of integrative activity, dating from the colonial period, encompassing the ill-fated Federation of 1958–62 and embracing in the 1960s the notion of regional free trade. In an area with such a history, many felt that some attempt to co-ordinate the foreign policies of the region's governments was long overdue when, in 1973, it was formally promulgated as one of the major objectives of the new Caribbean Community and Common Market (CARICOM) set up to replace the former free-trade area. To this end, Article 17 of the Community Treaty provided for the establishment of a Standing Committee of Ministers responsible for Foreign Affairs and required it to make recommendations to the governments of member states with a view to bringing about 'the fullest possible co-ordination of their foreign policies within their respective competences' and adopting 'as far as possible common positions in major international issues'.[2] The legal reference to the competence of regional governments initially confined representation on the committee to the four Commonwealth Caribbean states which were then independent, Jamaica, Trinidad, Barbados and Guyana, but the advancing process of decolonisation has since opened up membership to eleven of the member states of CARICOM, excluding now only Montserrat.

In the few years immediately following the Community's establishment, foreign policy co-ordination proved to be one of the least successful aspects of Commonwealth Caribbean regional integration. There were instances of joint action being taken and common policies being pursued, but equally there were obvious failures and examples of lack of co-ordination, and even of outright conflict, between the positions of different Community members on certain issues. The most important area of unity related to the negotiations with the European Economic Community, which led up to the signing of the Lomé Convention in February 1975. At the opening conference in Brussels in July 1973, Sonny Ramphal, then Guyana's Foreign Minister, informed the EEC that all the territories of the sub-region had chosen 'to sit together at this table under the single label of the "Caribbean Countries" '.[3] Although the Caribbean grouping was subsequently incorporated within an African, Caribbean and Pacific (ACP) negotiating front, it continued to behave as a united bloc amongst the ACP countries and has maintained a broad unity throughout all subsequent re-negotiation talks. Beyond this, the Commonwealth Caribbean stood solidly by the side of Belize in its long-standing dispute with Guatemala, contributing considerably by their diplomacy to the increasing support given to the Belizean cause at the United Nations in the latter part of the 1970s. At the United Nations itself, the independent Commonwealth Caribbean states worked together on many occasions to promote the case for a 'New International Economic Order', organised more in accordance with the interests of Third World states.[4] Lastly, in a significant move taken in July 1974, the Secretary-General signed an agreement with the Foreign Minister of Mexico on behalf of the whole Caribbean Community, establishing a joint Mexico–CARICOM Commission to explore possible areas of economic, technical and cultural co-operation. In the opinion of the technocrats in the Community Secretariat, this was the model of regional foreign policy-making which the Commonwealth Caribbean should in future seek to adopt.

Against these cases of joint action, however, there must be set certain counter-examples. Regional states have taken different attitudes towards the Non-Aligned Movement: Guyana and Jamaica under Manley were enthusiastic participants, Trinidad much less so, and Barbados not even a member. As we have seen, they developed relations of varying degrees of warmth with Cuba; they disagreed over the appropriate policy to adopt towards the different factions fighting for power in Angola; and, most seriously of all, they indulged in bitter public recriminations with each other over the underlying implications of Venezuela's activist foreign policy towards the Caribbean in the mid-1970s. Trinidad saw in this a threat to recolonise the region, most of the other territories an opportunity for the development of a fruitful economic partnership. What this particular conflict revealed more generally was a growing tendency on the part of CARICOM states to negotiate deals with other countries or groups of countries on a bilateral basis, without prior consultation with their regional partners. This development was a serious one because the negotiation of such external deals by individual member countries of a regional grouping inevitably compromises the integrity and effectiveness of the whole collective unit in all its areas of operation.

In general, in the early days of CARICOM, it was not possible to say much more in evaluation of the movement towards the enactment of a joint regional foreign policy than here it existed and here, as yet, it did not. The approach was pragmatic and the results reflected this. Critics did, however, note that such co-ordination as was achieved was worked out largely in meetings between heads of government, trade ministers or ambassadors – in other words, entirely informally in respect of CARICOM's institutions.[5] The impact of the Standing Committee of Ministers responsible for Foreign Affairs was initially almost negligible. In the first six years or so of the Community's existence it met only four times – inaugurally in November 1973, again after a gap of fully two and a half years in March 1976, again in January 1979 after an even longer interval, and then again a few months later in July 1979 – and cannot be said at any of these meetings to have achieved very much beyond the enunciation of vague statements of general principle. By the end of the decade, Commonwealth Caribbean governments were being widely urged to take this aspect of the integration movement more seriously, with the result that the foreign ministers at their fifth meeting in February 1980 at last turned their attention to the preparation of more effective procedures of operation. They made several recommendations: that matters of interest to the region to be discussed at forthcoming international forums should be first debated at a regional level; that responsibility for convening caucuses prior to these meetings should be assigned to particular member states on a rotational basis; that delegations in foreign capitals should institutionalise their informal consultations; and that more documentary support should be given to the Foreign Ministers Committee.[6] With the acceptance of these proposals, the formal arrangements for foreign policy co-ordination within CARICOM were much strengthened and were deemed adequate for their purpose in 1981 by the so-called 'Group of Experts' charged with preparing a strategy for Caribbean integration for the ensuing decade.

CARICOM and the CBI

The first meeting of the Foreign Ministers Committee to be convened after this attempt at reform took place in Grenada in June 1981, at a time when talk of a US 'Mini-Marshall Plan' for the Caribbean was just beginning to appear credible. Indeed, the Nassau meeting between Haig and his Canadian, Venezuelan and Mexican counterparts took place a week or so later. In their formal communiqué, the ministers made no reference to such a proposal, but took the opportunity to fire a warning shot across the bows of the Reagan administration by officially noting their concern at the economic aggression being waged by the United States against Grenada. They were particularly alarmed by American attempts the month previously to stipulate that a US grant to the Caribbean Development Bank to help the least developed countries in the Commonwealth Caribbean should not be disbursed to that island. The bank's directors had voted unanimously to reject the grant on the grounds that it would contravene that aspect of the bank's charter which prohibited it from interfering in the political affairs of any member country. Whatever they felt about the particular merits of Grenada's revolution, and many were very critical, the region's governments were not prepared to see one of their number isolated by an external power. As the foreign ministers put it, they condemned any such effort 'to subvert Caribbean regional institutions built up over long years of struggle'.[7]

It would be fair to say, therefore, that even before details of the proposed Caribbean Basin aid plan became known, governments in the Commonwealth Caribbean were more than a little suspicious of the sincerity of President Reagan's concern for the social and economic development of their region. The one continuing exception was Edward Seaga of Jamaica, who can claim to have been the first politician to call for the preparation of such a plan and who welcomed its provisions as they were gradually revealed. Leaders of the smaller states in the Eastern Caribbean were much more dubious of its potential benefits, as they indicated at a special meeting of foreign ministers, held in Kingston in 1981 to consider the region's collective response. A similar note of healthy scepticism was apparent in the CARICOM Secretariat's announcement at the time of the meeting that 'the Caribbean was getting ready not just to be the subject of consultations but to negotiate, if the other side was serious, a package which would be responsive to their clearly identified national and regional objectives'.[8]

With the need to defend their own interests in the forefront of their minds, the ministers formulated a set of principles and guidelines as a basis for the commencement of CBI negotiations. These declared the governments' intention to insist that:

(i)   participation in the programme should be open to all territories in the region;

(ii) the programme should respect the sovereignty and integrity of states, the integrity of regional institutions and their autonomous character;

(iii) the programme to be formulated should be truly reflective of national goals and priority areas for development and that the criteria used in granting aid should not be based on political or military considerations;

(iv) the programme should be directed towards strengthening ongoing regional integration and co-operation, and encouraging wider and more intensive co-operation and exchange particularly in the industrial, financial, technical and trade areas in order to get maximum economic and development benefits at minimal cost through joint efforts; and

(v)   wherever possible the programme should utilise regional institutions and indigenous resources and expertise.[9]

On the substance of what the Commonwealth Caribbean required from an aid plan, the meeting emphasised the need to pay special attention to balance of payments and foreign-exchange problems and to provide increased technological, institutional and managerial capacity to supplement the region's development effort. The foreign ministers were also at pains to point out that outside investment, which even at that stage seemed so central to Washington's vision of the CBI, should be directed both to the public and private sectors, as each had a mutually supportive role to play in the process of development. In this respect, they made the important point that neither domestic nor private investment would flow where infrastructure was woefully inadequate. Finally, to make sure that the region's case was fully worked out, the meeting set up a CARICOM technical group, chaired by a senior official of the Trinidad government, Frank Rampersad, to prepare the detail of the Commonwealth Caribbean's submission to the prospective donor countries.

Having established their own position, the CARICOM ministers immediately proceeded to a further meeting where they were joined by the foreign ministers of Haiti, the Dominican Republic and Suriname. This was a novel move, designed to extend the process of foreign policy co-ordination in the Caribbean to the whole range of regional territories. This meeting broadly endorsed the principles for negotiation adopted by the CARICOM ministers and widened the membership of the technical group to include the non-Commonwealth territories. The implementation of a joint response to the CBI was further advanced a month later when, in Santo Domingo in the Dominican Republic, officials of the 'wider Caribbean' group of countries met with representatives of the governments of El Salvador and Honduras for an exchange of views prior to a consultative meeting with US, Canadian and Venezuelan diplomats.

Rampersad's technical report on the CBI constituted a valuable contribution to the debate. It described in graphic terms the situation facing the Caribbean and set out starkly the region's needs:

> The governments of many of the Caribbean countries are now unable to meet their current expenditures out of current revenues. Their large balance-of-payments deficits mean that it is often impossible to acquire essential spares and supplies to keep their limited productive capacity at a tolerable level of operation. Unemployment exceeds 15% and is rising, and outbreaks of social and political instability are becoming more frequent.

> These countries need an urgent injection of emergency assistance in the form of aid and market access to prevent further deterioration in the present bad position; that assistance must be provided *within the next six to nine months*. Beyond that and over the medium-term they require a sustained flow of resources in the form of official development assistance, private investment geared to producing

goods and services for export and assured markets.[10]

The sums it placed on these needs were US $580 million in emergency aid and US $4.7 billion over the period 1982-6, both far in excess of the scale of assistance proposed under the CBI. In an observation which would not have struck a sympathetic chord with the political philosophy of the Reagan administration, the report further stressed that governments in the Caribbean continued to have an inescapable responsibility to assume a prime moving role in promoting economic development. It saw the CBI proposals to stimulate the flow of private investment to the region only as a complement to official development plans.

For all the considerable efforts of Caribbean governments, both at sub-regional and full regional level, to bring negotiating pressure to bear upon the formulation of the CBI, there is no evidence to suggest that they had any impact upon US thinking. By this time, Mexico, Canada and Venezuela had withdrawn from the discussions and the initiative, as set out by President Reagan in his OAS speech in St Lucia in February 1982, was a unilateral US offering to the region, deployed very much on a 'take-it-or-leave-it' basis. From the outset, as many had feared, it divided the region, splitting even the Commonwealth Caribbean states. Following Reagan's flattering reference in his speech to Jamaica as a country that was 'making freedom work',[11] Seaga was quick to applaud the package of proposals. The plan, he said, was 'bold, historic and far reaching in concept, especially in the stimulation of trade and investment'.[12] He also indicated that he would not object to Grenada's exclusion, since other countries would be taking care of its needs. In the rest of the region, however, the reaction varied from disappointment to bitter condemnation.

Two principal lines of criticism emerged. The first, already articulated in the technical report, expressed concern at the emphasis placed on investment and trade, rather than direct development aid. It was revealed in the reported comment of three of the most conservative political leaders in the whole of the Commonwealth Caribbean: Tom Adams of Barbados, Vere Bird of Antigua and Kennedy Simmonds of St Kitts-Nevis. Adams simply asked: 'who could comfortably have built the international airports of the Caribbean without official development assistance? Who could now carry out major oil conservation or rehabilitation in a small poor country without official development assistance?' Bird responded in this way to a favourite American metaphor on the subject of development: 'there is no disagreement with Washington's dictum that the region's poor countries must pull themselves up by their own bootstraps. But first we must have the straps with which to pull up the boots.' And Simmonds spelled out the economic problems of the smallest regional states in vivid detail: 'our people will not be satisfied merely to be hewers of wood and drawers of water. For investors we have to provide adequate electrical power, telecommunications, sewage disposal, roads and port facilities. The money for these can only come from aid or local taxes – and with our small populations, even the most stringent tax measures cannot realise enough to satisfy our development needs.'[13] In addition, rein-forcing each of these complaints, there was – in full keeping with Caribbean political culture – a barely disguised jealousy that Jamaica had been particularly favoured in the proposed allocation of supple-mental assistance under the CBI, being granted five times as much as all the Eastern Caribbean islands put together.

The second most frequently expressed criticism of the initiative was related to Washington's preoccupation with the Communist threat and its insistence on the exclusion of Cuba, Nicaragua and Grenada from being beneficiaries. The divisiveness of this aspect of the proposal disturbed several Commonwealth Caribbean governments, but was attacked in the most vitriolic fashion, as might have been expected, by the Grenadian Prime Minister, Maurice Bishop, himself. At a rally in March 1982, celebrating the third anniversary of the revolution, he denounced the CBI as the 'con game of the century' and a 'prostitu-tion'[14] of the original aid plan that had brought the four would-be donors together in Nassau the previous year. The proposals could bring no lasting benefits to the Caribbean and would only serve to undermine the unity which the region had worked so hard to create. Recalling the various principles laid down by the CARICOM Foreign Ministers meet-ing in September 1981, which included the demands that there should be no exclusions and no political or military component to the pro-gramme, he suggested that every one of them had been 'ignored, violated or broken'[15] by the terms of the CBI.

It was a timely reminder to his fellow Commonwealth Caribbean leaders, since a CARICOM Foreign Ministers meeting was due to assemble at the end of March with a view to giving the region's official reaction to the CBI proposals. It had the benefit of the assessment of the Rampersad report, but also had somehow to reconcile the different positions already taken up by member governments as far apart politi-cally as those of Jamaica and Grenada. The divisions could be seen in the communiqué, which equivocally observed that 'while the US proposal did not adequately address all of the issues or fulfil expectations for a comprehensive plan for the development of the economies of Caribbean states, it nonetheless would make a positive contribution'.[16] The former unity could only be salvaged in respect of the governments' collective disappointment that 'there were no specific elements of supporting their own inter-governmental institutions such as CARICOM and the Caribbean Development Bank'[17] and their complaints about the information-sharing proposal which a recipient country under the CBI was required to enter into as part of a bilateral executive agreement with the United States. The principle that participation in the CBI should be open to all CARICOM countries was also reaffirmed, but everybody knew that Jamaica, for example, was not going to forego the benefits of the programme for this cause. On the most important test of foreign policy co-ordination yet faced by the region, ranks had been comprehensively split.

Issues of Security and Peace

On the related issues of security and peace in the region, the Commonwealth Caribbean has also tried to assert a local point of view, arguing against the predominant external perception of the region's security in terms of East–West conflict. According to a statement issued by the Community Secretariat, the CARICOM countries see their security problems in very different terms, namely:

(i)   internal stresses due to the high expectations of their peoples, unacceptable levels of unemployment and the assertion of identity;

(ii) incursion or threats of incursions by mercenaries, a situation to which several of these island states, irrespective of their position on the political spectrum, have been exposed;

(iii) in the case of Belize and Guyana, territorial claims by powerful neighbours; and

(iv) the need to insulate the area from the effects of conflicts from outside.[18]

In short, security was mainly perceived as a problem of development.

For President Reagan, of course, development is seen primarily as a problem of security, a reversal of emphasis which provided some uneasy moments during the course of a 'working holiday' spent by the President in the Commonwealth Caribbean in April 1982. He travelled first to the favoured territory of Jamaica, where he allowed himself to indulge to the full his taste for anti-Communist rhetoric, declaring that Cuba was on the 'road to serfdom' and again applauding Seaga for 'rescuing' Jamaica from a government that was 'virtually under Communist control'.[19] In Barbados, however, the same sort of talk did not receive such as warm welcome. Reagan only invited to meet him there the leaders of Antigua, Dominica, St Kitts-Nevis and St Vincent. The Prime Ministers of Grenada, Belize and St Lucia were ostentatiously excluded and the Trinidadian Prime Minister, George Chambers, declined to attend. Yet even the highly pro-Western figures he did entertain were not impressed to hear the President refer to Grenada as bearing 'the Soviet and Cuban trademark, which means that it will attempt to spread the virus among its neighbours'.[20] He had misjudged the softening of attitudes which had taken place towards Grenada in the Eastern Caribbean since the revolution in 1979. Leaders in neighbouring territories no longer felt frightened for their own positions and were ready to work with Bishop within a Commonwealth Caribbean framework. It was also made plain to Reagan that these states did not share his perception of Cuba as the main threat to the freedom and stability of the region. Indeed, Tom Adams went to far as to indicate to the President that life would be a lot easier for all the little islands of the Eastern Caribbean if Washington and Havana could sort out some of their differences and thereby ease the cold-war tensions which imbued the region's affairs. These various rather cool reactions to Reagan's anti-Communism were very revealing, for they showed that conservative leaders in the Commonwealth Caribbea have, in fact, been rather more sophisticated in their response to the reality of 'ideological pluralism' in the region than have their supposedly more worldly allies in Washington.

As indicated earlier, this did not mean that they disregarded the question of security. For some time, Barbados had been trying to reach agreement on the signing of a joint security and military co-operation pact with Dominica, St Lucia, Antigua and St Vincent, finally managing to secure their assent in October 1982. According to the Memorandum of Understanding, the signatory governments agreed to 'prepare contingency plans and assist one another on request in national emergencies; prevention of smuggling; search and rescue; fishery protection; customs and excise control; maritime policing duties; protection of off-shore installations; pollution control; natural and other disasters and threats to national security'.[21] Although such a defence force can be interpreted as having anti-subversive or anti-revolutionary implications, it manifestly cannot be seen as a means of defending the Eastern Caribbean against attack by any of the major powers whose armies and navies manoeuvre in the region. In respect of this threat, the Commonwealth Caribbean region as a whole has begun to embrace the concept of the Caribbean as a 'zone of peace'. This idea was first discussed at the CARICOM Foreign Ministers meeting in February 1980. A committee of officials was subsequently set up to consider the matter and work continues on the task of formulating an appropriate declaration. Supporters of the idea feel that it would contribute to the de-escalation of military tension in the Caribbean.

The CARICOM Summit

With the political crisis surrounding the region still undiminished, the Third CARICOM Heads of Government Conference took place at Ocho Rios in Jamaica in November 1982. It was a more significant event in the affairs of the Commonwealth Caribbean than is immediately apparent, because it was the first meeting of the governing body of the Caribbean Community to have been held in seven years. As such, it was an important opportunity for the region's governments to put behind them previous divisions and disagreements, including those that had arisen over the CBI.

The most contentious issue facing the conference concerned the position to be accorded to Grenada in the Community's activities. In the weeks before the summit, Adams had frequently expressed the view that the Community's leaders should consider changing the CARICOM Treaty so as to commit its members to the maintenance of parliamentary democracy and the defence of human rights. His suggestion was immediately supported by Seaga. At the conference, Adams formally proposed an amendment to the Community Treaty which would have committed member states 'to the principle of political liberty and the protection of the fundamental rights and freedoms of the individual through adherence to the principle of the rule of law and practice of free, fair and regular elections'.[22] Bishop retorted that fundamental human rights should also be deemed to include the right to life, a job, education, good roads, electricity and piped water. The debate was only resolved by means of private dialogues outside formal conference sessions, in which it seems that George Chambers was particularly influential. Chambers reported that Bishop has personally given him an undertaking to hold elections in Grenada, although not necessarily of a Westminster type; added to which, during the conference the Grenadian government released some twenty-eight political detainees, in a move obviously designed to defuse further criticism of its record by Adams, Seaga and their followers. In the event, the conference decided to make no alterations to the CARICOM Treaty, but to adopt instead a statement on human rights to be known as the Declaration of Ocho Rios. It omitted the original Barbadian call for free and fair elections and specifically included the Community's commitment to 'the political, civil, economic, social and cultural rights of the peoples of the region',[23] as well as to the concept of ideological pluralism and the right of all states to choose their own path of development. Within the Caribbean, the agreement has been interpreted as a victory for Grenada and a defeat above all for the United States, which many believed to have been the instigator of the whole manoeuvre. It has been noted that the idea of trying to force Grenada out of CARICOM emerged only after President Reagan's April visit to the Caribbean and that there was an unusually strong US diplomatic presence in Ocho Rios during the summit. Some commentators have even cast doubt upon the seriousness with which Adams, if not Seaga, actually backed the proposal for the revision of the Treaty which they put to the conference.

The peace and security of the Caribbean was the other major political issue to preoccupy the conference. The heads of government called for international action to control the activities of mercenaries, expressed familiar concern at the heightening of tension in the region caused by the recent intensification of US military manoeuvres in the Caribbean, but were understandably most alarmed by the threats of direct aggression made by outside powers in pursuit of territorial claims against two Community members, Belize and Guyana. As was expected, the meeting reaffirmed its traditional support for the territorial integrity of Belize by attacking the Guatemalan government for reneging on its promise to abandon the dispute. Concern exists in the region about the extent of Belize's dependence upon the protection of the remaining British garrison, but there is little enthusiasm for the establishment of a regional or Commonwealth security force to assist. There is also no expectation, given the general orientation of the Reagan administration to the process of political change in Central America, that the United States can be induced to bring pressure upon the right-wing Guatemalan government to drop its claim upon Belize. Indeed, it has since lifted its embargo on arms sales to Guatemala.

The same condemnation was not, however, applied to Venezuela's claim upon Guyana. To the disappointment of the Guyanese President, Forbes Burnham, the final communiqué noted the 'unqualified undertaking' of the Venezuelan government to eschew the use of force in connection with the dispute and merely urged the two countries to 'continue their pursuit of a peaceful settlement of the controversy in accordance with the terms of the Geneva Agreement of 1966',[24] thereby contravening the Guyanese position that to accept any suggestion of negotiations was to lend credibility to the Venezuelan claim. The reasons for the adoption of this conciliatory stance are twofold. The first is the extent to which several CARICOM countries have come to rely upon Venezuelan economic assistance; the second is the poor human-rights record of Burnham's own government. Despite all the attention given to Grenada in this context and the publicity generated by open letters written by human-rights pressure groups to all the heads of government detailing the many violations of democracy in Guyana, the situation was not openly debated by the conference. However, it did almost certainly contribute to the reticence with which the other Commonwealth Caribbean leaders endorsed Guyana's resistance to Venezuela's demands.

The final issue of significance considered by the conference was the long-running saga of the CBI. By this time Commonwealth Caribbean governments were distinctly exasperated at the slow progress which the initiative was making in the US Congress. In the Eastern Caribbean, there was some relief that the supplemental assistance for their sub-region had been increased to US $20 million, but concern that even the limited gains which they had anticipated from the trade and investment provisions were being whittled away by congressional amendments. Privately, many of the leaders of the smaller states felt that they had been 'conned'. At the time they kept quiet, for fear of impeding the passage of the Bill, but as soon as it became clear that the legislation was going to fall their frustrations spilled out into the open. They were scathingly voiced by Eugenia Charles, Prime Minister of Dominica, who apart from Seaga had been perhaps the most avid supporter of the CBI in the region. 'The Caribbean has been expecting action on this programme since 1981', she said. 'Our people will say to us, their leaders, that you are jokers, and the US is the biggest joker of them all.'[25] The eventual passage of the CBI in August 1983 will obviously have allayed some of these criticisms, but it will not have entirely repaired the damage done to the reputation of the United States in the Commonwealth Caribbean by its earlier handling of the initiative.

An object lesson in how to handle its vulnerable southern neighbours was given to the United States by Canada in February 1983. The occasion was a novel gathering of heads of government of Commonwealth Western-hemisphere countries in St Lucia. From the first moments of the conference, the Canadian Prime Minister, Pierre Trudeau, identified himself with the region's support for ideological pluralism as the guiding framework for the conduct of international relations in the Caribbean. He declared that when a country chose a socialist path of development, it was not automatically injected into the Soviet orbit and reminded the meeting that Canada's development aid was disbursed on a non-discriminatory basis and was as high as that of any country in the world. Moreover, his government had continued to provide assistance to Grenada despite US hostility. Regional governments welcomed this approach and have always been gratified that in its aid programme Canada has sought to promote efforts at regional integration and given support to multilateral regional institutions such as the Caribbean Development Bank, the University of the West Indies and indeed CARICOM itself. In marked contrast to the methods of the present US administration, diplomacy of this sort positively assists the Caribbean in its various attempts to pursue development unimpeded by the constraints of geopolitical conflict.

Notes

1. W.G. Demas, *West Indian Nationhood and Caribbean Integration* (Caribbean Conference of Churches Publishing House, Bridgetown, 1974), p. 7.

2. *Treaty establishing the Caribbean Community*, Chaguaramas, 4 July 1973, Article 17 (1).

3. S.S. Ramphal, *Just, Enlightened and Effective Arrangements: New Approach to Relations with the European Economic Community* (Ministry of Foreign Affairs, Georgetown, 1973), p. 4.

4. For a discussion of these efforts, see D. Benn, 'The Commonwealth Caribbean and the New International Economic Order' in A.J. Payne and P.K. Sutton (eds.), *Dependency under Challenge: The Political Economy of the Commonwealth Caribbean* (Manchester University Press, Manchester, 1984), pp. 259–80.

5. See A.J. Payne, *The Politics of the Caribbean Community 1961–79: Regional Integration amongst New States* (Manchester University Press, Manchester, 1980), pp. 221–2.

6. See Group of Caribbean Experts, *The Caribbean Community in the 1980s* (Caribbean Community Secretariat, Georgetown, 1981), p. 86.

7. *Press Release no. 46/1981. Sixth Meeting of the Standing Committee of Ministers of CARICOM responsible for Foreign Affairs* (Caribbean Community Secretariat, Georgetown, 1981).

8. *CARICOM Perspective*, no. 9 (1981), p. 1.

9. 'Memorandum by the Caribbean Community (CARICOM) Secretariat' (86/81–82/FM) in *Fifth Report of the Foreign Affairs Committee of the House of*

Commons: Caribbean and Central America, together with an Appendix; part of the Proceedings of the Committee relating to the Report; and the Minutes of Evidence taken before the Committee with Appendices (HMSO, London, 1982), p. 304.

10. Ibid., p. 306; italics in original.

11. President Reagan, 'The US Caribbean Basin Initiative', speech to the Organisation of American States, St Lucia, 24 February 1982, p. 8.

12. *Latin America Regional Report: Caribbean*, RC–82–03, 26 March 1982, p. 1.

13. Ibid., RC–82–01, 15 January 1982, p. 6.

14. Ibid., RC–82–03, 26 March 1982, p. 3.

15. Ibid.

16. *Press release no. 16/1982. Seventh Meeting of the Standing Committee of Ministers of CARICOM responsible for Foreign Affairs* (Caribbean Community Secretariat, Georgetown, 1981).

17. Ibid.

18. 'Memorandum by the Caribbean Community Secretariat' in *Fifth Report of the Foreign Affairs Committee*, p. 303.

19. *Caribbean Contact*, May 1982.

20. Ibid.

21. Reproduced in ibid., December 1982.

22. Ibid.

23. *Press release no. 52/1982. Third Conference of the Heads of Government of the Caribbean Community. Attachment II. The Ocho Rios Declaration* (Caribbean Community Secretariat, Georgetown, 1982).

24. Ibid.

25. *Latin America Regional Report: Caribbean*, RC–83–01, 21 January 1983, p. 7.

8 CONCLUSION: THE PRESENT AND FUTURE STATE OF THE CRISIS

The Caribbean is now plainly the scene of considerable international competition for influence. The extent and variety of the powers which have had to be discussed in order to present a full picture of the geo-political conflicts that surround the region confirm beyond doubt the break-up of the traditional model of Caribbean international relations. The view of the region as an unchallenged preserve of the United States, with relatively amenable client-state governments, tolerating the avun-cular presence of extra-continental European powers which retain residual sovereignty over parts of the area, is but a historical relic. As we have seen, the present situation is one of great complexity and fluidity. The attempted reassertion of US hegemony, the ideological challenge of Cuba, the differing roles played by Britain, France and the Netherlands, the new presence of the European Economic Community, the greater activism of Venezuela and Mexico, the latent power of Brazil and, not least, the response to those pressures of the Caribbean countries themselves – all these factors have combined together to create a turbulent theatre of conflict in the Caribbean. The overriding impression is also of a struggle which has yet to be resolved and which could still move in different directions. The current crisis thus expresses the uneasy passage of the region from an old order, which has now dis-integrated, to a new one of which the profile remains to be deter-mined.

The key to an understanding of the crisis lies in a grasp of its origins. The traditional model of international relations in the area did not break down under the attack, either open or subversive, of any external power, whether it be the Soviet Union or Cuba. It is important to emphasise this. It fell apart under the pressure of the development impasse which confronted the region at the end of the 1960s and lasted throughout the 1970s. Initially, the problem was conceived as one of 'growth without development'; latterly, as a lack of growth itself. Following the sharp rise in oil prices in late 1973, the health of the Caribbean economy was rendered critical. As it struggled to recover, familiar patterns of politics were undermined in one territory after another, to the point where, to external observers, the instability of the region was its most notable characteristic. The United States was forced

153

to take notice, whilst other powers seized the opportunity to assert their influence, including socialist Cuba, with all the implications that this had for Western perceptions of security. Out of the inadequacies of the political economy of the Caribbean, there thus flowed the manifold rivalries and conflicts between regional and extra-regional powers which constitute the new character of international relations in the area.

As such, the Caribbean crisis is classically the product of what one might call North-South-East-West politics. It emerged out of the problem of development and underdevelopment (the North-South dimension), but has been transmuted into a sub-plot of the new cold war (the East-West dimension). In this sense, it is typical of the new breed of international crises whereby Third World regions, which have an intimidating array of indigenous social, economic and political problems still to be solved, are forced to stand service simultaneously as arenas of indirect superpower confrontation. In the Caribbean the situation is further complicated, and the range of participant actors correspondingly extended, because the area is unique in the Third World in belonging to both of the great North-South systems to have grown up in this century — the American hemispheric system with the United States as metropolis and Latin America and the Caribbean as periphery, and the European imperial system with Britain, France and the Netherlands, and now the EEC, as metropolis and Africa, the Caribbean and the Pacific as periphery. This matrix of relationships is fundamental, because the character of the present international crisis in the region has been shaped by the interplay of the many different links and associations with the outside world which the Caribbean has accumulated in the course of its history.

Conceived in these terms, the prospects for the establishment of a new and settled order in Caribbean affairs do not seem to be encouraging. The one certainty is that the underlying problem of securing greater economic development in the region will remain as intractable as ever throughout the rest of the 1980s. International interest rates remain high, commodity prices low, and the mild economic recovery foreseen in the industrialised countries will be insufficient to benefit weak Third World economies. In these circumstances, Caribbean countries will continue to face enormous difficulties.[1] In Guyana, the point of virtual economic collapse has been reached; in Jamaica, the economy has already failed to meet certain IMF performance tests, despite the tutelage of the pro-Western and much favoured Seaga regime; and even in Trinidad and Barbados, the two economic 'success-stories' of the Commonwealth Caribbean sub-region, serious economic cut-backs are now being experienced. Outside the region, the financial difficulties of debtor countries like Mexico, Brazil and Venezuela limit their capacity to offer help. In the industrialised countries themselves, the recession has induced a similar reluctance to spend large sums of money on development and has given rise to a growing tendency towards protectionism in the face of competitive exports from developing countries. A concerted reinflation of the world economy by its leading members would help everybody, but for political reasons this appears as unlikely as ever, following the failure of the Williamsburg summit of June 1983 to agree upon its necessity. In short, virtually all the economies of the Caribbean can be expected to suffer increased unemployment, widening balance of payments deficits and greater external debts over the coming few years. This means that the attendant international crisis will not, as it were, solve itself. The social and economic conditions which fostered the competition for influence in the first place will continue to sustain it, even if some of the aspiring powers, Cuba not excluded, are themselves weakened by the consequences of the recession.

Attention must therefore turn to the actions of the main protagonists, in particular those of the United States. As has been argued throughout, the United States is, and in the foreseeable future will continue to be, the prime determinant of the character of international relations in the Caribbean. Its geographical position, its enormous economic, political and military power, and its perception of the Caribbean as part of its own security zone dictate that pre-eminence, regardless of the behaviour of any other power concerned with the region. This is not to say that the United States has the future of the Caribbean in its hands, but simply to point out that the direction of US policy bears most heavily on the development and potential resolution of the crisis. In this connection, two scenarios for the future emerge, one based on the extrapolation of present trends in US foreign policy, the other built around an alternative approach which is being discussed in Washington, but which is alien to the philosophy of the present Reagan administration.

The first scenario assumes that the US policies of the last three years will continue in the same vein for the rest of President Reagan's first term and into a second. As explained, the administration's aim is to reassert the traditional hegemony of the United States over the Caribbean, to which end all its policies are bent. It is difficult, however, to see how it can hope to achieve this end. The CBI, even though it has now been finally passed, cannot be expected to secure the loyalty of more than a few of the tiniest states in the Eastern Caribbean. The Jamaican government, for example, should already be coming to realise that deference to Washington is not a certain passport to economic development. Neither have the administration's bitter attacks upon Cuba succeeded in intimidating that state. The Cuban leadership is used to US economic and political aggression and historically has had its resolve hardened by such policies. It will not give in now.

It is also significant that extensive US diplomacy has failed to win for its approach the backing of any of its major allies, with the single exception of the Thatcher government in Britain. The Mitterrand government in France is openly doubtful, Mexico has been consistently critical, the Venezuelan government has retreated from too close an alignment with US policies, Canada condemns attempts to equate the adoption of socialist strategies of development with automatic acquiescence in the policies of the Soviet Union, and the EEC has refused to bow to US pressure to fall into line. The list is long and revealing. With British support, the US can seek to extend its military hold upon the Caribbean, but in so doing it might risk the ultimate folly of a confrontation with the Soviet Union and could not realistically expect to stem the process of change in the region for more than a few years. When it surfaced again, the probability is that it would be more virulent and possibly more violent.

From the point of view of the United States, therefore, the charge that can be levelled against the present administration's Caribbean policy is not only that it damages the prospect of development in the Caribbean (which might presumably be viewed in Washington as a secondary consideration), but also that it does not serve US interests very successfully. Above all, the United States desires a peaceful Caribbean which does not have revolutions or socialist governments or large numbers of migrants who want to flee to Miami. Yet its present policies do not at any point address the deeper social and economic problems which give rise to these manifestations of changing times. All that is presently being achieved is the exacerbation of tension and conflict in the region, the promotion of an atmosphere of suspicion and hostility towards the United States on the part of even moderate governments, and the further retardation of the moment when a reasoned stability can again settle upon Caribbean affairs.

Yet an alternative scenario can be discerned which suggests that the gloomy and possibly fateful implications of the first are not inevitable. The basic requirement is a recognition in the United States that some relative loss of influence is to be expected in a rapidly changing world, and that this need not be detrimental to the protection of any fundamental US interests in the Caribbean. The case for this sort of approach has been well argued recently in a pamphlet called *The Americas at a Crossroads*, published as the summary of an 'inter-American dialogue' between 46 eminent scholars, diplomats, politicians, business leaders and international administrators from North America, Latin America and the Caribbean. At the outset, the signatories confirmed their unanimous acceptance of two critical points: first, that the basic roots of insecurity in the hemisphere were 'primarily economic, social, and political, not military' and, second, that 'the sources of insecurity are mainly internal to each nation, and that external influences are secondary'.[2] In their view, the solution therefore lay in 'economic and social development and political dialogue, not in weapons or military advisers'.[3] On the sensitive question of security, they suggested that US and regional perceptions of the problem were not intrinsically irreconcilable and that some basis of compromise could be reached around the norms of self-determination and non-intervention. In this respect, they openly criticised US policy under Reagan:

> We all favor keeping Latin America and the Caribbean out of the East–West conflict to the greatest extent possible. It does not serve that purpose for the United States to oppose changes in the region simply because they diminish US influence and hence are perceived as advantageous to Cuba and the Soviet Union, unless they are clearly related to basic security concerns. We believe that the United States can better achieve its long-term interest in regional stability, one shared by Latin Americans, by exercising measured restraint in the projection of its own power.[4]

This last notion — the exercise of measured restraint in the deployment of US power — underpinned the approach of the whole report and provides a basis on which to build the outlines of an alternative US policy towards the hemisphere.

The acceptance by Washington of such a guiding principle would open up a whole series of new possibilities. As the report of the 'inter-American dialogue' specifically suggested, it could lead to the establishment of a US–Soviet understanding on the Caribbean and Central America. Within this, the Soviet Union and Cuba might pledge not to deploy strategic or conventional combat forces to any part of the region and the United States, the Soviet Union, Cuba and indeed all

governments in the region might at the same time pledge not to intervene or interfere in the internal affairs of another nations of the area or
give support to revolutionary or counter-revolutionary movements
seeking to overthrow existing governments. Acceptance of the principle
should also lead to the opening of a new dialogue with Cuba, initially
on a variety of economic and technical matters, but subsequently on
more politically contentious matters, and should certainly have generated
an end to US attempts to isolate and intimidate the revolutionary government in Grenada. By its very absurdity, the case of Grenada best
illustrated the case for US restraint in its approach to the Caribbean. For all the scares that have been raised by the Reagan administration, the new airport is no threat to US interests: it was being built quite
openly and with the help of several Western companies and is badly
needed for tourist purposes. As former US ambassador to the Eastern
Caribbean, Sally Shelton, told a congressional committee in April 1983,
'it is incongruous that the most powerful nation on earth should be so
disturbed and so threatened by a small island of 110,000 people whose
main export is nutmeg'.[5] She proposed the holding of high-level talks
with the Bishop government and the ending of provocative military
manoeuvres in Caribbean waters, declaring for the benefit of the hard-
liners that 'we can achieve our goals far more easily and effectively by
stressing our respect for the national sovereignty of the nations of the
Caribbean and by supporting their economic development than by a
revival of an obsolete policy of gunboat diplomacy'.[6]

As she indicated, a new US policy of measured restraint should take
up again the question of encouraging Caribbean economic development.
The CBI drew attention to this problem, but proposed no meaningful
solution. For all the domestic objections that would arise, the US
should seek to put together – in close consultation with *all* the countries of the region – a major package of government-to-government
assistance on concessionary aid terms. Encouragement of private-sector
investment is not enough. The US could afford such a programme and
would find the money well spent in terms of the protection of its wider
interests in the region. Indeed, the US could learn from Cuba in this
respect, for it is in part by the provision of badly-needed economic
assistance that Havana has gained influence in the Caribbean. The irony
is that the US has more to offer in this way than Cuba will ever have,
if only it could learn to respond to the economic needs and political
demands of Caribbean countries without insisting upon rigid ideological
conformity. It urgently needs to display a genuine tolerance of ideological pluralism in the Third World and a greater awareness that the

process of development inevitably throws up radical and nationalistic politics.

These are some of the major changes of approach which a US government should adopt if it seriously wanted to try to defuse the international crisis in the Caribbean. In present political circumstances, it is virtually impossible to conceive of the Reagan administration moving in these directions. However, several prominent US Democrats were party to the 'inter-American dialogue' and can be said in this report to have put down markers for the Caribbean and Latin American policy of a future Democratic administration. If US policy was to be restructured in broadly these terms in the not-too-distant future, it would in all probability find a ready response, both inside and outside the region. Caribbean governments could not but respond to the aid programme and would be grateful of the opportunity to pursue development according to indigenous priorities without fear of disapproval and de-stabilisation from the watchful giant to the north. For its part, the Cuban leadership has long seen the case for an economic *rapprochement* with the United States, and it is significant that the Bishop government in Grenada went on asking for assistance from Washington throughout all the rebuffs it received. All the countries in the region would also benefit from a relaxation of East–West conflict and a de-escalation of military activity. Externally, such a change in the direction of US policy would make the negotiation of a genuinely multilateral initiative to promote the economic development of the region a real possibility. The EEC, Mexico, Venezuela, France and Canada would endorse it and give it their support. Even in Britain, it would be welcomed by that strand of political opinion which produced the broadly liberal recommendations of the Foreign Affairs Committee of the House of Commons, when it reviewed British policy towards the Caribbean.

In sum, it almost seems as if it is only the right-wing governments of the United States and Britain which have yet to open their eyes to the consensus which has emerged in opposition to their policies and which could, if followed, arrest the slide towards increasingly bitter and dangerous international conflict within the Caribbean. In Britain, the Thatcher government has just been re-elected, but in the United States there is a presidential election due on 6 November 1984. Whether or not the Caribbean will be an issue in the campaign remains to be seen. What is certain is that the United States will continue to be an issue in the politics of the Caribbean. The people and governments of the region cannot hope to achieve their social and economic goals in a political environment so heavily imbued with cold-war tensions. Their reduction is thus a priority in the pursuit of development in the Caribbean. Unfortunately, the region's political leaders can themselves only contribute marginally to the achievement of this immediate end. It is the leadership of the United States which has the power to bring the international crisis of the Caribbean to an end.

Notes

1. For a discussion of the present economic situation in the region, see Caribbean Development Bank, *Annual Report 1982* (Caribbean Development Bank, Bridgetown, 1983), pp. 28–48.
2. Report of the Inter-American Dialogue, *The Americas at a Crossroads* (Woodrow Wilson International Center for Scholars, Washington 1983), p. 40.
3. Ibid.
4. Ibid., p. 42.
5. *Caribbean Contact*, April 1983.
6. Ibid.

EPILOGUE: THE US INVASION OF GRENADA

The armed invasion of Grenada by United States forces in October 1983 constituted a tragic new climax to the international crisis of the Caribbean. It demonstrated to the whole world the intensity of the political conflicts which had grown up in the region and dramatically illustrated the facility with which they could develop into open violence and warfare.

The immediate events which led up to the invasion were initiated when sharp internal differences between members of the People's Revolutionary Government of Grenada began to emerge into the open. There had always been a division of opinion within the PRG leadership between a broadly social democratic element, committed primarily to the task of national reconstruction following the disastrous maladministration of the Gairy era, and a Marxist element, intent upon the eventual socialist transformation of the society. During the first four years of the revolution agreement was achieved around the necessity for reform of the bureaucracy, the educational system, the health and social services generally and the building of the new airport. Virtually no action was taken to further the collectivisation of the economy; indeed the small commercial elite in the island greatly benefited from the government's proper management of the state finances and the increased demand for goods generated by the spending power of the local airport workers and those employed in the newly-established agro-industries. Inevitably, as time went on, dissatisfaction grew among the more impatient Marxist elements in the leadership at the moderate pace of revolutionary change adopted by the PRG. They were also suspicious of Bishop's continued attempts to improve Grenada's relations with the United States in the face of repeated snubs meted out to him by Washington and of his apparent support for the holding of a Western-type election as a means of legitimising the regime, and they resented what they felt to be his increasingly autocratic style of leadership.

Matters came to a head over this last issue. At a meeting of the central committee of the ruling New Jewel Movement in mid-September, the left faction, headed by the Deputy Prime Minister and Finance Minister Bernard Coard, called for a more effective sharing of power by which Bishop would continue to lead the masses but Coard would assume responsibility for the army and the party. Bishop argued against the practicalities of such a collective leadership and asked for time for further consideration since he was about to embark on a mission to Hungary and Czechoslovakia in search of aid and technical assistance. On his return in the middle of October he found himself facing an ultimatum from Coard, which he refused to accept, whereupon – amidst charge and counter-charge from each faction concerning assassination plots – he was placed under house-arrest.

Coard resigned in an attempt to show that he was not simply engaged in a personal power struggle, but still appeared to be the major figure behind the scenes as the left faction sought to reconstitute the government in conjunction with the army. Protests were mounted against Bishop's arrest and a call made for a general strike as a means to register popular discontent. The situation seemed to have been stabilised when on October 19 a large crowd of Bishop's supporters marched to the Prime Minister's official residence where Bishop was being held and freed him after only token resistance from his military guards. He was carried in triumph to army headquarters, where he demanded that the garrison lay down its arms. At this point other soldiers arrived, opened fire on the crowd causing several deaths, and took Bishop and three of his ex-Cabinet ministers inside the fort, where they were shot in a coldly brutal manner. A 'Revolutionary Military Council', headed by General Hudson Austin, was subsequently proclaimed as the new government. Austin was himself a long-standing member of the New Jewel Movement and had been Minister of Labour, Communications and Works in the PRG. However, his main support came from a group of radical younger officers who had been members of the so-called Organisation for Educational Advance and Research, a Marxist 'party within the party', headed by Coard. The coup thus brought to power not only a military regime alien in the politics of the Commonwealth Caribbean, but a government considerably more left-wing than its civilian predecessor.

Maurice Bishop's murder unavoidably focused international attention upon Grenada, forcing the conflicts within the country to the forefront of the political debate about the Caribbean. Although many in the West were quick to assume that the evil hand of international communism lay behind the military take-over and the subsequent killings, there is no evidence to confirm the direct involvement of such forces. The assumption of power by the army was the end-result of a domestic struggle over the direction of the revolution, whilst the actual shooting of Bishop and the others appeared to be a product of circumstance carried out in the heat of the moment. The reaction of the Soviet Union and Cuba to the whole series of events was also very different. Although regretting the violence, the former applauded the coup, interpreting it as a deepening of the revolution. Cuba, on the other hand, much closer to the realities of the Caribbean, was greatly disturbed. In an official statement issued immediately after the killings were announced, it declared that 'no doctrine, principle, or proclaimed revolutionary position, and no internal split, justifies such brutal procedures as the physical elimination of Bishop and the renowned group of honest and dignified leaders killed with him'. In these changed circumstances, its relations with Grenada would have to be submitted, it said, to 'deep and profound analysis'.

In the rest of the Caribbean too the position of Grenada was urgently reviewed, but with differing responses. At a meeting of the Organisation of Eastern Caribbean States, the six-island grouping of the smallest Leeward and Windward Islands, a very aggressive line was adopted and a call made for external assistance to help restore order to Grenada. By contrast, an emergency gathering of CARICOM heads of governments a day later took a more cautious position, deciding provisionally to expel Grenada from the organisation and institute trade and other sanctions against the new military regime but failing to agree upon the necessity for armed intervention. It seems that Jamaica, Barbados and those smaller Eastern Caribbean states which possessed right-wing governments were in favour, Trinidad and Guyana strongly opposed, and Belize and the Bahamas neutral. Yet, even as these meetings were taking place and the case for and against an external intervention was being debated in the Commonwealth Caribbean, a United States armada of two aircraft carriers and ten warships was bearing down on Grenada, ostensibly to prepare to evacuate the thousand or so US citizens (many of them medical students at an offshore university) who lived on the island, but in reality to stand by in readiness to invade.

The Reagan administration's hostility to the revolutionary regime in Grenada had long been evident. For over three years it had opposed and harassed Bishop and his colleagues without succeeding in breaking their nerve and without convincing the rest of the world that Grenada, even with its new airport, constituted a threat to US national security. As much as it might have wanted to take direct action to bring the regime down, and plans were definitely made, it could not find the appropriate opportunity to do so. The wider significance of the brutal murder of Bishop and the outrage this action so widely provoked was that it gave the Reagan team the opening they had been searching for. Responding, so it was claimed, to a formal request to intervene issued by the OECS states, the United States landed a large force of marines on the morning of 25 October. They were nominally supported by a token force of soldiers and policemen from four of the OECS states – Dominica, Antigua and Barbuda, St Lucia and St Vincent – plus Jamaica and Barbados.

Speaking on television, with the Prime Minister of Dominica, Miss Eugenia Charles, supportively at his side, President Reagan asserted that the United States had taken 'this decisive action' for three reasons:

> First – and of overriding importance – to protect innocent lives, including up to 1,000 Americans whose personal safety is, of course, my paramount concern. Second, to forestall further chaos, and third, to assist in the restoration of conditions of law and order and of governmental institutions to the island of Grenada where a brutal group of leftist thugs violently seized power.

This justification was disingenuous, to say the least. No evidence existed to suggest that the lives of American citizens on Grenada had been in any way endangered by the internal struggle for power in the country. Talks were still taking place about their evacuation and Cuba in a diplomatic note delivered to the US before the attack had offered its assistance in ensuring their safety. Shorn of this pretext, the rest of Reagan's argument, including the much-publicised OECS invitation, constituted an attempt to create a moral and political defence of what was in reality United States interference in the domestic affairs of an independent sovereign state. As most non-American observers immediately pointed out, the attack was a blatant breach of the United Nations charter, the OAS charter (of which both the United States and Grenada were signatories) and of all the normal conventions of international law.

As such, the invasion was widely condemned all over the world, not only by expected opponents of the United States, such as the Soviet Union and Cuba, some hundreds of whose citizens were at the sharp end of the US attack by virtue of their involvement in the airport project, but also by a whole host of traditional allies with interests in the Caribbean. France, the Netherlands, Canada, Mexico, Venezuela and Brazil, to name only some of the most prominent, all came out in opposition; so too did those Commonwealth Caribbean states like Trinidad which had refused to endorse the idea of military intervention at the CARICOM meeting; and so too, more surprisingly, did the

Thatcher government in Britain, which had hitherto been the Reagan administration's closest supporter in the Western alliance. The participation of Britain in the operation had, in fact, been sought by some of the Caribbean states, but they had received a negative response. The British government felt that an invasion of what was, after all, a Commonwealth state would damage the West's claim to moral superiority in international affairs when inevitable comparisons were made with the Soviet invasion of Afghanistan, and it did try rather ineffectually to dissuade the United States from its plans. In an attempt to limit the damage done to its 'special relationship' with Washington, the government refused actually to condemn the attack once it had started and ordered its representatives at the United Nations to abstain on a Security Council resolution deploring the US aggression. Although ultimately vetoed by the United States, this resolution – which had, in fact, been sponsored by a Commonwealth Caribbean country, Guyana – was passed by eleven votes to one with two other abstentions apart from Britain, thereby giving some measure of the scale of international opposition to the US action.

The overwhelmingly critical reaction to President Reagan's initial justification of the invasion served to expose more fully the real politics that lay behind the US decision, namely the desire to achieve at least one 'victory' in the world-wide anti-Communist crusade to which his administration was dedicated. In the context of this world view, Grenada appeared to offer the perfect opportunity – a small island close to the United States, a blood-stained left-wing regime with Cuban and Soviet connections, and seemingly little risk of serious casualties if intervention was decided upon. Revealingly, in a further statement to the nation made on the third day of the landings whilst fighting was still taking place on Grenada, Reagan shifted his line of argument in this direction. 'We got there just in time', he declared, asserting that Grenada was a 'Soviet–Cuban colony being readied as a major military bastion to export terror and undermine democracy'. US propaganda subsequently exaggerated the number and the role of the Cubans on the island, most of whom were construction workers, and claimed that all the resistance their forces were meeting was coming from them rather than from Grenadians. Much play was also made of captured warehouses full of ammunition and alleged Cuban plans to take over the island and establish a military base there, the significance and veracity of which was called into question as soon as independent journalists were allowed into Grenada. The propaganda was nevertheless effective in justifying the intervention in the eyes of the American public and legitimising a massive build-up of US forces in Grenada in the aftermath of the invasion.

However, to anyone who was not a supporter of President Reagan's politics, the implications of the whole Grenada affair were gravely alarming. In the short-term it will have strengthened the 'hawks' within his administration and made more likely the pursuit of equally aggressive policies towards Nicaragua or even Cuba itself, with all its attendant dangers for world peace. It may well also have helped the chances of his re-election should he decide to stand again for the presidency. The adoption of the more sensible and sensitive US approach to the problems of the Caribbean, favoured by that body of opinion represented in the recent report of the 'inter-American dialogue' and by many allies of the United States, thus seems as remote as ever. For all this, the lesson of the Grenadian invasion is clear: not until such a change of policy is effected will real freedom and tranquillity be restored to Grenada and the Caribbean people as a whole.

APPENDIX

Basic Data on the Countries of the Caribbean

The following notes contain brief comparative data on the various countries of the Caribbean. The population figures are estimates for 1980. The figures concerning the economy are estimates for gross domestic product and per-capita income in 1978, and are given in US dollars. The dates in brackets are dates of independence.

Anguilla

Area: 35 sq. miles. *Population:* 6,500. *Capital:* The Valley.
Economy: GDP $3.8 million; per capita $584.
Political status: British Colony.

Antigua-Barbuda

Area: 170 sq. miles. *Population:* 75,500. *Capital:* St John's.
Economy: GDP $73.1 million; per capita $1,001.
Political status: Independent (1 November 1981).

Bahamas

Area: 5,380 sq. miles. *Population:* 236,000. *Capital:* Nassau.
Economy: GDP $1,044.5 million; per capita $4,924.
Political status: Independent (10 July 1973).

Barbados

Area: 166 sq. miles. *Population:* 250,500. *Capital:* Bridgetown.
Economy: GDP $533.6 million; per capita $2,152.
Political status: Independent (30 November 1966).

Belize

Area: 8,864 sq. miles. *Population:* 144,857. *Capital:* Belmopan.
Economy: GDP $166.5 million; per capita $896.
Political status: Independent (21 September 1981).

British Virgin Islands

Area: 59 sq. miles. *Population:* 12,000. *Capital:* Road Town.
Economy: GDP $31 million; per capita $2,600.
Political status: British Colony.

167

Cayman Islands

Area: 100 sq. miles. *Population:* 17,340. *Capital:* George Town.
Economy: GDP $94 million; per capita $5,529.
Political status: British Colony.

Cuba

Area: 44,218 sq. miles. *Population:* 9,883,000. *Capital:* Havana.
Economy: GDP $15,400 million; per capita $1,711.
Political status: Independent (20 May 1902).

Dominica

Area: 290 sq. miles. *Population:* 78,000. *Capital:* Roseau.
Economy: GDP $36.9 million; per capita $479.
Political status: Independent (3 November 1978).

Dominican Republic

Area: 18,703 sq. miles. *Population:* 5,621,000. *Capital:* Santo Domingo.
Economy: GDP $5,700 million; per capita $1,140.
Political status: Independent (27 February 1844).

French Guiana

Area: 35,135 sq. miles. *Population:* 65,000. *Capital:* Cayenne.
Economy: GDP $140 million; per capita $2,222.
Political status: French Overseas Department.

Grenada

Area: 133 sq. miles. *Population:* 108,000. *Capital:* St George's.
Economy: GDP $61.3 million; per capita $584.
Political status: Independent (7 February 1974).

Guadeloupe

Area: 686 sq. miles. *Population:* 320,000. *Capital:* Basse-Terre.
Economy: GDP $1,100 million; per capita $3,459.
Political status: French Overseas Department.

Guyana

Area: 83,000 sq. miles. *Population:* 829,000. *Capital:* Georgetown.
Economy: GDP $496.9 million; per capita $608.
Political status: Independent (26 May 1966).

Haiti

Area: 10,714 sq. miles. *Population:* 5,739,000. *Capital:* Port-au-Prince.
Economy: GDP $1,240 million; per capita $260.
Political status: Independent (1 January 1804).

Jamaica

Area: 4,411 sq. miles. *Population:* 2,250,000. *Capital:* Kingston.
Economy: GDP $2,729 million; per capita $1,299.
Political status: Independent (6 August 1962).

Martinique

Area: 425 sq. miles. *Population:* 311,000. *Capital:* Fort-de-France.
Economy: GDP $1,350 million; per capita $4,326.
Political status: French Overseas Department.

Montserrat

Area: 39 sq. miles. *Population:* 12,000. *Capital:* Plymouth.
Economy: GDP $10.4 million; per capita $972.
Political status: British Colony.

Netherlands Antilles

Area: 383 sq. miles. *Population:* 248,000. *Capital:* Willemstadt.
Economy: GDP $800 million; per capita $3,187.
Political status: Part of the Kingdom of the Netherlands.

Puerto Rico

Area: 3,421 sq. miles. *Population:* 3,187,570. *Capital:* San Juan.
Economy: GDP $12,300 million; per capita $4,032.
Political status: Self-governing Commonwealth in association with the
United States.

St Kitts-Nevis

Area: 104 sq. miles. *Population:* 49,000. *Capital:* Basseterre.
Economy: GDP $35.2 million; per capita $704.
Political status: Independent (19 September 1983).

St Lucia

Area: 238 sq. miles. *Population:* 122,000. *Capital:* Castries.
Economy: GDP $87 million; per capita $737.
Political status: Independent (22 February 1979).

St Vincent

Area: 150 sq. miles. *Population:* 114,000. *Capital:* Kingstown.
Economy: GDP $47 million; per capita $456.
Political status: Independent (27 October 1979).

Suriname

Area: 63,251 sq. miles. *Population:* 402,000. *Capital:* Paramaribo.
Economy: GDP $820 million; per capita $2,110.
Political status: Independent (25 November 1975).

Trinidad and Tobago

Area: 1,980 sq. miles. *Population:* 1,059,825. *Capital:* Port of Spain.
Economy: GDP $3,896 million; per capita $3,485.
Political status: Independent (31 August 1962).

Turks and Caicos Islands

Area: 166 sq. miles. *Population:* 7,436. *Capital:* Cockburn Town.
Economy: GDP $9.5 million; per capita $1,301.
Political status: British Colony.

United States Virgin Islands

Area: 132 sq. miles. *Population:* 118,960. *Capital:* Charlotte Amalie.
Economy: GDP $520 million; per capita $4,406.
Political status: United States territory.

Sources

The Caribbean Community in the 1980s (Caribbean Community Secretariat, Georgetown, 1981)

The Caribbean Handbook 1983-4 (West India Committee, London, 1983)

The World in Figures (Economist, London, 1981)

Encyclopedia of the Third World (Mansell Publishing House, London, 1982)

International Financial Statistics (IMF, Washington, 1982)

SELECT BIBLIOGRAPHY

Ambursley, F. and Cohen, R. (eds.), *Crisis in the Caribbean* (Heinemann, London, 1983)

Axline, W.A., *Caribbean Integration: The Politics of Regionalism* (Frances Pinter, London, 1979)

Beckford, G.L. (ed.), *Caribbean Economy: Dependence and Backwardness* (Institute of Social and Economic Research, Kingston, 1975)

Bender, L.-D., *Cuba vs United States: The Politics of Hostility* 2nd edn (Inter American University Press, San Juan, 1981)

Blasier, C. and Mesa-Lago, C. (eds.), *Cuba in the World* (University of Pittsburgh Press, Pittsburgh, 1979)

Bond, R.D. (ed.), *Contemporary Venezuela and its Role in International Affairs* (New York University Press, New York, 1977)

Brewster, H. and Thomas, C.Y. (eds.), *The Dynamics of West Indian Economic Integration* (Institute of Social and Economic Research, Kingston, 1967)

Bryan, A.T., 'Mexico and the Caribbean: New Ventures into the Region', *Caribbean Review*, vol. 10, no. 3 (1981)

Brzezinski, Z., *Between Two Ages* (Viking, New York, 1970)

Commonwealth Caribbean Regional Secretariat, *From CARIFTA to Caribbean Community* (Commonwealth Caribbean Regional Secretariat, Georgetown, 1972)

Connell-Smith, G., *The Inter-American System* (Oxford University Press, New York, 1962)

Cosgrove Twitchett, C., *A Framework for Development: The EEC and the ACP* (George Allen and Unwin, London, 1981)

Crassweller, R.S., *The Caribbean Community* (Pall Mall, London, 1972)

Cross, M., *Urbanization and Urban Growth in the Caribbean* (Cambridge University Press, Cambridge, 1979)

Da Breo, D.S., *The Grenada Revolution* (Management Advertising and Publicity Services, Castries, 1979)

De Kadt, E. (ed.), *Patterns of Foreign Influence in the Caribbean* (Oxford University Press, London, 1972)

Demas, W.G., *West Indian Nationhood and Caribbean Integration* (Caribbean Conference of Churches Publishing House, Bridgetown, 1974)

—— 'The Caribbean and the New International Economic Order', *Journal of Interamerican Studies and World Affairs*, vol. 20, no. 3 (1978)

Dinerstein, H.S., *Soviet Policy in Latin America* (Rand, Santa Monica, 1966)

Dominguez, J.I. (ed.), *Cuba: Internal and International Affairs* (Sage, Beverley Hills, 1982)

—— 'Cuban Foreign Policy', *Foreign Affairs*, vol. 57, no. 1 (1978)

—— 'The United States and its Regional Security Interests: the Caribbean, Central, and South America', *Daedalus*, vol. 109, no. 4 (1980)

Donaldson, R.H. (ed.), *The Soviet Union in the Third World: Successes and Failures* (Westview Press, Boulder, 1981)

Duncan, W.R., 'Caribbean Leftism', *Problems of Communism*, vol. 27, no. 3 (1978)

Ecumenical Program for Inter-American Communication and Action, *Puerto Rico: A People Challenging Colonialism* (EPICA, Washington, 1976)

Feinberg, R.E. (ed.), *Central America: International Dimensions of the Crisis* (Holmes and Meier, New York, 1982)

Girvan, N. and Jefferson, O. (eds.), *Readings in the Political Economy of the Caribbean* (Institute of Social and Economic Research, Kingston, 1971)

Gonzalez, E., 'Complexities of Cuban Foreign Policy', *Problems of Communism*, vol. 26, no. 6 (1977)

Gouré, L. and Rothenberg, M., *Soviet Penetration of Latin America* (Miami Centre for Advanced International Studies, Miami, 1975)

Grant, C.H., *The Making of Modern Belize: Politics, Society and British Colonialism in Central America* (Cambridge University Press, Cambridge, 1976)

Group of Caribbean Experts, *The Caribbean Community in the 1980s* (Caribbean Community Secretariat, Georgetown, 1981)

Guy, J.J., 'Venezuela: Foreign Policy and Oil', *The World Today*, vol. 35, no. 12 (1979)

Heyman, T., 'Chronicle of a Financial Crisis: Mexico, 1976-82', *Caribbean Review*, vol. 12, no. 1 (1983)

Ince, B. (ed.), *Contemporary International Relations in the Caribbean* (Institute of International Relations, St Augustine, Trinidad, 1979)

Kegley, C.W., Jr and Wittkopf, E.R., 'The Reagan Administration's World View', *Orbis*, vol. 26, no. 1 (1982)

Kirkpatrick, J., 'US Security and Latin America', *Commentary*, vol. 71, no. 1 (1981)

Latin American Bureau, *The European Challenge: Europe's New Role in Latin America* (Latin America Bureau, London, 1982)

LeoGrande, W.M., 'Cuban-Soviet Relations and Cuban Policy in Africa', *Cuban Studies*, vol. 10, no. 1 (1980)

Lewis, G.K., *The Growth of the Modern West Indies* (Monthly Review Press, New York, 1963)

—— *Notes on the Puerto Rican Revolution* (Monthly Review Press, New York, 1974)

Lewis, V.A. (ed.), *Size, Self-Determination and International Relations: The Caribbean* (Institute of Social and Economic Research, Kingston, 1976)

—— 'The Caribbean in Emerging World Political/Economic Trends', *Caribbean Quarterly*, vol. 25, no. 3 (1979)

Linowitz, S. *et al.*, *The Americas in a Changing World* (Commission on United States-Latin American Relations, Washington, 1974)

Loescher, G.D. and Scanlan, J., ' "Mass Asylum" and US Policy in the Caribbean', *The World Today*, vol. 37, no. 10 (1981)

Long, F. (ed.), *The Political Economy of EEC Relations with African, Caribbean and Pacific States* (Pergamon Press, Oxford, 1980)

Lowenthal, A.F., 'The Caribbean Basin Initiative: Misplaced Emphasis', *Foreign Policy*, vol. 47 (1982)

Lowenthal, D., *West Indian Societies* (Oxford University Press, London, 1972)

Maingot, A.P., 'Cuba and the Commonwealth Caribbean', *Caribbean Review*, vol. 9, no. 1 (1980)

Manigat, L.F. (ed.), *The Caribbean Yearbook of International Relations 1975* (A.W. Sijthoff, Leyden, 1976)

—— (ed.), *The Caribbean Yearbook of International Relations 1976* (A.W. Sijthoff, Leyden, 1977)

Manley, M., *The Politics of Change: A Jamaican Testament* (André Deutsch, London, 1974)

—— *Jamaica: Struggle in the Periphery* (Third World Media, London, 1982)

Millett, R. and Will, W.M. (eds.), *The Restless Caribbean* (Praeger, New York, 1979)

Mishin, S., 'Latin America: Two Trends of Development', *International Affairs* (Moscow), no. 6 (1976)

Newton, D.J., 'Mexico's Uneasy Progress', *The World Today*, vol. 38, no. 10 (1982)

Nicholls, D., *From Dessalines to Duvalier: Race, Colour and National Independence in Haiti* (Cambridge University Press, Cambridge, 1980)

Pastor, R., 'Sinking in the Caribbean Basin', *Foreign Affairs*, vol. 60, no. 5 (1982)

Payne, A.J., *The Politics of the Caribbean Community 1961-79: Regional Integration amongst New States* (Manchester University Press, Manchester, 1980)

—— *Change in the Commonwealth Caribbean* (Royal Institute of International Affairs, London, 1981)

—— 'The Rise and Fall of Caribbean Regionalisation', *Journal of Common Market Studies*, vol. 19, no. 3 (1981)

—— and Sutton, P.K. (eds.), *Dependency under Challenge: The Political Economy of the Commonwealth Caribbean* (Manchester University Press, Manchester, 1984)

Pearce, J., *Under the Eagle: US Intervention in Central America and the Caribbean* (Latin America Bureau, London, 1981)

Perry, W., *Contemporary Brazilian Foreign Policy: The International Strategy of an Emerging Power* (Sage, Beverley Hills, 1976)

Philip, G., 'Mexican Oil and Gas: The Politics of a New Resource', *International Affairs*, vol. 56, no. 3 (1980)

Preiswerk, R. (ed.), *Documents on International Relations in the Caribbean* (Institute of Caribbean Studies, University of Puerto Rico, Rio Piedras, 1970)

—— 'The Relevance of Latin America to the Foreign Policy of Commonwealth Caribbean States', *Journal of Interamerican Studies and World Affairs*, vol. 11, no. 2 (1969)

Ramsaran, R., 'The US Caribbean Basin Initiative', *The World Today*, vol. 38, no. 11 (1982)

Report of the Inter-American Dialogue, *The Americas at a Crossroads* (Woodrow Wilson International Center for Scholars, Washington, 1983)

Smith, W.S., 'Dateline Havana: Myopic Diplomacy', *Foreign Policy*, vol. 47 (1982)

Smouts, M.-C., 'The External Policy of François Mitterrand', *International Affairs*, vol. 59, no. 2 (1983)

Stevens, C. (ed.), *EEC and the Third World: A Survey 3. The Atlantic Rift* (Hodder and Stoughton, London, 1983)

Sutton, P.K. (ed.), *Forged from the Love of Liberty: Selected Speeches of Dr Eric Williams* (Longman, Port of Spain, 1981)

Theberge, J.D. (ed.), *Soviet Seapower in the Caribbean: Political and Strategic Implications* (Praeger, New York, 1972)

Thorndike, A.E., 'The Concept of Associated Statehood with Special Reference to the Eastern Caribbean', unpublished PhD thesis, University of London, 1979

Valenta, J.R., 'The Soviet–Cuban Alliance in Africa and the Caribbean', *The World Today*, vol. 37, no. 2 (1981)

Wallace, E., *The British Caribbean: From the Decline of Colonialism to the End of Federation* (University of Toronto Press, Toronto, 1977)

Wesson, R. (ed.), *Communism in Central America and the Caribbean* (Hoover Institution Press, Stanford, 1982)

—— (ed.), *US Influence in Latin America in the 1980s* (Praeger with Hoover Institution Press, Stanford, 1982)

Williams, E., *From Colombus to Castro: The History of the Caribbean 1492-1969* (André Deutsch, London, 1970)

INDEX

Costa Rica 2, 54, 58, 62, 85, 113
Council for Mutual Economic Assistance (COMECON) 70
Council of the Americas 64
Cross, Malcolm 5
Cuba 1–4, 7, 13, 15–16, 24, 28, 30,
 32, 67–87, 134, 140
 relations with Britain 95–8
 relations with Colombia 131–2
 relations with France 95–8
 relations with Grenada 19–20,
  55, 64, 138
 relations with Mexico 123–9
 relations with US 36–7, 39–41,
  43, 45, 47–50, 52–6, 63, 145,
  147, 153–9
 relations with Venezuela 116,
  118, 120–1
Czechoslovakia 69

de la Madrid Hurtado, Miguel 129–30
Demas, William 9, 138
Den Uyl, Joop 105
Díaz Ordaz, Gustavo 124
Dijoud, Paul 101
Dominica 1, 4, 6, 21–3, 93, 101,
 108–9, 147, 150
Dominican Republic 1–3, 6, 27, 134
 domestic politics 4, 31–2
 economy 7–8, 38, 40, 120
 foreign policy 84, 87, 89, 108–10,
  116–18, 130, 137, 143
 relations with US 45, 50, 55, 58,
  61, 124, 143
Douglas, 'Rosie' 21–2
Duarte, Napoléon 121

Echeverría, Luis 124–6
El Salvador 30, 52, 54, 58, 60–1,
 63, 84, 103, 121, 127–8, 143
Ethiopia 48, 70, 77, 83
European Economic Community
 (EEC) 89–92, 107–11, 139,
 154, 156, 159
 relations with Grenada 19, 54, 95

Falklands/Malvinas Islands 61, 86–7,
 99, 121
Fascell, Dante 44
Figueiredo, Joâo 134
Ford, Gerald 41, 43, 73, 75
France 3, 5, 26–7, 79, 89, 99–104,
 107, 110, 138, 156
French Guiana 2–3, 5, 99–101, 104,
 108, 113, 137

Gairy, Eric 18–20, 81, 93
Giscard d'Estaing, Valerie 26, 100–1
Godber, Joseph 93
Gonzalez, Edward 74–7
Gonzalez, Felipe 89
Goulart, Joâo 134
Granma 87
Grenada 1, 3, 24, 68, 84, 120, 127,
 138, 151
 domestic politics 4, 18–20, 93
 relations with Britain 87, 94–8
 relations with Commonwealth
  Caribbean 21–2, 30, 141, 144,
  148–9
 relations with Cuba 80–3
 relations with EEC 19, 54, 95,
  108–10
 relations with France 101–3
 relations with US 48, 50, 52,
  54–6, 63–4, 145, 147–9,
  156–9
Guadeloupe 1, 5, 6, 26–7, 79, 99–
 101, 104, 108–9, 137
Guatemala 2, 37, 52, 61
 dispute with Belize 29–30, 96,
  119, 125, 139, 149
Guevara, Che 89
Guyana 2–3, 6, 44, 96
 dispute with Venezuela 115, 117,
  121–2, 146, 149–50
 domestic policies 4, 11–14, 92
 economy 7, 15, 38, 154
 foreign policy 54, 68, 84, 108,
  124–5, 131, 139–40
 relations with Brazil 113, 133–5
 relations with Cuba 79–83
 relations with US 40, 42, 50
Guzman, Antonio 31–2, 45, 47

Haig, Alexander 56, 60, 141
Haiti 1, 6, 39
 domestic politics 4, 27–9
 economy 7–8, 10, 17
 foreign policy 84, 87, 108–10,
  116, 130, 137–8
 relations with US 50, 55, 58, 61,
  143
Heath, Edward 93
Heng Samrin 83
Herrera Campins, Luis 119–21
Holland *see* Netherlands, The
Honduras 2, 58, 61, 143

Inter-American Development Bank
 117